Loose Cannons

LOOSE CANNONS

101 MYTHS, MISHAPS, AND MISADVENTURES OF MILITARY HISTORY

GRAEME DONALD

LYONS PRESS
Guilford, Connecticut
An imprint of Globe Pequot Press

To Rhona

First published in the UK in 2009 by Osprey Publishing

First published in the USA in 2011 by Lyons Press, an imprint of Globe Pequot Press

Designed by Myriam Bell Design

Library of Congress Cataloging-in-Publication Data is available on file.

ISBN 978-0-7627-7794-5

Printed in the United States of America

10 9 8 7 6 5 4 3 2 1

CONTENTS

Contents

INTRODUCTION

While it was tremendous fun researching the material for this book, it must be said that it was equally alarming to discover just how many significant moments in military history turned out, on closer inspection, to be glamorized blunders of mind-boggling proportions. Furthermore, research revealed many iconic figures who either had feet of clay or penchants and peccadilloes best kept from their adoring public. Many of the famous and inspiring quotations associated with the great and the good never graced the lips of those to whom they have been widely attributed. Most alarming of all were the numbers of blood-soaked wars fought over meaningless trifles, and the amount of money squandered on the development of weapons more dangerous to those using them than to any enemy.

To take that last category first, all married people are to one degree or another influenced by their spouses. This is fine unless it is World War II, you are leader of the most powerful nation on earth, and your other half has a friend with a plan to pattern-bomb Japan with millions of pyrotechnic fruit bats; the total cost of Eleanor Roosevelt's convincing husband Franklin to take seriously the bat bomb mooted by her imaginative dentist can only be guessed. And what of the Russian Army's disastrous misapplication of the experiments of their own compatriot, the psychologist Ivan Pavlov? Determined to turn dogs into anti-tank weapons, they conditioned the mutts to eat underneath tanks. The intention was to turn them loose during armored engagements while wearing explosive backpacks, hoping that they would run under and destroy the German tanks. Great in principle, but the conditioning was too successful and the dogs only associated the underneath of *Russian* tanks with food. In more recent times, the CIA's sanctioning millions of dollars to turn Russian Embassy cats into mobile listening posts, complete with aerials inside their tails, takes some beating. Why, in addition, would developed nations go to the brink of war over a pig, or other countries actually lock swords over an old bucket or even the loss of a football match?

In this book you will also find a section dealing with misattributed quotations. When it comes to lofty declarations associated with major battles and pivotal moments, many of these transpired to be invented after the events or the deaths of those to whose memory they are pinned. Extraordinary personalities, it seems, are not allowed to slip their mortal moorings muttering an inanity about an unpaid utility bill, or some other banality; some appropriate exit lines have to be coined. Paul Revere never rode through the New England night shouting "The British are coming"; Wellington never said "Up, Guards, and at 'em" at Waterloo, where he equally never heard "The Guard dies but never surrenders" from any French commander. General MacArthur never promised "I shall return," and although an action rather than a quote, Russian Premier Nikita Khrushchev never banged his shoe on the desk at the United Nations (UN). Of all the entries in this section of the book, the latter came as the greatest shock; I am sure that anyone over fifty would bet confidently that they had in their youth seen some old monochrome news footage of him, standing in a cheap grey suit, banging his United Nations desk with his shoe, but it is a folk memory.

All too often, horrendous screw-ups have to be spun to heroic status by administrations reluctant for the public to know the truth; the World War II evacuation of Dunkirk and the fall of Singapore are two fine examples of that process. Other events, such as the so-called Battle of Britain, the fiasco at the Alamo and the Storming of the Winter Palace during the Russian Revolution, have been, to one degree or another, blown out of proportion to serve as morale-boosters or rallying cries, and woe betide any who question their status as such. Sometimes history has no choice but to present ineptitude as heroics, as was the case with Teddy Roosevelt's fabled charge up San Juan Hill at the head of his Rough Riders during the Spanish-American War of 1898. Not only were the Rough Riders on foot, Roosevelt having been unable to make proper transport arrangements for their horses, but he led his "cavalry" up the wrong hill. Roosevelt actually charged the nearby Kettle Hill by mistake, but the myth of his assault on San Juan was enough to propel him into the White House.

At other times, historical characters are unsettled by loose cannons riding abroad when they should have been home in bed. Although the aforementioned Paul Revere is still celebrated for his night-time ride to Concord on the eve of the Revolutionary War, aiming to warn all there that the British Army was headed their way, he never completed the task. At some point in the journey he crossed the unsung Sam Prescott, sneaking home from a midnight tryst. Thinking it a great way to cover his tracks, Prescott joined the venture, and when Revere was arrested en route it was the amorous Prescott who completed the task with the message: "The regulars are out!"

In our first section, to which we shall now turn, we examine the lesser-known facts concerning the bad, the mad and the mediocre. Benito Mussolini never managed to make the trains run on time; Rasputin was "taken out" by British Intelligence; Hitler lived in Liverpool for about six months in 1913 to dodge conscription into the Austrian Army; despite all the cinematic hagiography eulogizing the much-hyped Che Guevara, he was nothing but a nasty little killer, named Ernesto Lynch. The self-orchestrated death of Gordon of Khartoum launched the Thomas Cook travel business to the world; Dr. James Barry, the high-profile inspector-general of British Army Hospitals throughout the Crimean War, afterwards turned out to be a woman; there was no such person as "Tokyo Rose"—she was instead a figment of overactive American imaginations; and Napoleon's personal priest gave the emperor a post-mortem penisectomy. All said and done, I hope you have as much fun reading this book as I had putting it together.

THE GOOD,
THE BAD, AND
THE DEADLY

Ambulance Belle

Perhaps it was because he was essentially raised as a girl by his mother that Ernest Hemingway spent his life trying to out-macho everyone. Grace Hemingway managed to convince herself that "Ernestine" was in fact the twin of her beloved Marcelline. Dressing and tressing them the same, she held Marcelline back from school for a full year so the "girls" could commence their education together. It is perhaps little wonder that he constantly spoke of his involvement in conflict and wars, although his presence in the combat zone was mainly that of an observer.

Hemingway was full of tall tales of his derring-do during the Spanish Civil War (1936–39), but he was there only as a correspondent for the North American Newspaper Association (NANA). And a very focused reporter he was too. He fervently reported the misdeeds and atrocities of the revolutionary fascists and demanded that others in the pack followed suit. When John Dos Passos refused to toe Hemingway's line and continued to cover the atrocities of the equally brutal republicans, the two writers went their separate ways. Hemingway was already irked by Dos Passos' presence because he, along with his friend E. E. Cummings, really had served as an ambulance driver in World War I. According to his version of events, not only was he a heroic ambulance driver in wartime Italy, running maverick missions into fire zones where no other driver dared go, but he was also the first American wounded in that theater and collected such injuries rescuing the wounded from under the very muzzle of enemy fire.

In fact, his entire involvement with the American Red Cross in Italy ran from June 4 to July 8, 1918, during which time he only drove an ambulance twice, and neither time in action. After a brief induction in Milan, he was attached to Section Four at Schio, a town located some fifteen miles to the north of Vicenza and thus well removed from any action. Section Four had twenty-three ambulances, each with a crew of two, but the lack of any action in the area earned it the nickname of The

Schio Country Club as only three crews were put on standby on any one day. At some point before June 22, Hemingway was transferred to the canteen services at Fossalta which, on the Piave River in the Province of Venice, was very close to the action. Here he was in charge of a bicycle to ferry cigarettes and chocolate to the men in the trenches. On the night of July 8, he was going about such duties when he was blown off his bike by shrapnel from a mortar fired from the Austro-Hungarian positions; that much is true, but the extent of his injuries and what happened next was spun into a yarn that is still believed by some today.

According to Hemingway, despite the 227 pieces of shrapnel that had riddled his legs and lower body, he abandoned his "ambulance" to rescue an Italian soldier injured in the same blast. Now under heavy machine-gun fire, he tossed the man over his shoulder and began running for the Italian lines. Almost at once a bullet "shattered' his right knee but, brushing aside such inconsequential injuries, he recovered himself and his patient to sprint the last 100 yards to safety. Although he was indeed wounded by stray shrapnel that night, Hemingway seems to be the only one who remembers these events and, despite all attempts, no one was able to track down any wounded Italian dragged from the jaws of death by a young American. Either way, he was invalided out to Treviso and thence to Milan where he was awarded the *Croce di Guerra* by an Italian government which, not believing a word of the story either, was nevertheless keen to exploit the publicity at home and abroad.

Still only nineteen, Hemingway later told anyone open enough to listen that, with a body looking like a second-hand dartboard, he hobbled off to fight with the Arditi until the close of the war. Their name translating as "the bold," the Arditi were the world's first true Special Forces and would not have entertained the idea of taking on a raw recruit, especially one with a shattered knee and another 227 holes in him. In truth, his recovery dragged on for five months and then he boarded the *Giuseppe Verdi* on January 4, 1919, when it sailed from Genoa for New York. He was by then sporting a rather flamboyant Italian cape and a wholly unnecessary cane to support his "shattered" knee.

Hemingway's first published novel, *The Sun Also Rises* (1926), examined the footloose and rudderless generation dealing with the aftermath of World War I and, although this popularized the epithet of "Lost Generation" for such people, he did not coin it. He heard it first from Gertrude Stein, who had picked up the expression in France where it had been inspired by *enfants perdu*, lost children, the French military nickname for the first wave of attacking infantry, which had little chance of survival.

Carry on Doctor

There are many examples in history of women enlisting in the military services, despite contemporary prohibitions against female soldiers. The most frequently cited example is Hannah Snell, who lived well on her claims to have served as an eighteenth-century British Marine. No woman, however, was more successful in her deception than the audacious Miranda Barry, who played out her entire life as a man in the British Army, achieving the rank of inspector-general of British Military Hospitals.

To say that Barry's early life is shrouded in mystery is something of an understatement. Born Margaret Bulkley in 1795 in the quarters of army surgeon George Worgan at Old Train Barracks in Belfast, she was perhaps the niece of or otherwise related to the artist James Barry, hence the later pseudonym. Either way, she was raised by her mother and her circle of bohemian friends, which included Barry himself, Venezuelan revolutionary General Francisco de Miranda and David Erskine, 11th earl of Buchan, a dedicated if eccentric proponent of women's rights and education. There were also peripheral links to more stable and powerful figures such as Lord Fitzroy Somerset (Raglan) and Lord Charles Somerset, later governor of the Cape Colony (South Africa) and commander-in-chief of His Majesty's Forces. In short, Margaret was raised with some seriously influential strings to pull in later life.

At some point the child assumed the name of Miranda, doubtless after the Venezuelan general who, along with Erskine, convinced the girl that if she really wanted to study medicine and get on in life then she would have to dress and live like a man. (It would be another fifty years before women were allowed to practice medicine in the UK.) What might have started as a joke or perhaps some misguided sociological experiment by Erskine now set the pattern of her life. Adopting the name James Barry, she entered Edinburgh University in 1809 and, a brilliant student, emerged in 1812 with a medical degree after writing her final thesis in Latin on herniorrhaphy, a thesis dedicated to Lord Buchan. Still only seventeen, Britain's first ever female doctor joined the Army Medical Department where "he" (from now on we will use the male pronoun to avoid confusion) proved extremely able but unpopular. Barry could be blunt to the point of callous indifference, but those upon whom he unleashed his acerbity felt they had no choice but to tolerate the humiliations because of the influence he so obviously wielded throughout Whitehall and London at large.

Next he completed a civilian attachment to London's Guy's Hospital, where he showed an unusual expertise in obstetrics and gynecology, and instituted highly innovative programs of what today would be called preventative medicine. By now in full uniform and by all accounts a very handsome young man—if a trifle slight of build—Barry was posted to the Cape Colony (remember the Lord Somerset connection) in 1815 to serve as assistant surgeon at Table Bay Military Hospital. Wasting no time on niceties, he immediately got off to a bad start with the senior medical officer, Major McNab, who was expecting him to join the team as a junior. Barry soon put him straight on that issue, before loftily informing his boss he would not be requiring the quarters assigned him as he would be staying at the governor's house.

Over the next thirteen years, he and Governor Charles Somerset grew very close—unusually so, in fact. Cape society rattled with gossip of a homosexual affair, as the truth was not even guessed at. Perhaps the relationship did extend to the physical; upon death, Barry was discovered to have stretch marks, and in 1819 he had suddenly left the Cape to return to England where he went into hiding for a time. He also went absent without leave in 1829 from his Jamaican posting, yet on neither occasion was he reprimanded or required to explain his absence.

Nevertheless, Barry became very much the Cape crusader, instituting healthcare services for ordinary soldiers and their families that were way ahead of their time. On July 25, 1820, for example, he performed the Cape's first successful Caesarean section on the wife of Thomas Munnik, a prominent merchant who named the boy Barry in the surgeon's honor. Yet his private life was a mess. Doubtless a bisexual, Barry was an outrageous flirt with any pretty face in his social circle and once had to fight a pistol duel with one Captain Cloete, aide-de-camp to the governor, who objected to Barry getting over-cozy with his lady friend; neither was seriously injured and they subsequently became close friends.

The outbreak of the Crimean War in 1854 saw Barry with the ranks of brigadier-general and inspector-general of Military Hospitals, achievements no doubt bolstered by Fitzroy Somerset, who was by then Lord Raglan and in charge of British forces in that peninsula. Here too Barry left his mark, instituting basic health and hygiene regimes that dramatically decreased the horrendous death rate in the field hospitals. After his tour of duty in the Crimea, Barry went to Canada, again as inspector-general of British Military Hospitals, but by now he was sixty and not in the best of health.

In 1859 he was invalided back to England where, on July 25, 1865, he died. His secret was revealed when Sophia Bishop, the maid attached to his lodgings, ignored his wish to be buried in the nightshirt he was wearing, and proceeded to lay him out. She had already seen more than enough by the time army surgeon Major McKinnon arrived to buy her silence and issue a docket stating Barry was a male who had died of dysentery.

In next to no time, Barry's Marylebone home was besieged by Victorian England's equivalent of "men in black," who arrived in unmarked carriages to remove all his papers, possessions and even his pet dog,

Psyche. To his manservant, John, there was a generous pay-off with a one-way ticket back home to the West Indies before he was bundled into one of the waiting carriages. And that might have been the end of the matter had Bishop not smelled a guinea or two in her story. Thinking she had been short-changed by the army, she sold her story to Dublin's *Saunder's News Letter*, and the *Manchester Guardian* picked up on the item. The registrar-general demanded that Doctor McKinnon present himself under oath to be quite specific over the details on the death certificate, and the cat was well and truly out of the bag. But by this time, Barry had already been buried in London's Kensal Green Cemetery with full military honors and all his records vanished from the War Office.

Castro's Cuban Heel

Names can be so important to image. Just as the well-dressed of Covent Garden in London prefer to attend a performance of *La Traviata* by Giuseppe Verdi instead of *The Slut* by Joe Green, it is doubtful that generations of disaffected youth would have flocked to the banner of Ernesto Lynch, middle-class kid from the right side of the tracks in Argentina.

Che Guevara's family line traces straight back to the Lynches of Galway, Ireland, a family of substance at the center of lucrative trade between Ireland and Spain that ran from the 13th to the 17th centuries. In times of hardship or famine, most Irish migrants headed to North America, but those from Galway, with established Spanish connections, headed for Spain and South America and the first of Che's line to do so was Patrick Lynch (b. 1715), who moved to Argentina via business connections he had in Bilbao. Che's grandmother, Anna Lynch, was born in 1861 and her son, Ernesto Guevara Lynch, married in 1927 and had five children, another Ernesto Guevara (Che) arriving in 1928. Most sources state his date of birth to be June 14, but his birth certificate was doctored by his parents to bring conception within the bounds of respectability. (His mother later made no secret of this, or that his real date of birth was May 14, 1928.) As a kid his nickname was Chancho (Pig), on account of his abhorrence of washing or changing his clothes. "Che" was a nickname given him by the Cubans because of his habitual use of that Argentinean interjection which can mean anything from "hey!" to "pal."

Convinced by his father that the "blood of Irish rebels ran in his veins," Che does seem to have been proud of his Irish heritage. He is known to have visited Dublin in 1964 on his way to New York, and on March 13 the following year he stunned drinkers in Hanratty's Hotel on Limmerick's Glentworth Street when he sauntered in for a pint or three of Guinness. His Prague–Cuba flight had been interrupted owing to engine trouble and after touchdown in Ireland he spent his time in the company of Arthur Quinlan of the Dublin-based *Sunday Tribune*, who took him on a pub crawl ending back at *The White Horse* on the corner of O'Connell and Glentworth. According to Quinlan, Guevara was blind drunk and covered with shamocks from the pre-St Patrick's Day celebrations by the time he got back to the airport. But what of the face that launched a thousand T-shirts?

The iconic shot of Guevara was taken by Alberto Korda, official photographer to Castro and the Cuban Revolution. On March 4, 1960, Havana had been rocked by an enormous explosion when a French freighter loaded with munitions for Cuban forces blew up in the harbor. The incident was believed by some to have been an act of sabotage by the United States, and the memorial service to the dead, in which Castro gave one of his notoriously long-winded speeches, turned into something of an anti-American demonstration attended by the likes of Simone de Beauvoir and Jean-Paul Sartre. At some point, Guevara made an appearance, and as he moodily scanned the crowd Korda took a casual snap that lay in the bottom of a drawer until Guevara's death, when publisher Giangiacomo Feltrinelli became involved.

The son of an aristocratic family, Feltrinelli was something of a champagne communist, expelled from the Italian Communist Party for smuggling Boris Pasternak's novel *Doctor Zhivago* out of Russia and into Italy, where he published the first edition in 1957. Always in the right place at the right time, Feltrinelli was in Bolivia when Guevara was killed in October 1967 and immediately secured the rights to his Bolivian diaries. The only photographs the Bolivians had of Guevara were taken on his surrender, and they showed a scruffy and emaciated scarecrow of a man, so Feltrinelli flew to Cuba to get something more suitable for the dust jacket, where he met up with Korda.

Korda refused payment for the photo, providing it was used to present Guevara and the Cuban Revolution in a positive light. His original negative was due for some serious doctoring and image enhancement before achieving its iconic status. Korda had snapped Guevara staring down at the crowd from the elevated platform whereas the popular version has the subject staring slightly upward, wistfully and idealistically, at some distant horizon. Furthermore, in 1968 when *Vogue* fashion photographer, Don Honeyman, was examining the image prior to solarizing it, he noted incongruities and subsequently reported: "I worked over the image for several days but couldn't seem to get the same idealistic gleam in Che's eyes. I finally compared the first Che with the second, and discovered that some canny designer, presumably at the original Italian printers, had made Che slimmer and his face longer, by about one-sixth. It was so effective that I, too, stretched him, and it worked like a charm. It doesn't really do to have a revolutionary who's too plump."

And as for Guevara, man of the people, his masquerade falls at the first fence. Guevara was an extremely dangerous man whose death brought a smile to all who knew the reality. Had the young Ernie Lynch not fallen in with Fidel and Raul Castro in Mexico City in the summer of 1955, he would in all likelihood have continued his life of anonymous wanderings. Armed with forged documentation professing him a doctor (it is a myth of his own making that he was medically qualified), Che managed to get himself accepted as medical officer to the Cuban Revolutionary Forces, even though he just about knew that bandages went sticky side down. During the crossing from Yucatan to Cuba, he was found slumped in a cabin, almost comatose from seasickness and asthma, prompting Fidel Castro to pronounce him useless and suggest chucking him over the side.

About a year into his tenure in Cuba, Castro suggested in a conversation with Lazaro Asencio, "Know what I am going to do with Che Guevara? I'm going to Santo Domingo and see if Trujillo kills him." Raphael Trujillo, dictator of the Dominican Republic, was annoyed with Castro for aiding rebels in his country, so it would have been a dangerous mission had it happened. But the point is that Che was not exactly top of Castro's love list and never had been; the notion of them as comrades-in-arms or friends of any kind is pure fantasy.

As soon as his feet hit Cuban soil, Che's darker side emerged. On January 28, 1957, he wrote to his wife that he was "Here in the Cuban jungle, alive and bloodthirsty." His diary for the same month eulogizes the value of "unbending hatred" to "push a human being beyond his natural limitations, making him into an effective, violent, selective and cold-blooded killing machine." Guevara was certainly at ease with killing, especially when the victims were gagged and bound so he could taunt them before shooting them in the head. In fact, he appeared to so enjoy killing people trussed up like chickens that he used to record the details of the entrance and exit wounds and anything he stole from his victims. After he had casually shot one Eutimio Guerra, whom he suspected of passing on information, he wrote: "I ended the problem with a .32 caliber pistol, in the right side of his brain . . . His belongings were now mine." To attract the suspicions of Che was a death sentence; Jamie Costa Vazquez, one of the original Yucatan-Cuba group, later revealed that Guevara's mantra was "If in doubt, kill."

Once the Communist-backed Revolutionary Forces were in control, Guevara ran the San Carlos de la Cabana fortress, into which he crammed nearly one thousand "enemies of the revolution" where there was space for only about two hundred. Just how many were killed here, either by Guevara in person or by firing squad, is unclear, but when he was finally captured in Bolivia in October 1967, where he was leading a guerrilla force, he did not query the figure of two thousand personal shootings, only arguing that they had all been CIA-backed enemies of the revolution. Apart from his own hands-on killings, whenever he attended firing squads—which was often—he insisted on delivering the final pistol shot to the head himself; by his own admission he had a "thing" about shooting people in the head. Countless statements by guards and prisoners at La Cabana also give matching accounts of him prankishly firing indiscriminately through the barred windows of the cells from time to time to "keep the prisoners on their toes." Interviewed later at his home in Puerto Rico, Javier Arzuaga, the Basque chaplain assigned to La Cabana, recalled how he often tried to intervene, especially in the case of children and boys not yet sixteen, but Guevara was inflexible. Eventually tiring of this turbulent priest, Guevara made it clear to Arzuaga that he should leave Cuba or "When we take our masks off, we will be enemies." Although slightly enigmatic, the clarity of the threat was enough for Arzuaga, who took the hint and fled.

Apart from the executions, Guevara set up concentration and labor camps to hold the ever-burgeoning number of "dissidents." To qualify as a dissident was not difficult, as this catch-all term embraced vagrants, drunks, *Roqueros* (those caught listening to "Yankee Imperialist rock-music"), gays, Jehovah's Witnesses and anyone who disagreed with the letter of Che's thinking. He even tried at one point to impose a Taliban-like morality police force to "regulate the interaction" between men and women and the use of alcohol. Castro was quick to quash this move, knowing that even the Cubans would rise up mob-handed if anyone messed with their "rum 'n rumba."

Having murdered so many of those he had come to liberate, Guevara turned his attention to the economy which, sadly for Cuba, suffered equally in his care. Guevara brought the island to its knees with hare-brained schemes that inflicted far more damage to the economy than anything the American embargo achieved. At one point, he brought in a fleet of snowplows from Czechoslovakia to mechanize the harvesting of the sugar crops, which destroyed the plantations and set the Cuban sugar business back five years. By 1964 the Kremlin had had enough of Che and his madcap schemes; indeed, Humberto Fontova, a man who has written extensively of post-revolutionary Cuba, conjectures that Khrushchev's sudden capitulation at the end of October 1962 over the Missile Crisis was likely due to his horrified realization that Guevara really wanted to start a war. Talking to the *London Daily Worker* in November 1962, Guevara said, "If the missiles had remained we would have used them against the very heart of the US, including New York City . . . the victory of socialism is well worth millions of atomic victims." It seems Khrushchev was right to be concerned. In an attempt to ensure the crisis went the distance, Guevara planned a terrorist bombing of Macy's, Gimbels, and Bloomingdale's stores and Grand Central Terminal with 1,100 pounds of TNT (five times the amount used in the 2004 Madrid bombings that killed 191 and injured 1,700) on the day after Thanksgiving, November 23, the busiest shopping day in the American retail calendar. Fortunately the FBI foiled the plan, and with it Guevara's intention of implicating the Russians in the atrocity to bring about a full East–West confrontation and perhaps the nuclear holocaust of which he spoke so glibly.

Enough was enough. The Kremlin told Castro they would stop payrolling him if Guevara remained so, increasingly resentful of the international star Guevara had become, Castro readily agreed. Guevara resolved to make his impending departure from the Cuban stage appear an issue of political integrity and, unable to see the folly of his plan, on December 17, 1964, he embarked on a sort of farewell tour that peaked in Algeria. There, on February 24, 1965, he made the biggest mistake of his life with a speech denouncing the Russians as "accomplices of the imperialist exploitation." He returned to Cuba on March 14 and was placed under virtual house arrest, with the very real possibility of being handed over to someone like himself for disposal. Realizing that he had to make every word count, this is when he penned his cringe-inducing "Farewell to Fidel" letter in which, after much toe-curling prose about what a hero Castro was, Guevara asked to be relieved of all posts, offices and even his Cuban citizenship so he could fulfill his destiny as some sort of shadowy emissary, taking Castro's revolutionary principles to other lands, never to return. In short, he was begging for his life in exchange for his quitting Cuba for good, at the same time placing in Castro's hands a letter absolving him of blame for whatever happened next.

Guevara first went to the Congo, teaming up with two other homicidal figures, Laurent-Desire Kabila and Pierre Mulele, but soon bored of their struggle to overthrow the equally murderous and corrupt Mobutu regime. Realizing he had buried himself in a backwater, Guevara let it be known he would like to go back to Cuba but Castro, horrified by the prospect of his return, made public the "Farewell" letter proclaiming Guevara's desire to roam the globe, never to return. So, condemned to the life of a wandering revolutionary by his own florid prose, Guevara sulked a while in Dar es Salaam and Prague before taking himself off to Bolivia, where he was killed on October 9. Tracked to his base in the country's eastern lowlands, he and his rather grandly named National Liberation Army were ambushed in the Yuro Ravine, where Guevara exhorted his hapless minions to "fight to the last man and the last bullet." He, on the other hand, seems to have been quite enthusiastic in his surrender. With the firefight still in full swing, Guevara, only used to shooting at unarmed people, crawled up the ravine toward the Bolivian soldiers shouting, "Don't shoot; I'm Che; I'm worth more to you alive." He threw out his weapons and went meekly to the Bolivian camp, where he offered to treat their wounded; asked if he was a doctor, he answered, truthfully for the first time, "No; but I do have a little medical knowledge."

Unfortunately for Guevara, the Bolivians did not concur with his self-evaluation and thought him better dead than grandstanding at some expensive trial. Annoyed he had not died in the battle, they radioed back news of his capture and awaited instructions. They soon received a message telling them to initiate Operation *Five-Hundred/Six Hundred*—"Five Hundred" was the code for Guevara and "Six Hundred" meant "execute." Some of the Bolivians drew straws to see who got the job of riddling him with bullets to make it look like he had died in the firefight, and Sergeant Mario Teran took the short straw and an M-2 carbine to do the job. On October 10, doctors Moisés Baptista and José Martínez Cazo of the Hospital Knights of Malta, Vallegrande, Bolivia, both signed a death certificate stating "on October 9 at 5:30 p.m., there arrived Ernesto Guevara Lynch, approximately forty years of age, the cause of death being multiple bullet wounds in the thorax and extremities." At least they got his name right.

The continued adulation of a man who thought blacks "indolent," South Americans "small-minded-animals," Mexicans "a rabble of illiterate Indians," and that anyone who played or listened to pop music should be shot is itself an enduring mystery.

Cicero—Warts and All

One of the most bizarre and underrated figures of World War II was Elyesa Bazna, born in Kosovo to a family of Albanian Muslims, leaving home in his teens to seek ill-gotten gains in Turkey. After various shady dealings he landed the job of valet to the Yugoslav ambassador to Turkey, but left under a cloud to work for the German consul, from which he was sacked for reading through confidential mail. By 1942 he was again a valet, this time to Sir Hugh Knatchbull-Hugessen, British ambassador to Turkey, who did not have him fully screened. When this oversight was picked up, MI5 (the UK counter-intelligence and security agency) gave Bazna deeper scrutiny and pronounced him "too stupid to be a spy." In October of that year, while Sir Hugh was taking a bath, Bazna took impressions of his boss's keys and had one of his criminal associates make a set.

On October 21, Bazna began to photograph every sensitive document that came through the embassy, whether it was stored in the safe or the now not-so-secure diplomatic bag. When he had established a nice little portfolio of secrets—fifty-six documents in all—he made contact with Ludwig Moyzisch, an attaché at the German Embassy, and negotiated a job-lot price of £20,000. Moyzisch codenamed him "Cicero" for the "eloquence" of his merchandise, presumably unaware that the Roman orator's family endured that surname to celebrate an ancestor with a massive wart on the end of his nose, shaped like a *cicer*, Latin for "chickpea." At the time, this codename was unknown to Bazna, who related to the Germans under his own chosen codename of "Pierre."

Berlin was not sure what to make of Cicero; the quality of his material was so good that they were naturally suspicious. It is known that at some point he sold Moyzisch some documents relating to the D-Day landings, but exactly how sensitive and detailed these were is argued to this day. After these had been transferred to Berlin, Moyzisch told Bazna that Hitler was so pleased that he was going to give him a villa in Germany and a handsome pension after the war. In fact, the bulk of opinion in Berlin was that Cicero was so good that he had to be a plant. He had accurately forewarned them of the Allied air raids on Sofia, Bulgaria, in December 1943 and early 1944, but the opinion in Berlin was that this had just been a taster to lead them up to some sucker punch.

Bazna continued his operations until late in the spring of 1944, by which time he had amassed something in the region of £500,000, perhaps $17 million at today's values, making him the highest-paid spy in history at that time. But the times were changing, and rapidly. Turkey was turning against Germany (it would break all diplomatic ties in August and declare war on Germany in February 1945) and Moyzisch's secretary, Nele Kapp, daughter of the German consul-general in Sofia, turned out to be an American agent. Fearful of exposure, Bazna packed up his ill-gotten gains and slipped away to South America to build a hotel and retire in luxury. With the Gestapo hot on her heels, Kapp made it safely to America where she eventually settled in California. And through sheer bad judgment of one individual, the British had already thrown away their chance to identify the leak in Ankara and learn a great deal more besides.

In August 1943, closet anti-Nazi German diplomat, Fritz Kolbe, was sent as a courier to Berne in Switzerland, where he took the chance to

visit the British Embassy to offer his services as a source of information. The military attaché, Colonel Henry Cartwright, thought Kolbe
was a plant (there had been earlier incidents of Gestapo agents posing
as anti-Nazis) and, denouncing him as a cad, had him thrown physically
into the street. Dusting himself off, Kolbe nipped round to the American Embassy where he was better received and assigned Allen Dulles as
a handler. Demanding not a penny for his services and later hailed by
the Americans as the most important intelligence source of the whole
war, Kolbe told the Americans the identity of Cicero and much more
through the thirty-one hundred documents he passed to them.

Bazna, meanwhile, was locked in highly animated talks with his bank
in Argentina after being told that the money he had deposited with them
was counterfeit; the Germans had been paying him with their famous
forged £5 notes all along. He returned to West Germany after the war,
but failed in his rather ridiculous lawsuit demanding that the new government make good the payment. Moyzisch also returned to Germany
to write *Operation Cicero* (1950) before disappearing into obscurity, leaving Bazna to write *I Was Cicero* (1962) before he died, a penniless night-
watchman in Munich. Kolbe eventually settled in America to sell power
saws for a living, while Dulles would later become head of the CIA.

The Fat Controller

Forenamed Benito on account of his father's misplaced admiration for
Mexican president Benito Juarez, Mussolini was a thug from the very
beginning. He was thrown out of his first boarding school by the monk
he had just stabbed in the backside with the same knife he had previously used on fellow pupils. The mere mention of his name today will
elicit a chorus of comments celebrating his getting the trains to run on
time. It seems not.

The train myth is tied up with the *Marcia su Roma* (March on Rome)
fable that supposedly took place on October 28, 1922. As Mussolini would

have it told, he sat tall on a white stallion to lead a column of thirty thousand fascists in a march on the capital to seize power. In fact, he was formally invited by King Victor Emanuel III to come out of hiding in Milan and form a government. Far from any march, Mussolini and his small entourage of thugs made the journey by train, first class all the way, and kept everyone waiting because, like all Italian trains of the day, his was running hours late.

Once in Rome he summoned the international press and, in a jovial mood, told his audience that all would be fine now that he was in control. "Even the trains will run on time" he wisecracked, knowing the Italian railway system to be a well-established joke. This comment appealed to the journalists, who repeated it so much that it became a truth. Mussolini was in no way being serious—even he knew that world domination would be a piece of cake compared with re-organizing the Italian railways. According to Carlo Crova, then general manager of the Italian State Railways, the infamous levels of incompetence and inefficiency continued unchanged throughout Mussolini's tenure and at no time did Il Duce himself offer to do anything about it.

Most detrimental to Italy's war effort, however, was the man's capacity for self-delusion, especially when it came to the size and capabilities of the Italian Air Force. Heavily influenced by General Giulio Douhet, an Italian military theorist who predicted that all modern wars would be contested by bombers alone, Mussolini was convinced that—with the right kind of bomber—he could wipe London off the map in six days. Already in syphilitic megalomania before the beginning of World War II (having contracted the disease as a young man), Mussolini was highly attracted to the image of his reaching out and zapping enemy cities with a wave of his hand, and he particularly liked Douhet's prediction that all Italian bombers would be hidden from ground fire by their own smoke-screens. The sane might have asked how the smoke would stay with the plane in flight, or why enemy gunners could not just fire blindly into the middle of such a spectacle, but not Benito, who lied to Hitler so often about the size of the Italian Air Force and airplane production capability that he actually began to believe his own tales.

Not wishing to end up swinging from a lamp-post, assorted Air Ministry officials and air marshals played along, even organizing for entire squadrons to be flown from one airfield to the next to be counted again and again when Mussolini went on tour to drool over his imagined 8,530 airplanes. The true figure was in fact about 400 bombers and 100 fighters, with maximum production capability perhaps 60–70 aircraft per month instead of the 500 that Mussolini proclaimed. Throughout the entire war the Italians produced only 11,508 planes, fewer than they did in World War I and pitiful compared with America's output of 297,199 aircraft throughout a shorter involvement in World War II.

Come September 1943, when Italy signed an armistice with the Allies, even the myopic could read the proverbial writing on the wall. Mussolini had been ousted from government the previous July, by which time his air force had been blown out of the sky and a staggering 1,476,987 Italians had already rushed to surrender. (Italy's most crushing defeat came during Operation *Compass* in the Western Desert in December 1940–February 1941. One flustered British Guards officer famously radioed for instructions after finding himself in possession of "Five acres of officers and two hundred acres of other ranks.") Mussolini had been rescued by Hitler and was installed as the puppet leader of the German-controlled "Italian Social Republic" in the north of the country. In April 1945, with Germany just days away from final defeat, Mussolini and his girlfriend, Clara Petacci, made a bid for Switzerland but were caught by partisans and, shot out of hand, their bodies were hung upside down in a square in Milan. For days the dead couple were shot at and generally abused, then she was dumped somewhere and he was buried in an unmarked grave in the Musocco cemetery to the north of the city, but not for long. The following Easter someone resurrected him, and a suitcase containing Benito's bones was passed from one neo-fascist group to another while the police brought up the rear. The suitcase was finally reclaimed and held in secret locations by successive administrations for ten years until 1957, when permission was given for the body to be laid to rest in a marble crypt in Mussolini's home town of Predappio.

From Bad to Wirz

That conditions in the Confederate-run POW camp at Andersonville, Georgia, constituted an atrocity is beyond dispute, but where the ultimate responsibility lay for those murderous conditions is very much open to debate. After the end of the Civil War in 1865, the camp commander, Captain Henry Wirz, attained the dubious distinction of being the first man to stand trial for war crimes, but the overwhelming balance of evidence would seem to underpin Robert E. Lee's opinion that the trial was nothing but a judicial lynching.

Frail and sickly, Wirz was a Swiss national who practiced medicine in Kentucky and Louisiana before joining the 4th Louisiana Infantry. He was invalided out of active service after the battle of Seven Pines in 1862 and assigned to the staff of Brigadier-General John Winder, who held overall responsibility for various prison facilities. Close to Winder's own HQ was Camp Sumter, the Confederate name for Andersonville, to which he appointed Wirz as commander on March 27, 1864, although he didn't actually take up the post until April 12.

Neither designed nor intended to hold more than 10,000 people, the camp had been set up by Captain Richard Winder, son of Brigadier-General Winder, and received its first prisoners on February 17, 1864. Within a week, Winder fils was sending out frantic demands for more supplies to cater for the mushrooming population in his care. Throughout the relevant period, Winder père maintained his HQ at Andersonville, so he can hardly have been unaware of the disaster unfolding under his very nose, but his only positive action was to pull his son out of the hellhole and send in Wirz to carry the can. The tide of new prisoners peaked at 31,678 in July 1864 after which, through death and transfers, the numbers dwindled to about 10,000. Most of these were sent home in the massive prisoner exchange of March 1865 to leave the camp all but deserted. In the fourteen months the prison had been open, it received a total of 45,000 prisoners, 13,000 of whom died from disease, malnutrition, exposure or casual violence.

Wirz remained at the camp until arrested on May 7, 1865, by Captain H. E. Noyes, attached to the staff of General James Wilson, and transported to Washington for trial. The Union had really wanted to show-trial General Winder, but he eluded them with a fatal heart attack, leaving Wirz in the frame. The trial lasted from August 23 to October 23, when he was convicted on all charges and hanged on November 10 in Washington's Old Capitol Prison where he was buried, without rites, next to the conspirators of the Lincoln assassination. The court martial was only too diligent in its determination to exclude evidence likely to cloud the issue of Wirz's predetermined guilt.

The first charge, of which Wirz was inevitably convicted, accused him of "combining, confederating and conspiring together with Jefferson Davis, Howell Cobb, John Winder, R. B. Winder and W. S. Winder [another son of Brigadier-General Winder], Isaiah White, Randolph Stevenson and others to impair and injure the health and to destroy the lives of large numbers of Federal prisoners at Andersonville." In other words, Wirz had presided over a death camp. His defense, headed by the eminent Louis Schade, pointed out that if such a conspiracy had existed then there would, by necessity, be a wealth of telegraph messages and diary entries to back up the allegation, but this point was swept aside. The prosecution further leveled thirteen specimen charges of Wirz's personal and hands-on brutality which, together with lurid and perjured testimony from a procession of hand-picked and groomed witnesses, painted a picture of the man gleefully presiding over the horrors, cackling maniacally while variously shooting, clubbing or beating prisoners to death for his own twisted entertainment. The wound Wirz received at Seven Pines had shattered his right wrist, leaving him in constant pain and quite unable to beat or club anyone; any attempt on his part to pistol-whip a man or fire but a single shot would have left him in agony for days, but when Schade attempted to put forward such awkward facts he was overruled.

As with so many other officially organized frame-ups, the Union conspirators were so confident of the outcome that they became sloppy with their facts and figures. Specimen Charges 1–4 inclusive had Wirz variously shooting, stomping and beating assorted prisoners to death on specific dates and times yet, despite these brutal and sadistic acts taking place in front of thousands of witnesses, no one could actually name the victims of Wirz's rampages. Charge 5 had Wirz leaving a man to die in the stocks on August 20, 1864, despite irrefutable evidence he was on sick leave for the whole of that month. Charge 6 had Wirz again using the stocks for slow killing, but this time on February 1, 1864, before the camp was even open and six weeks before he himself arrived. Charge 7 laid out a gruesome incident in which Wirz allegedly had a group of prisoners march in chains until dead yet, again, no names or details were forthcoming despite this incident supposedly happening in broad daylight in front of the whole camp.

Charges 8 and 9 put a new word into the English language. These claimed that Wirz had ordered a sentry to shoot dead two other (nameless) prisoners who had strayed into the no man's land that existed between the outer stockade and another line running parallel some 18 feet into the camp. Any man entering that buffer corridor around the camp was assumed to be attempting escape and liable to be shot. This was the "deadline" of which the court made so much that the press picked up on it as a new term for a cut-off point. Whether Wirz had done this on May 15, 1864, it would in no way constitute a war crime since all POW camps, Northern and Southern, had such a line and imposed the rule unwaveringly. Charge 10 had Wirz shooting prisoners, again while absent in August 1864; charge 11 had him setting dogs onto prisoners, again unnamed; charge 12 described another deadline incident and charge 13 had him holding a cowering man with his left hand to pistol-whip him to death in the mud; medical evidence showing that it had been over two years since Wirz could move his right arm to any degree was, of course, ruled inadmissible.

Star witness for the prosecution was the exotically named Felix de la Baume, who seems to have been omnipresent in the camp and experienced no difficulty in moving with lightning speed across a compound packed like a sardine can to witness every one of Wirz's crimes. In reality a Union deserter named Felix Oeser, he had been set up with a nice job in the Department of the Interior before the trial began. Then there was Dr. Joseph Jones, a Confederate doctor who had made a tour of inspection at Camp Sumter and accurately recorded the horrors in a report. Willing to testify, he was shocked to find out that snippets of his report were taken out of context and twisted to implicate Wirz. Any attempts he made to clarify the issue were quashed; he was required only to answer yes or no as to whether the extracts read out came from his report.

In fact, Wirz had done everything he could to improve conditions in the camp, including on one occasion boarding a train he knew to be carrying General Richard Taylor, the departmental commander on an inspection tour of Georgia. Bursting unannounced into the general's compartment, he somewhat forcefully put his problems regarding the lack of food, blankets, medicines and wagons to haul fuel. He left Taylor with copies of all the requests for supplies he had previously sent and Taylor, whose offer of testimony was rejected out of hand, later wrote: "I knew nothing of this Wirz, who I then met for the first and only time, but he appeared earnest in his desire to mitigate the conditions of his prisoners." Wirz had also stamped out the activities of a group known as the Raiders, gangs of Union prisoners who robbed their fellow inmates of anything and everything. He cabled his superiors to get permission to hold proper trials and issue punishment, an effort which was hardly in keeping with the image of a gun-toting psycho. If Wirz was indeed a monster, keen to bring about the deaths of as many of his charges as possible, why would he stop the Raiders at all? Or, as a man who loved to dole out punishment on the spot as and when he saw fit, why would he go through the proper channels to sort out a group he could gun down himself before breakfast? As it was, after a fairer trial than he himself received, the six ringleaders—Patrick Delaney, Charles Curtis, William Collins, James Sarsfield, John Sullivan and A. Munn—were hanged, not by Wirz but by eager volunteers from the Union prisoners themselves. Theirs are the only graves at Andersonville set apart from the rest and with no flag or decorations.

Ultimately, no one could help Wirz or his charges. The Union's reworked Anaconda Plan (see "Louisiana Anna," page 36), which destroyed the rail and transport network to inhibit the movement of goods, was strangling the South. Nothing was getting through the Union naval blockades and, to further impoverish the South, the North had ceased all exchange of prisoners, forcing the enemy to cope with large numbers of unwanted mouths to feed. Besides, conditions and death rates in many Union camps were no better than Andersonville. The most horrendous Union-run camp was Elmira in New York State where over 9,000 half-naked and starving wretches were packed into a camp designed to hold 5,000. Punishments ranged from being starved to death in sweatboxes to being strung up by the thumbs for the entertainment of the locals, who paid 15 cents a time to watch the fun from observation towers. In all, 3,000 died there.

It must also be remembered that Wirz's trial took place in the witch-hunt days after the assassination of Lincoln, so he didn't stand a chance. Even after his death he was ridiculed in the press for not being man enough to face his end with dignity, instead trying to get his wife, Elizabeth, to smuggle in a cyanide pill to help him cheat the rope. The story first appeared in the *New York Times* of November 11, 1865, in an account by General L. C. Baker who claimed to have foiled the ploy after suspecting something had been transferred during the goodbye kiss. Baker claims his coup of eagle-eyed diligence took place on October 27, a day that Mrs. Wirz was nearly one thousand miles away from Washington. His descendants, most notably Colonel Heinrich Wirz of the Swiss Army, have repeatedly but unsuccessfully tried to clear the family name, and hold a memorial service for Captain Henry every year at Andersonville.

Jane's Fighting Quips

Born Martha Jane Cannary or Canary, the woman remembered as Calamity Jane was no feisty Indian-fighting Army scout with her pouting charms tightly restrained by her 7th Cavalry uniform; the wholesome pertness projected by Doris Day in *Calamity Jane* (1953) is nothing short of laughable. Tall—approaching six feet—the real Calamity Jane was so weather-beaten and masculine of appearance that, on the rare occasions she did wear a dress, she looked like a desperado in drag. The *Black Hills Daily Times* once described her as looking like a Sioux Indian. Never attached to any army unit in any capacity, she frequently turned to prostitution to fund her prodigious capacity for whisky. Between 1876 and perhaps 1882 she was also something of a regular in the brothels of Dora DuFran and it was the dubious pleasures of her bed chamber which produced her nickname; *Jane* is a long-standing Americanism for a prostitute so "useless hooker" might be a more accurate, if unkind, interpretation of her soubriquet. The fact that her middle name was indeed Jane was a happy coincidence.

Permanently befuddled by drink, she did organize the ghost-writing of a couple of pamphlets, which are responsible for most of the misconceptions regarding her life, but she was always careful to claim association with dead characters who, safely in the graves, could not rise up to call her a liar.

According to these pamphlets, Calamity first enlisted in the U.S. Army at Fort Russell in Wyoming in 1870 and stayed there to serve under Custer, but there is no record of either of them ever having been at Fort Russell. (Women were not permitted to enlist, only to attach themselves to a regiment as laundresses or cooks.) She also claimed to have scouted and ridden point (advance recon) for Custer's regiment during the Arizona campaigns, a series of punitive expeditions mounted against the Apache nations. However, these only started in earnest in 1876, the year of Custer's death, so he was never involved in the wars, which dragged on until the apprehension of Geronimo in 1886. Besides, Elizabeth Custer wrote with pride at having been the only woman ever to ride with her husband's regiment and labors that point in her *Boots and Saddles* (1885). But that same book does mention a woman who *did* fight with Custer's command on several occasions, and it wasn't Calamity Jane.

Apparently, the Custers' personal laundress and seamstress, Mrs. Nash, perhaps of Mexican blood, was something of a star. Apart from keeping the Custers' clothes crisp and clean, she could cook, bake, made her own dresses, and married or entered into arrangements with a succession of troopers and NCOs. She was also first-choice midwife for any woman whose time fell due while with the regiment. If under attack, all marveled at the agility with which Mrs. Nash grabbed a rifle and sprang gazelle-like to the battlements, where her ability to pick off a fast-moving rider at several hundred yards impressed the hell out of all who fought alongside her. There was nothing, it seemed, to which she could not turn her hand. When she died in Fort Lincoln, North Dakota, in 1878, her last wish, to be buried straightaway in the clothes she lay in, was ignored. Those who laid her out discovered she was in fact a man—and a rather hairy one at that. The veil she habitually wore was not for the reasons of demure modesty she always claimed, but to hide the moustache. By this time known as Mrs. Sergeant Noonan, her then "husband" shot himself in the fort's blacksmith's shop when he realized the game was up. But back to Calamity.

By 1873 she was supposedly under the command of one Captain Egan, whom she had rescued single-handedly at Goose Creek after he lay wounded by Indians who were about to finish him off. According to her, this is how she gained her nickname. Egan, in manly gratitude, supposedly proclaimed: "I name you Calamity Jane, the heroine of the plains." Not only are there references to her as Calamity Jane long before 1873, but such a nickname hardly resonates with the sentiments of a man grateful for being snatched from the jaws of death. Nor was she resident scout at Fort Laramie, Wyoming, where she claims to have first met Wild Bill Hickok. She only struck up a vague acquaintance with him in July 1876 on a wagon train bound for Deadwood—the town where he was killed on August 2 the same year, so there was hardly time for the pair to establish the intimate bond of which Calamity later made so much.

Hickok really had operated as an Army scout, and most of Calamity's yarns are reworkings of his adventures put into print after he was dead and buried. His real name was James, but after he killed one Jack McCanles for repeatedly calling him "duck-bill" because of his protruding upper lip and buck teeth others, quite content with the standard number of holes in their bodies, modified the soubriquet. Nor was he much of a gunslinger either. Poor eyesight, compounded by early-onset glaucoma, often led him to shoot at the wrong man—when he was marshal of Abilene in 1871 he shot his own deputy, Mike Williams, in the head (twice!) while trying to quell a street riot. Be that as it may, in Calamity's last venture into print, just before her death, she claimed to have been the love of Hickok's life—they had married in secret and produced a child; pretty good going for a four-week scrape.

Fortunately for a later fraudster, Calamity did indeed drift into Deadwood in 1895 with an orphaned girl for whom the locals organized a collection to fund the child's education at the nearby (and extant) St. Martin's Convent in Sturgis. To the disgust of all who contributed, she promptly ditched the kid in the street and spent the money on an almighty drinking spree. But this incident, combined with Calamity's claims to have been Hickok's wife and mother to his child, was enough to encourage a woman, calling herself Jean Hickok McCormick, to tout herself around in 1941 as the result of that imaginary passion. Failing to spot the glaring flaws in the bundle of clumsy forgeries she presented to substantiate her claims, the *Billings Montana Gazette* splashed her across the front page and CBS picked up on the story for an edition of the series *We the People*. Despite Hickok's only known descendant, Martha Dewey, coming forward to prove McCormick a liar who was not even born until four years after Hickok's death, she continued to do well out of the imposture, simply because people *wanted* to believe her. Her yarns inspired the aforementioned Doris Day film, and the main storyline of Larry McMurtry's book *Buffalo Girls* (1990) was made into a film in 1995.

Having worn out her welcome in every town throughout the Dakotas, Calamity ended her days washing sheets in Dora DuFran's brothel in Belle Fourche, South Dakota, where the bottle finally killed her.

Kentucky 'Fraid Chicken?

Unknown until the age of thirty-one and dead by forty, it is something of a miracle that Kentucky-born Jim Bowie achieved the reputation he enjoys to this day. Most think of him as a straight-shooting hero who carved out his place in history with his grit and rough-diamond goodness—but reputations could be cheaply won in Bowie's times, and usually at others' expense.

Bowie began a criminal career in 1818 when, still only twenty-two, he and his brother Rezin went in for a bit of smuggling with the notorious pirate, Jean Lafitte. Next, he became involved with the illegal slave trade in an admittedly rather clever way. After 1808, the importation of new slaves into America had been outlawed, but Lafitte and others were still trafficking into a compound on Galveston Island, then a haven of free enterprise favored by those with scant regard for the petty irritations of the law. Bowie bought slaves from Lafitte and, having transported them over to the mainland, he had Rezin report him to the customs for the reward. The slaves would then be impounded as contraband, but the same law also required Bowie to be paid half the value that the slaves would have realized at auction, had he been able to sell them on the open market. Having taken possession of the contraband, the customs were obliged to offer the slaves up for sale, at which point Bowie would buy them back at a knock-down price, having made it clear that other bidders might meet with a nasty accident. Now armed with paperwork declaring the slaves a bona fide purchase from an official customs sale and thus legal, Bowie was free to move them on to the slave markets of New Orleans to double his money. He and Rezin worked this scam so many times that, in the end, the custom house officials they favored simply shuffled the paperwork, took their cut and bid the Bowies bon voyage.

By 1825 James and Rezin had amassed something in the region of $100,000 from such shenanigans and so, joined by their younger brother Stephen, the trio turned their attention to fraudulent land scams, which boiled down to selling land they didn't own. In 1827 alone, the Arkansas Superior Court handled 126 claims from disgruntled purchasers who had been fleeced by the Bowies and their forged land grants. It was also in the September of that year that James Bowie came to wider attention after he rode into Natchez to watch a duel between Samuel Wills and Dr. Thomas Maddox who, for reasons long forgotten, had agreed to shoot it out on a sandbar. Both men were too drunk to hit a barn door and, after firing off a few wild shots, they decided to patch up their differences over a drink. This should have been the end of the matter. However, there was bad blood between some of the spectators and seconds—especially between Bowie and Norris Wright, sheriff of Rapides Parish—and a rather ugly melee ensued during which Bowie, having been shot and stabbed, killed said sheriff with a large butcher's knife he just happened to have about his person.

Even in the Mississippi of the day, killing a sheriff raised a few eyebrows, but Bowie's plea of self-defense was accepted by the jury (which may or may not have been intimidated), leaving Bowie enough of a dark celebrity to prompt the production of so-called Bowie knives, which bore no resemblance to the machete-like thing he had wielded at Natchez. (In fact, a Bowie knife is nothing more than a stylized bayonet, most of which were made in Sheffield, England, engraved with the criminal's name and shipped out to America to cash in on a new fashion.) Bowie, who made nothing out of this trade, used his new "standing" to expand his fraudulent land dealings into other states. By 1830, he had assumed Mexican citizenship so he could resume his questionable land dealings in Texas after making that his permanent home. Indeed, right up to his death at the battle of the Alamo in 1836—where Colonel Travis noted him to be extremely quarrelsome, obstreperous and "roaring drunk all the time"—Bowie was a decidedly shady operator with a great many out-of-pocket businessmen after his blood. Most accounts agree that Bowie was either dead or dying of typhoid when the Alamo fell, this being twisted by some to bolster up claims that, while others died like heroes, Bowie was found hiding under his bed, dragged out and shot. This is completely at odds with the vast majority of accounts of the man; he was most definitely a liar, a thief and a cheat, but cowardice does not seem to be a charge that anyone could lay at his door.

The Liar, the Witch, and the Wardroom

The supporters of Helen Duncan are still clamoring for a pardon to clear her name, claiming she was prosecuted as a witch on the express instructions of Winston Churchill. Found guilty, her nine-month sentence was, according to her supporters, a callous ploy by a War Office determined to keep her on ice to prevent her "powers" revealing details of the forthcoming D-Day landings. In fact, her trial is rightly famous for being the only time that a branch of the British forces, in this case the Royal Navy, targeted a clairvoyant and set up a sting operation to put her out of business and into jail.

Duncan attracted controversy from first to last. When the London Spiritual Alliance denounced her as a fraud in 1931, she tried to overcome this hindrance to her earning capacity by presenting herself for testing at the National Laboratory of Psychical Research. Aware that her favorite method of producing manifestations in darkened rooms involved her regurgitating cheesecloth, the institute's fraud-finder general, Harry Price, surprised her with a pre-test X-ray, which prompted Duncan to run screaming from the building. In 1934, she was prosecuted in Edinburgh as a fraudulent medium after being caught waving around a stockinet vest in the dark to convince her audience they had a visitor from the other side. She paid the fine to avoid the alternative of one month in prison.

By 1941 Duncan's specialty was war widows, claiming to have a hotline to dead sailors from the sinkings of HMS *Hood* and the HMS *Barham*. HMS *Hood* had exploded, hit by a shell from the *Bismarck*, on Saturday, May 24, 1941, leaving only three surviving crew members. Duncan's supporters claim she knew about it long before the official announcements, telling clients of its sinking while the event was still being kept secret by concerned authorities. Yet there was no shroud of secrecy; the *Times of London* carried news of the disaster on the Monday. The loss of HMS *Barham*, torpedoed off the coast of Egypt on November 25, 1941, was indeed kept quiet for a while, but letters of condolence were sent out to the families of the 861 dead, asking them to keep the secret until the official announcement. So, allowing for perhaps ten people in each family, there were about nine thousand people who knew of the sinking; if each of them told only one other person, there were twenty thousand people in the country aware of the sinking, and so on—hardly a guarded secret. In short, news of the sinking spread like wildfire; Duncan simply picked up the gossip and decided to turn it into profit. Bear in mind that all of this was at the tail end of 1941 and Duncan was not even arrested until 1944, so the "terrified establishment" was certainly taking its time.

By 1944, Duncan was plying her trade in Portsmouth, where it was the Navy alone who, tired of her dealings with vulnerable widows and orphans, decided to put her out of business. Operating with the full blessing of the Admiralty, two local Navy lieutenants, Worth and Fowler, hatched a plan with police officers Cross and Taylor whereby they would attend Duncan's séances and pounce when her "ectoplasm" appeared. After a trial attendance to familiarize themselves with the layout of the room and the location of the light switches, they were ready. On the night of January 19, 1944, they attended again and when Constable Cross lunged at the floating form and called for the lights, he was found to have a grip of a shamefaced Duncan and a few yards of cheesecloth. She was promptly arrested and charged under Section 4 of the 1824 Vagrancy Act, which covered the activities of fraudulent mediums and fortune tellers. In view of her track record for such offenses, the magistrate sent her for trial at the Old Bailey so she could be charged under Section 4 of the 1735 Witchcraft Act, which provided for heavier penalties and longer prison terms. She was also charged under the Larceny Act for "accepting money by falsely pretending that she was in a position to bring about the appearance of the spirits of deceased persons." Found guilty, she was sentenced to nine months in prison.

Much of the fuss surrounding Duncan rests on two major misconceptions, the first being that she was prosecuted for being a witch. At the opening of the trial on March 23, the prosecution, led by John Maude, went to great lengths to make it clear that witchcraft had nothing to do with the matter, despite it being the name of the act under which Duncan stood charged. The case, he stressed, was one of fraud and larceny—nothing else. The Witchcraft Act had in fact been drawn up to eliminate belief in witches, and its introduction meant that no one could thenceforth be tried as a witch in Britain; they could only be tried for pretending to be one for financial gain. The second misconception is that the authorities had to invoke anachronistic legislation to prosecute her and that she was the last person to be so charged. This claim simply is not true. Until it was replaced by the more modern-sounding Fraudulent Mediums Act of 1951, which read pretty much the same, the Witchcraft Act saw plenty of use. On the very day that Duncan was leaving prison another woman, Jane York of Forest Gate, East London, was likewise charged and the president of the Redhill Spiritualist Church was formally cautioned that he was treading very near the line.

Helen Duncan was released on September 22, 1944 and managed to steer clear of further prosecutions until November 1956, when the police raided a private seance in West Bridgford, just outside Nottingham, having been tipped off that she was practicing again. While charges were being considered, Helen Duncan died. Churchill's reaction to Duncan's prosecution was to brand it "obsolete tomfoolery."

Lord and Lady Haw-Haw

William Joyce was not a British citizen, but born on Herkimer Street in Brooklyn, his Irish family moving to Galway soon after, where William became involved in the troubles of Irish politics at an early age. The target of an IRA assassination attempt before his 16th birthday, Joyce moved to the United Kingdom in 1921 to finish his education and by 1932 was a leading member of Oswald Mosley's British Union of Fascists (BUF). In 1933 he was invited to accompany Mosley on a trip to Germany and, in need of a passport, he falsely declared himself a British citizen to get one—a petty fraud that later cost him his life. By the end of that year he was Mosley's deputy, but all may not have been as straightforward as it seemed.

It now transpires that Joyce maintained close links to Maxwell Knight, who in the 1930s was a leading light of British Military Intelligence (BMI) and head of its Section B5b. Back in the 1920s, Maxwell too had been a card-carrying member of various fascist organizations, through which he and Joyce had become friends. B5b's purpose was to monitor the activities of fringe political groups and one of Knight's agents, the future author Ian Fleming, later modeled James Bond's "M" on his old boss. There was definitely some kind of working relationship between Joyce and Maxwell, although other branches of MI5 bugged Joyce's phone and generally kept tabs on him. In August 1939, Maxwell tipped off Joyce that he was about to be detained under Defense Regulation 18B, allowing Joyce and his wife, Margaret, to escape to Germany.

Friendless and broke, Joyce had a chance encounter with fellow Mosleyite Dorothy Eckersley, who reckoned she could get him a job with Rundfunkhaus, the German propaganda radio station from which even the likes of P. G. Wodehouse made some very ill-advised broadcasts. That Eckersley had contacts in such a realm is of little wonder, since she had been married previously to Captain Peter Eckersley, a foundation stone of the BBC who, come World War II, joined BMI to combat enemy propaganda radio efforts. Joyce was an instant hit, as indeed was Margaret herself when later involved in the shows. The couple were fêted by Hermann Göring and lived in the fast lane of Berlin's decidedly louche society.

Once Joyce had won sufficient trust, he was allowed to alter Joseph Goebbels' awful scripts that required him, for example, to talk of torpedoes hitting "ships" kettles' instead of their boilers. He proved to be a real star, and not just to the Germans — it is a mistake to write him off as a wartime joke in the UK. His broadcasts covered all of the UK and Ireland, rapidly winning an audience that, in 1940, was estimated by a BBC survey to number about 6 million. A later Mass Observation study put his audience at about twenty-six million and noted that his popularity crossed all social bands. He wasn't just popular, however, he was effective as well; 32 percent of his listeners admitted, quite openly, that they looked to his broadcasts for a balance against what they heard on the BBC. About as many said that they looked to Joyce for information before it was released at home. One broadcast, for example, told the UK of the German taking of Amiens and Arras in 1940 some fifteen hours before the news was released at home. Only 7 percent said they listened to giggle at his unusual voice. As to his effectiveness, another Mass Observation poll revealed, rather disturbingly, that 17 percent of the population thought Britain was fighting the war to save the Jews and their money.

But was he Lord Haw-Haw? Originally the nickname of Lord Cardigan, the individual who led the disastrous "charge of the Light Brigade," bestowed for his barking, upper-class laugh, it was redirected in 1939 by the *Daily Express* radio critic who wrote under the pseudonym of Jonah Barrington. Yet he was not talking about Joyce, but about the star performer of the German radio station, Norman Baillie-Stewart, who did affect an upper-class English bark while Joyce, then playing second-fiddle to Baillie-Stewart, had a more downmarket and nasal twang. As Joyce's broadcasting star eclipsed that of Baillie-Stewart, people became confused between the two.

As Berlin crumbled toward the end of the war, Joyce made his last and very drunken broadcast on April 30, 1945, before he and Margaret went on the run, only to be caught at Flensburg near the Danish border. The pair were returned to the UK for trial, where it soon became obvious that Joyce was to hang, come what may. Baillie-Stewart, apparently detained in some rather fetching Lederhosen and an embroidered chamois leather shirt, pretending to be a lumberjack, received only five years' imprisonment despite his track record of treachery; before the war he had done five years in the Tower of London for selling military secrets to the Germans. Pearl Vardon, a schoolteacher from Jersey who attached herself to a German officer during the occupation of the Channel Islands and returned to Germany to broadcast from Rundfunkhaus, received nine months, and the writer P. G. Wodehouse had a smack on the wrist and a knighthood. American stars of Nazi radio fared pretty much the same. Mildred Gillars, AKA Axis Sally, did only twelve years inside before disappearing into a convent to teach German. The worst American offender, Robert Best, also escaped the electric chair, despite being so vehement that even the Nazis thought him over the top—on the night of July 14, 1942 a couple of SS officers had to drag him off-air for good.

Joyce, on the other hand, was fast tracked to the gallows. As an American citizen beyond the jurisdiction of British courts in matters of treason, the prosecution hung on the risible thread of the passport he had obtained fraudulently in 1933, and the fact that it might have been valid when he started broadcasting from Rundfunkhaus. As the British historian A. J. P. Taylor so wryly observed, the normal penalty for falsifying a claim on a passport form was then £2, not the hangman's noose. Even if the passport was valid when Joyce started broadcasting, he was second fiddle to Baillie-Stewart, who got only five years. But none of this smoke really matters; you need a lot more than a fraudulently obtained passport to qualify as a British citizen. There was a deal; everyone wanted to silence whatever it was that went on between Joyce, Maxwell and BMI before the war. Joyce was told that he could keep his mouth shut, take the fall alone and leave Margaret in the clear, or blab and take her with him. Although a deeply unpleasant pair, there can be no doubt about the strength of the bond between them, and it seems from released documents that this was the lever brought to bear on Joyce.

Before his trial in the autumn of 1945, the press was given free rein to whip up public support for the lynching. Even Oswald Mosley, whose beloved Nazism was no longer chic, tried to grab himself some merits by mounting the parapets to scream traitor at his old colleague. With the trial finally under way, everyone remarked how the normally loquacious and keen-to-banter Joyce remained completely silent throughout, not uttering so much as a single word from start to finish. Within hours of qualifying as the last man to hang for treason in the UK, on January 3, 1946, Margaret was taken from her cell in Holloway Women's Prison and told she was leaving the country. Whisked away before the press got wind of her inexplicable departure, an early morning flight took her from Croydon to Brussels where she was simply turned loose. Major J. F. E. Stephenson of BMI informed her new hosts: "It has been decided by the authorities in the UK not to prosecute this woman, in effect on compassionate grounds. There is no lack of evidence implicating her in the treasonable activities of her late husband; but the authorities do not think she need be punished further, and would like her to be returned to Germany as a German subject." So, the American Joyce was hanged as an English traitor while his equally guilty English wife—born in Manchester in 1911—was released as a German citizen because she had taken German citizenship in 1940. Baillie-Stewart had done likewise in the same year, which is how he avoided charges of high treason—he called into question the whole issue of what constituted treason. William Joyce had also taken German citizenship in 1940, but nothing was going to save him. Out of the thirty-two British who worked the airwaves for the Nazis, only William Joyce was hanged and only Margaret Joyce was allowed to walk. She later returned to London, and died there in 1972.

Louisiana Anna

Anna Carroll was such a smart cookie that she had to be airbrushed out of history to hide the fact that, while Union generals sat debating how best to conduct the Civil War, a middle-aged woman pulled their collective chestnuts out of the fire with a battle plan to bring the South to its knees.

Equipped with a legally trained, creative and analytical mind, Carroll was the daughter of Thomas Carroll and served as his aide after masterminding his 1830 campaign to secure the governorship of Maryland. Her great-grandfather, Charles Carroll, was the longest surviving signatory of the Declaration of Independence, so it is safe to say that politics ran in the family blood. In 1852, she was central to the campaign for the re-election of President Millard Fillmore, whose proposal of marriage she turned down. With a sudden change of heart, the Whigs dropped Fillmore's candidacy for that of national hero General Winfield Scott, a man whose path Carroll soon crossed herself. And, crucial to her saving the Union's bacon, she had met the rail magnate Cornelius Garrison in 1856 and so impressed him with her knowledge of the railroad system (on which she had written several papers) that he hired her as his assistant to re-vamp the existing network and plan how best to expand it. Although he took all the credit, fortunately for the Union she did all the work and capped off her endeavor with her first major political paper, *The Star of the West* (1857), in which she laid out the importance of the rail network as the sinews that bound the Union together, but could equally bring it to division. Come the outbreak of the Civil War, her value did not escape President Lincoln who made her part of his so-called Kitchen Cabinet think tank and it was here that she really showed her mettle.

At the beginning of the war, Winfield Scott, otherwise known as Old Fuss and Feathers for his pompous vanity, was commander-in-chief of the Union Army but, too fat to get on his horse or into a train, he offered effective command of the Federal army to Robert E. Lee. Yet Lee soon resigned his Union commission to go to the South and head up the opposition. Scott's next gaffe came in the form of his strategy to slowly strangle the South with what the press ridiculed as the Anaconda Plan. He proposed a blockade of all Confederate ports, in conjunction with a massive thrust down the Mississippi to divide the South. This force was to be followed by a more sedate army whose job it would be to secure and consolidate strategic points in the wake of the advance. But the Union press and its readership of armchair generals were in no mood for slow-burn solutions; they wanted blood and guts—other people's, of course. And the plan did indeed have two major flaws: the Mississippi was not deep enough to allow the passage of the ironclads so essential to the speed and effectiveness of the dividing thrust, and the Union Navy did not have nearly enough ships to mount and sustain a blockade of the Confederacy's three thousand miles of coastline.

On November 1, 1861, Scott was replaced by General George McClellan. Having himself sat back and mocked the glaring holes in the Anaconda Plan, which contributed to the putting out to pasture of his predecessor, one would think that McClellan would have profited from the experience. Instead he put forward his Grand Strategy, which proposed that an army of about 300,000 men invade Virginia from the sea to capture Richmond and other major Southern cities. Could no one in Washington count the ships they had on roster? The number of ships required to shift a third of a million troops, horses, ordnance and other supplies was way beyond the Union's capability. On January 6, 1862, Lincoln met with the Congressional Committee for the Conduct of the War and informed them he was in receipt of a viable plan that was neither the work of the War Department or any ranking officer. When pushed for the identity of its author, Lincoln boxed clever and avoided giving any direct answers.

As early as 1861, Lincoln had appointed Anna Carroll as aide to Thomas Scott, assistant secretary of War, and in the middle of that year he had sent her to St. Louis to study the Mississippi Valley area, a task that only confirmed in her mind the futility of the Anaconda Plan and its reliance on that river. Diverting from her assigned task, she started gathering information from two main sources, the senior librarian of the Mercantile Library who, ironically, was the brother of Confederate general Joe Johnston, and a riverboat pilot called Charles Scott. Protracted conversations with the latter revealed that the Tennessee and Cumberland rivers were not only ironclad friendly and open to supply ships the year round, but would also be virtually impossible for the

Confederacy to defend. Carroll also dismissed any notion of trying to block the Confederate ports and thought beyond that. Any supplies brought into a Confederate port would then have to be shifted, so if the Southern rail network was crippled at strategic points to impede the east-west movement of men and supplies, the South would be stymied. Control of the Tennessee and the Cumberland rivers would give the necessary access to the east-west Confederate rail network at significant junctions such as Chattanooga and Nashville, and who better to plan pinpoint strikes on the network than the woman who designed it. She prepared her report, which was channeled through to Secretary of War Edwin Stanton, who was instructed in January 1862 by Lincoln to forge ahead with Carroll's Tennessee River Plan. It proved pivotal to Union victory.

Having welcomed Carroll's plan with "overwhelming relief, joy and hope," Lincoln determined to get things moving as swiftly as possible and, as early as February 2, 1862, a considerable number of troops and a flotilla of ironclads were heading down the Tennessee to take Fort Henry and, if successful, to move on Fort Donelson on the Cumberland. Both forts had been built to defend Tennessee and the deep South from invasion and both fell, Fort Henry on February 6 and Fort Donelson on the 16th. As Carroll had predicted, this initial strike opened the South to further punitive expeditions and a task force centered on three warships—the *Tyler*, the *Conestoga* and the *Lexington*—pushed on as far as Florence, Alabama, capturing Confederate shipping, blowing up munitions stores and knocking out crucial bridges of the Memphis and Ohio railroad. Meanwhile, again in accordance with Carroll's plan, Union troops were already marching on Vicksburg in Mississippi. The two major waterways of the Confederacy were now in Union hands, forcing the Confederate forces to withdraw from western Kentucky altogether. And that was just the beginning.

Despite her undoubted contribution to the outcome of the war, Carroll never received the recognition she deserved. The trouble was, she was a woman. It would never do for the press to get wind of the fact that, while the Union high command sat around whistling "Dixie," a woman had put their game in order. She did not receive any share of her rightful credit, which was instead heaped on the undeserving shoulders of others, notably General Grant who, to Carroll's disgust, played to the gallery and lapped up the unearned adulation. However, not everyone deserted her. Carroll's struggle for a pension and recognition was backed by Thomas Scott who, on May 1, 1872, presented the following to the Chairman of the Senate:

My Dear Sir:

I take pleasure in stating that the plan presented by Miss Carroll, in November, 1861, for a campaign upon the Tennessee River and thence South, was submitted to the Secretary of War and President Lincoln. And after Secretary Stanton's appointment, I was directed to go to the Western armies and arrange to increase their effective force as rapidly as possible. A part of the duty assigned me was the organization and consolidation into regiments of all the troops then being recruited in Ohio, Indiana, Illinois and Michigan, for the purpose of carrying through this campaign, then inaugurated. This work was vigorously prosecuted by the army, and, as the valuable suggestions of Miss Carroll, made to the Department some months before, were substantially carried out through the campaigns in that section—great successes followed, and the country was largely benefited in the saving of time and expenditure. I hope Congress will reward Miss Carroll liberally for her patriotic efforts and services.

Eventually, in 1881, she was finally awarded a derisory pension of $50 per month with no acknowledgement of her enormous contribution, but by now 66 years old she was too tired and broke to remonstrate. She died on 19 February 1894 and was buried in the Old Trinity Church, Church Creek, Maryland, under a headstone that merely proclaimed her to have been "a gifted woman." After pressure from those who knew the truth, this meager epitaph was expanded to the more fitting: "Maryland's Most Distinguished Lady. A Great humanitarian and *close friend of Abraham Lincoln. She conceived the successful Tennessee Campaign and guided the President on his constitutional war powers."*

Name of the Rose

There was no Tokyo Rose. No such person ever existed nor did anyone purporting to be such a character ever make a taunting broadcast to the Allied troops.

It is doubtful that there has been an incident of mass hysteria involving a greater number of people. Every soldier serving in the Pacific during World War II either believed wholeheartedly in the existence of such a person, or claimed they had endured her honey-voiced taunts of defeat and of the supposed infidelities of their loved ones back home. Despite the kangaroo trial and imprisonment of Iva Toguri d'Aquino in 1947, no Japanese broadcaster ever used the name Tokyo Rose.

In July 1941, Toguri went to Japan to tend a sick relative and was caught on the hop by the Japanese attack on Pearl Harbor in December. Having been born in America, she was regarded as a hostile alien, arrested when she refused to assume Japanese citizenship and only released on condition she take a job at Tokyo Radio. Here she met and married Filipe d'Aquino. The station broadcasted a propaganda program called *The Zero Hour*, which featured POWs forced to make capitalistic speeches, but Iva was simply an announcer of the show who regularly risked her life by slipping food and medicines to the prisoners. She also colluded in their attempts to undermine the venture by slipping in sarcastic allusions and double-entendres beyond the grasp of the Japanese monitors. It is fair to say that, in all her time at the station, Iva never made a single broadcast in any real sense of the word; she simply helped with the preparation of the show, introduced music and did a few links. She was also one of about a dozen other women who made broadcasts for the show.

Following the defeat of Japan, General MacArthur landed at Atsugi airfield on August 30, 1945 and he brought with him a host of reporters, each determined to interview General Tojo, former prime minister of Japan, and to track down the sinister-yet-sensual Tokyo Rose. Two of the leading lights of this pack, Clark Lee and Harry Brundridge, put out word that they would pay $250 to anyone who could put them in touch with Tokyo Rose and $2,000 to the lady herself for an exclusive interview. In post-war Japan, this was the kind of money that made the difference between survival and oblivion so, inevitably, one of Iva's colleagues, Leslie Nakashima, sold her name to Brundridge.

With the prospect of her payment being in the region of $40,000 at today's rate, Iva was all too willing to give an exclusive interview. However, to the newshounds' increasing alarm, she cackled with laughter at any suggestion of her being a cat-voiced femme fatale, having as she did a rather gruff and masculine voice. Brundridge's editors weren't stupid; they quickly spotted the fact that he had signed a contract with a nobody and refused to cover the $2,000 which they said would have to come out of his own pocket instead. Desperate to avoid such a crippling loss, Brundridge took all the tapes and transcripts to the Army Intelligence Corps commander, General Elliot Thorpe, and urged him to arrest her. And, just in case Thorpe failed to act, Brundridge arranged for the gullible Iva to give a mass interview to over three hundred reporters to place her in breach of their exclusivity agreement and so void the contract. The unwitting Iva happily gave her mass interview at the Yokohama Bund Hotel, and all present curiously noted that she reveled in her role, thinking she had become some sort of darling of the GIs. Iva had some notion that her efforts at subterfuge on the show had garnered her great praise in the country she thought of as home; she obviously hadn't the slightest idea who Tokyo Rose was supposed to be.

Back in America, Walter Winchell, the inventor of the gossip column, latched on to the story and made repeated demands for Iva to be tried for treason. The carrot-and-stick tactics of money and threats were brought to bear on two other US-born employees at Tokyo Radio, Kenkichi Oki and George Mitsushio, who were groomed and coached for weeks to get them word perfect for Iva's impending trial for treason.

When later admitting their perjury, they offered the mitigation that, having both renounced their American citizenship, they had to live in a Japan under American control, and it had been made abundantly clear how difficult life would be if they did not do as they were told. Even the carefully selected district judge, Michael Roche, later confessed his conduct was a disgrace. He consistently ruled out any evidence likely to "confuse the jury as to her guilt," and then steered them into a guilty verdict on the last remaining charge after they infuriated him with not guilty verdicts on the other seven.

Among the evidence Judge Roche disallowed was the testimony of Australian radio personality Major Charles Cousens, who hosted *The Zero Hour,* plus Army captain Wallace Ince and Filipino lieutenant Norman Reyes, two of the POWs forced to take part in the show. Their combined testimony proved that Iva did everything she could to help slip double meanings and sarcastic jibes into the shows, and pass the POWs basic medicines to take back to camp. Had any of these efforts been detected, she would most certainly have been executed by the Japanese. Furthermore, all three confirmed she had never said anything on air that could be considered actionable.

The defense also wanted to point out that, as early as August 1945, the Office of War Information had published a report in the *New York Times* saying: "There is no Tokyo Rose; the name is strictly a GI invention. Government monitors listening in twenty-four hours a day have never heard the words 'Tokyo Rose' over a Japanese-controlled Far Eastern Radio." It might also have "confused" the jury to hear that General Theron L. Cauldle, assistant attorney-general, had written a report to the attorney-general stating:

Considerable investigation has been conducted in this case and it appears that the identification of Toguri as "Tokyo Rose" is erroneous as her activity consisted of nothing more than the announcing of music selections. A few recording cylinders of her broadcasts and a large number of her scripts have been located, and they, as well as the transcripts of the broadcasts of her program which were monitored by the Federal Communications Commission do not disclose that she did anything more than introduce musical records. It is my opinion that Toguri's activities, particularly in view of the innocent nature of her broadcasts, are not sufficient to warrant her prosecution for treason.

Even six months *after* her arrest, the Eighth Army Legal Services was still reporting: "There is no evidence that she ever broadcast greetings to units by names or location, or predicted military movements or attacks indicating access to secret military information and plans, etc., as the Tokyo Rose of rumor and legend is reported to have done."

The few who spoke out in defense of Iva lived to regret it. The climate was not right to tell America that its returning heroes were behaving like a bunch of hysterical persecutors, so Iva was thrown to the wolves with a sentence of ten years' imprisonment and a $10,000 fine. America was determined to focus its recriminations on Iva to save itself from examining the real traitor of the war too closely. Few today would recognize the name of the aforementioned Mildred Gillars, who did broadcast extensively for the Germans as Axis Sally, usually signing off, "I love America but I hate Roosevelt and all his slimy-kike boyfriends." It was Gillars who taunted American troops with tales of defeat and infidelities at home, and in a honey-dipped sultry voice trained in minor acting roles in pre-war America. Quietly locked away while the venom focused on Iva, Gillars was a white middle-class woman from Maine, and America was not yet ready to see itself in the mirror.

After serving her time Iva settled in Chicago, but never gave up the fight to clear her name, finally gaining a full pardon in 1977 from President Ford. Iva finally died in 2006 aged ninety, having never once uttered so much as a single criticism or comment on her treatment. This unwavering loyalty to her country was recognized a few months before her death, when she was presented with the Edward J. Herlihy Citizenship Award by the American World War II Veterans Committee, which praised her for her silence throughout all she had suffered.

The Other "Nightingale"

So much has been written of Florence Nightingale that Mary Seacole, a woman who can justifiably claim to have made a difference in the lives of British soldiers in the Crimea, has been marginalized and overshadowed.

Born Mary Grant in Kingston, Jamaica, she was the daughter of a white British Army officer and a local Creole healer who ran one of the town's best residential rest homes for ailing and disabled European soldiers. Mary grew up helping and learning from her mother, not only in their own rest home but also at the military hospital in Up Park Camp, where she was later asked to oversee the nursing services after her part in fighting the island's 1850 cholera outbreak and the 1853 epidemic of yellow fever. She blamed the former on the arrival of a steamer from New Orleans, an insight that demonstrates her knowledge of the contagion theory. This theory was still being treated with skepticism by many, despite its validation when Dr. John Snow shut down the public water pumps in Soho's Broad Street, London, to curtail the 1854 cholera outbreak. He knew that the disease was spread by living organisms in the water and not by foul air, as Nightingale and other adherents of the miasma theory believed. Mary was also sufficiently savvy to shun the opiates so casually used by others, as she knew them to be both addictive and debilitating. By the time of the British involvement in the Crimean War (1854–56), she had nearly forty years of medical experience in military nursing and the combating of various diseases that would plague the British in the Crimea so at her own expense, she set sail for London to offer her services.

Armed with countless references and recommendations, she was surprised to find herself shunned; all doors remained closed, and even Nightingale refused to receive her for reasons that can only be conjectured. Undaunted, she mustered what little support and finance she could and made her own way to the war zone where, once again, Nightingale turned her down. Obviously, given the period of history, the color of Seacole's skin worked against her with many people, but given what she had to offer there must have been more to it than that. Perhaps many people simply saw her expertise and experience as a threat. Therefore, scrounging building materials from wherever she could find them, Seacole built her first refuge within a mile of the main British camp, on the supply road to Balaclava, and this New British Hotel opened to the sick and injured in March 1855. Funding herself by various catering ventures, Seacole was as familiar a face in military hospitals as she was in the thick of battle, tending the wounded where they lay. *Times* correspondent, Sir William Russell, was sufficiently impressed to state in his dispatch of September 14, 1855, that she was "a warm and successful physician who doctors and cures all manner of men with extraordinary success. She is always near the battle-field to aid the wounded and has earned many a poor fellow's blessing." Similar praise and recognition came from numerous other sources, including Dr. Sir John Hall, inspector-general of Hospitals, and Lady Alicia Blackwood, who happened to be a friend of the less-than-impressed Florence Nightingale.

When Sevastopol fell, Seacole arrived with the advance parties, tending to British and Russian wounded alike. However, the cessation of hostilities saw her stranded and virtually penniless after giving away her entire stock of food and drink to those who had nothing. Crippled by debt and ill health, she made it back to London in August 1856, where those who knew what she had achieved stepped up to the plate in droves. Fund-raising initiatives were launched by *the Times, Punch* magazine, Major-General Lord Rokeby, commander of the 1st Division in the Crimea, Prince Edward of Saxe-Weimar and the duke of Wellington, to name but a few. Yet against this backdrop, and for reasons best known to herself, Nightingale continued a campaign against Seacole so unfair and damaging that even her most ardent supporters now have little defense for her actions.

Following her return to England, Nightingale's health failed and she took to her bed, where she remained for the next fifty years of her life. When not busy writing letters demanding the change of sanitary regimes in hospitals and the improved training of nurses, Nightingale sent out damaging letters about Seacole, branding her a loose woman and a drunk. The (possibly Egyptian) young girl that Seacole took under her wing in the Crimea was hailed as the result of an illicit affair that

Seacole supposedly had with one Colonel Henry Bunbury in Jamaica. Yet the girl's age would place said affair at the time Seacole was nursing her dying husband, Edwin Horatio Hamilton Seacole who claimed to be, and maybe was, Vice-Admiral Nelson's godson, and there is no record of a Colonel Bunbury on the island at the time. Even as late as 1870, Nightingale would not drop the feud. She heard that Seacole had approached her brother-in-law, Sir Henry Verney of the National Society for the Relief of the Sick and Wounded, with an offer of help in the Franco-Prussian War of 1870–71. Nightingale immediately sent him a letter telling him to shun her as she "kept—I will not call it a "bad house" [brothel]—but something not very unlike it—in the Crimean War" and went on to brand Seacole a "woman of bad character."

When Seacole fell on hard times again in 1867, the prince of Wales, with help from the dukes of Edinburgh and Cambridge, set her up in comfort. One of her patients in the Crimea had been Prince Victor of Hohenlohe-Langenburg, Queen Victoria's nephew, and through that contact she became masseuse to the princess of Wales, who suffered from various arthritic and rheumatic conditions. So it is something of a mystery that Seacole was wiped from the history books after her burial in St. Mary's Cemetery in London's Kensal Green. Here, her grave was soon overgrown and lay forgotten until 1973, when the British Commonwealth Nurses' War Memorial Fund and the Lignum Vitae Club tidied up the site and provided her with a suitably impressive gravestone. Since then she has slowly gained the recognition she deserves, with various research institutes and foundations named in her honor, such as the Mary Seacole Research Centre, run by Leicester's De Montfort University in conjunction with the Royal College of Nursing.

Patch, Match, and Dispatch

Horatio Nelson may loom large in British lore, but he was shorter than Napoleon and not the nicest man you could meet on the quarterdeck.

Although he did lose the odd bit of himself throughout his career, he did not lose an eye and never wore an eyepatch. At the siege of Calvi in 1793, a cannonball struck a wall near him and splattered the right side of his face with hot gravel, causing some damage to his eye which, he would later claim, never fully recovered. A couple of days after the incident, he is on record as declaring his eye much better when reporting to his commander, Lord Hood, but later decided that the chance of another £200 a year for his "loss" was too good a chance to pass up. Nelson pressed his claim for a few years, but the Admiralty stuck to its guns and refused. Realizing that nothing was forthcoming, Nelson dropped the pretense and "recovered." To quote an article from the *Times* in 1804: "Lord Nelson is not blind in either eye. It is true that he, for a short period, lost the sight of one eye but it has been happily restored. He also has a speck in the other eye but that he could see with both at very great distant date we are assured from the very best authority—that of his Lordship's own information."

Hero of the seas he might have been, but Nelson was by all accounts rude, snobby, arrogant and incredibly vain—that last flaw no mean achievement for a chap who was but five feet four inches tall and barely had any teeth left by the age of thirty. He was a shameless self-publicist and ever willing to trade on his standing for a decent freebie. His affair with Lady Emma Hamilton has been portrayed in fiction as the turmoil of two noble souls torn between duty and their hearts. The reality was less appetizing. Not to put too fine a point on it, the lady was a tramp. The daughter of a Cheshire blacksmith, Amy Lyon, as she was properly named, was a prostitute by the age of fourteen and working various brothels in and around London. Through a lucky strike of circumstances, she became the consort of one Honourable Charles Greville. Keen to keep a rich widowed relative, Sir William Hamilton, distracted from seeking a wife who would jeopardize any inheritance that he stood to gain, Greville passed Lyon on as a temporary plaything to him. Before Greville could take her back, Emma outflanked him by marrying the old gent.

The Hamiltons moved to Naples, where Sir William was British ambassador. Emma first met Nelson in 1793, she a sprightly twenty-eight and Hamilton a washed-out sixty-three. To put it bluntly, Emma saw the ideal chance to swap horses. Hamilton was nearing the end of any useful life as far as she was concerned and Nelson's star was in the ascendant. They were perfectly matched; both were greedy, selfish, hungry for celebrity status and quite happy to trample over anyone in their way. Their liaison was put on hold while Nelson popped off to sink a few French warships, but he was straight back to her side in 1798 to pick up where they left off. Indifferent to the public humiliation he was causing his own wife and child back home, Nelson moved in with the Hamiltons to make a *ménage a trois* that became the scandal of Naples—a town that took some shocking. Contemporary observers described Nelson being "led about like a performing bear" by Emma and two sisters of the late Marie Antoinette.

Eventually, the three returned to England, intending to continue their cozy little arrangement, but found that the scandal had preceded them. They were publicly snubbed, most notably by King George III. Things were not much improved by Emma's being pregnant with Horatia and Nelson's callous "dumping" of his wife, Frances, who was not the shrew the pair tried in vain to portray her as. By 1803, Sir William was dead and the two were openly living together, taking perverse joy in flaunting themselves in public at every opportunity, while Frances Nelson maintained the dignified silence that won in the end. Nelson's behavior backfired when the codicil of his will regarding Emma and Horatia was loftily ignored. In keeping with his arrogance, he proclaimed them his bequest to the nation, which should not let them starve. But starve the woman did; all public honor, privileges and pensions went to Frances, leaving Emma to debtors' prison and thence to France, where she drank herself to death.

And so to Nelson's last words. Nelson did not die craving a kiss from Sir Thomas Masterman Hardy, nor did he say "Kismet, Hardy." In fact, after he was shot on the deck of HMS *Victory* by a French naval marksman during the battle of Trafalgar on October 21, 1805, Hardy remained on deck while Nelson was taken below, where he lived for another three hours. Recently discovered and validated as genuine is a letter written by Robert Hilton, surgeon's mate on HMS *Swiftfire*, a seventy-four-gunner of the British fleet at Trafalgar. He informed his family:

> *We hailed the Victory to inquire the health of Lord Nelson who we had heard was wounded at the commencement of the action when we received the melancholy information from Captain Hardy that this hero was no more. His dying words of this warlike Admiral were "I have then lived long enough." This unwelcome intelligence of his death troubled most sensibly those hearts that were but a moment previous elated with the success. Our gallant seamen now paused to pay tribute to the memory of so great a character.*

As soon as HMS *Victory* returned to port, portrait painter Arthur Devis went aboard to take statements from all there at the end and to make preliminary sketches of the precise spot where Nelson died on the orlop deck. Something must have been scrambled because the gold plaque marking the spot today is in the wrong place, by about twenty-five feet and to the left. *Victory*'s curator, Peter Goodwin, has studied all the original drawings and, after a ten-year battle, has finally managed to convince the Admiralty that the plaque should be moved.

Springtime for Hitler in Liverpool

Was he part Jewish and really named Schicklgruber; was he a teetotal vegetarian; was he a mono-testicular, bisexual fetishist riddled with syphilis; and did he visit pre-war Liverpool? Best start with the pivotal Maria Schicklgruber.

One of eleven children born to Johannes and Theresia Schicklgruber, Maria grew up in the tiny village of Strones, which used to stand somewhere to the north-west of Vienna. (As soon as he annexed Austria in 1938, Hitler had the place wiped off the map, along with all surrounding villages for good measure, so the precise location is uncertain.) In

1837 she registered the birth of a child, Alois, Hitler's father, at the church in Dollersheim, near Strones, the birth logged as illegitimate. It is the identity of Hitler's paternal grandfather that prompts so much speculation. Maria had at some time worked as a maid for the Rothschilds in Vienna, but theories that one of the Rothschilds succumbed to her peasant charms are without foundation. However, one historical line of inquiry vehemently contested among historians places her in the Jewish household of the Frankenbergers of Graz, once again employed as a maid. Leopold Frankenberger in later life acknowledged paternity of Alois; at the relevant time he would have been nineteen, she forty-two, and marriage quite out of the question. The theory goes that the Frankenbergers paid support to Maria until the child was fourteen, a full five years after she married Johann Hiedler at the church in Dollersheim. Maria and Hiedler had conducted an on-off relationship throughout the period that Maria was pleasuring the young Frankenberger, but perhaps Maria was canny enough to know that, whoever the father, her best option was to point the finger at the money.

Another possible indicator of young Frankenberger's paternity is the fact that Hiedler made no move after the wedding to adopt Alois, who was instead sent to live with Nepomunk, Johann's childless brother, who raised the boy as his own. An additional pointer to the "shame' of Jewish blood in the family is that someone later tried to fudge the parish records, altering them to show Johann acknowledging paternity in front of three witnesses on June 6, 1876. These forgers, however, paid no heed to detail—Maria had died in 1847 and Hiedler ten years later in 1857. The real question is why anyone would care enough to mount such pointless and futile fraud unless to distract from the accusation of Jewish heritage. (It should be pointed out that many major biographers of Hitler contest the Frankenberger theory, pointing out that there were actually no Jews whatsoever in Graz during the relevant period. Evidence presented by other historians, however, leaves it as an intriguing possibility.)

Nevertheless, by the age of thirty-nine Alois had abandoned the Schicklgruber tag and formally registered himself as Alois Hitler, so

Adolf never carried the trade-inspired surname that indicates a digger of cesspits. Thus history is the poorer for the want of old black and white footage of thousands of enraptured Nazis filling the Nuremberg nights with cries of "Behold the Shit-Pit-Digger!' But the full implications of the Schicklgruber–Dollersheim saga were yet to be played out.

Adolf was born in the Austrian town of Braunau am Inn (he did not become a German citizen until February 1932) and would later attend school in Linz with Ludwig Wittgenstein, which must have made for interesting times in the playground. By now Alois was a customs officer and on his third wife, Klara Pölzl. She had moved into the Hitler household as a maid at the age of sixteen and immediately began "comforting" Alois, her biological uncle, throughout his first marriage to a wealthy but ailing woman while he was also sleeping with another servant called Franziska Matzelberger. In January 1882, "Franni" gave birth to Alois Jr., but the happy couple had to wait for the first wife, Anna, to die before they could marry; he was forty-five and she twenty-one. The union legitimized Alois Jr., but when Franni died too, she was immediately replaced by the already pregnant and ever-attendant Klara. It was Klara who produced Wolfie, as Adolf Hitler was nicknamed. He later realized the political dynamite of being the issue of an incestuous and adulterous liaison and possibly "contaminated" with Jewish blood to boot. Such a heritage was far from ideal for a man who insisted that only those with unbroken and legitimate "Aryan" lineage stretching back to 1750 were fit to join his elite.

Hitler was determined to find out what records remained, who was still alive with their memory intact and, worst of all, what a good investigator could uncover. As the 1938 annexation of Austria drew ever closer, Dollersheim found itself hosting a contingent of undercover Gestapo officers who not only conducted their own guarded inquiries, but also kept the village tightly under wraps. Journalists who turned up asking the wrong sort of questions were treated to a one-way nature ramble. Most significantly, as soon as Hitler annexed Austria he ordered the evacuation and destruction of Dollersheim and Strones. The villagers were relocated throughout Germany and Austria and the village names were removed from the maps. The question of Hitler's Jewish heritage will be argued further; only Maria Schicklgruber knew for sure. But suspicions of this unacceptable truth trickled down through the family, as these things will. Hitler obviously thought there was something to hide at Dollersheim, whatever that might be, and Bill and Bridget, the Liverpool Hitlers, had yet to put in their contribution.

Hitler's older half-brother, Alois Jr., had fled Germany after trouble with the police, arriving in Dublin where, at the 1909 Dublin Horse Show, he met and wooed the seventeen-year-old Bridget Dowling. He told her that he was a wealthy Austrian hotelier in Ireland on business, but he was in fact a waiter at the city's Shelbourne Hotel. It must be hard to rate as the black sheep of a family that included Adolf Hitler, but Alois struggled valiantly all his life to prove worthy of the dishonor. Bridget's father told the con-man to be gone, but he and Bridget eloped to England and produced William Hitler on March 12, 1911, in Liverpool, where they had settled at 102 Upper Stanhope Street in the city's Toxteth district. After trying his hand at running a boarding house on Upper Parliament Street, a café on Dale Street and a "hotel" in the appropriately named Mount Pleasant district, Alois got grandiose notions of capturing the European market for disposable razors. He sent ticket money for his sister, Angela, and her husband, Leo Raubal, to come over from Germany to discuss the idea and their involvement.

According to Bridget, it was half-brother Adolf who quit his digs in Vienna to come in their stead, as he wanted to dodge conscription into the Austrian Army. According to Bridget, he arrived in November 1912 and stayed until the following April. While there are many who challenge her account, what is so implausible about someone, even Hitler, visiting relatives? Those who take issue with Bridget Hitler's memory place Adolf in Vienna for those months but, since his years in that city were spent in a succession of cheap rooming houses, who would notice his absence for so short a time. Taking Bridget at her word, we have the image of Hitler drinking (more of his "abstemious" nature later) in the local pubs and cheering on Everton football club from the very terraces he would later bomb to blazes; the house on Upper Stanhope was also destroyed on the last raid of the Liverpool Blitz on January 10, 1942. Adolf returned to mainland Europe followed by Alois who, in 1914, abandoned his family to explore the opportunities of the German World War I black market.

During the war, Adolf joined the German Army's 16th Bavarian Reserve Infantry and served as an HQ orderly and message-runner. He suffered a light shrapnel wound and later a slight exposure to gas, resulting in hysterical and temporary blindness. His comrades-in-arms are fairly unanimous in remembering him as unsociable and aloof, unless haranguing them on various political matters. They also remember him as a sycophant to officers, volunteering to do their laundry and other menial tasks. Despite serving four years in the same regiment—with the casualty toll producing field promotions by the sackful—he never advanced beyond the rank of corporal. Hermann Rauschning, head of the Danzig Senate, later stated that this was because his military record referred to disciplinary proceedings resulting from his being caught in a homosexual clinch with an officer. He also maintained that, while in Munich, Hitler was prosecuted under Paragraph 175 of the penal code dealing with sodomy. While Rauschning, whose refusal to institute certain Nazi Party measures resulted in his flight to Switzerland in 1936, later exaggerated grossly his importance within the Nazi structure in his books, which are peppered with inaccuracies and invented conversations with Hitler, he was not the only one to mention Hitler's homosexuality.

Hitler's recall of his war service was somewhat different. He was a fearless beast protecting his country, and was honored with the Iron Cross, First Class, for his relentless heroism, crowned by his single-handedly taking prisoner a detachment of French troops, complete with officers. Unfortunately, the records neglected to include any account of his heroism, or indeed his being awarded any such medal. Even he did not have the gall to parade himself with the Iron Cross until 1927, by which time it would have been a brave, if short-lived, soul who stood up to call him a liar. When doubts were whispered, the Nazi propaganda machine leapt to inept action. The *Völkischer Beobachter* of August 14, 1934, ran a cover story presenting the "authentic" documentation of his award dated October 4, 1918, However, to quell later mutterings the *Berliner Illustrierte Zeitung* of August 10, 1939, repeated the story with the same "authentic" documentation, this time dated August 4, 1918. Neither of the papers, nor anyone else ever produced proof of Hitler having won the Iron Cross, Second Class, without which the First Class could not be awarded.

Hitler was certainly prone to embellishment, but his favorite World War I yarn, about his life being spared by a British soldier who had him dead in his sights, is unfortunately true. It seems we have Private Henry Tandey, then of the Green Howards, to thank for all the fun of round two with Germany.

Five times mentioned in dispatches, Private Tandey was one of the most highly decorated British soldiers of World War I and distinguished himself on numerous occasions during the incredibly vicious fighting of September 1918 around the French village of Marcoing, about five miles south-west of Cambrai. At some point in the proceedings, a wounded and unarmed German corporal emerged from the smoke right in front of Tandey, who raised his rifle but declined to pull the trigger as the wretch just stood there waiting for the shot. After staring at each other for a while, both men nodded their understanding of what should happen next and the German limped away. Tandey later said that he could never have gunned down a wounded man, "so I let him go." In 1940 Tandey, as a resident of what was left of Coventry, told the press:

"If only I had known what he would turn out to be. When I saw all the people, women and children he had killed and wounded I was sorry to God I let him go."

Tandey had recognized Hitler throughout his rise to power, but Hitler would never have known his savior's identity had it not been for a famous portrait of Tandey aiding a wounded man after the battle of Ypres. The picture, by the celebrated Italian war artist, Fortunino

Matania, came to Hitler's attention and he immediately recognized the central character. In 1937 Hitler ordered his minions to make representation to the Regimental HQ of the Green Howards to obtain a copy of said painting, which was duly sent. All the relevant correspondence and grateful acknowledgement of receipt from Captain Weidmann, Hitler's adjutant, is extant.

In 1938, when Chamberlain made his doomed trip to Germany, he was entertained by Hitler and his coterie of thugs up at Berchtesgaden and the story revealed Hitler's desire for Chamberlain to contact Tandey and convey his message of thanks. William Whateley, Tandey's nephew, remembers the night of the call and the typical modesty of his uncle, who simply said that it had been the prime minister on the phone with a message from the Reichskanzler of Germany, before asking for another cup of tea. Major Roger Chapman, spokesman for the Green Howards, said of Tandey: "He was a remarkably brave man, small, only 5-foot-5 and intensely modest. He was no line-shooter. After a lot of research we have no doubts that he did meet up with Hitler and allow him to live, an act of compassion he came to regret twenty-two years later."

You can pick your enemies but not your family, and in 1933 Bill Hitler, Adolf's British-born nephew, paid his uncle a return visit from Liverpool to profit from the family connections. Hitler fixed him up with various jobs with banks and the Opel company, but young Bill was far more interested in swanning around Berlin society boasting of his connections. By 1938, Bill was something of a thorn in Hitler's side and his demands were getting increasingly petulant. He told Adolf that a high-ranking party job was what he really fancied. When Hitler said that this could not happen until Bill assumed German citizenship, Bill rightly suspected a trap and fled back to London, from where he contented himself with trashy articles such as "Why I Hate My Uncle" in *Look* magazine. In 1939 he and his mother were invited by William Randolph Hearst to tour America and he decided to stay, Bill later joining the Navy. After the war he changed his surname to Stuart-Huston, married, had four sons and settled down to suburban obscurity in Patchogue on Long Island. He died in 1987 and was buried beside his mother in the Holy Sepulchre Cemetery, Coram, New York.

Next—Hitler's much debated sexuality. The women in his life, though few in number, seem to have been uniform in their disposition to suicide, and it is unclear whether any of these relationships went as far as the bedroom. Even the ill-fated Eva Braun wrote that Hitler had told her "physical contact with me would be to him a contamination of his mission." (Braun tried suicide with a pistol in 1932 and pills in 1935.) The first to find herself the focus of Hitler's attentions was Stephanie Rabatsch of Linz in 1905 (Hitler was then seventeen) and she is significant only in that Hitler wrongly thought her Jewish, yet did not see this as a problem. His next known female dalliance would not be until 1929 when, in a disturbing reflection of his grandfather's antics, Hitler moved his niece, Geli Raubal, into his Berlin flat after packing off her mother, his half-sister Angela, to Berchtesgaden as resident housekeeper. Bill Hitler remembered Geli as a childlike figure, pouting around the flat in pleated skirts and white blouses with her hair in pigtails. Exactly what happened to her in 1931 is unknown; the pair had been rowing furiously in the days leading up to her "suicide," when she was shot through the lung with Hitler's own pistol. Suicides tend not to go for torso shots with a pistol, so if she was not shot by Hitler himself then possibly by some third party on his instruction. If the latter, then the prime suspect is Hitler's chauffeur and long-term friend, Emile Maurice, who the following year was suddenly appointed Oberführer of the re-formed and expanded SS.

The only woman with whom there might have been anything physical was the incredibly naive Unity Mitford, whose sister Diana married the jack-booting Oswald Mosley, founder of the BUF. By 1934 Unity was resident in Berlin and besotted with Hitler, who organized the murder of a Jewish family so she could have their apartment, a gesture the self-proclaimed "Jew-hater" found deeply touching. Ignoring the fact that World War II had broken out, Mitford stayed with the object of her desires until January 3, 1940, when she returned to England on a stretcher having sustained a gunshot wound to the head, from an uncertain cause. The wartime head of MI5, Guy Liddell, tried to get to her at the airfield, but even he was kept away by the incredibly well monied and connected Mitford machine and their tame home secretary, Sir John Anderson, who stymied every attempt to have her interned. But everybody there remarked how well she looked and, as Liddell's diary put it: "there were no outward signs of her injury. We had no evidence to support the press allegations that she was in a serious state of health and it might well be that she was brought in on a stretcher in order to avoid publicity and unpleasantness to her family." A few days later, he received a detailed report from the security officers who processed Mitford's return and they too asserted "there were no signs of a bullet wound." Such suspicions would seem borne out by the fact that she was up and leaping about within days. Suspicions about the real reason for her return are even more startling.

In late December 2007, Martin Bright, political editor of the *New Statesman*, wrote an article about the puzzling circumstances of Mitford's return to England. The article elicited a phone call from Valerie Hann, who told him that during the war her aunt, Betty Norton, ran a private maternity home called Hill View Cottage at Wiggington just outside Oxford, where "nice" girls, like Unity, went to have their mistakes resolved in private. Bright soon discovered that Unity's file in the National Archives was covered by the hundred-year rule—the highest restriction possible. He visited Wiggington to meet women who had either worked at the maternity home or had some member of the family do so, and they confirmed Unity's presence in the home in 1940. According to Hann, Betty Norton had confided that the child was a boy who was put out to adoption, and that Mitford had been quite matter-of-fact about Hitler's paternity. Bright's findings went to make the UK television documentary *Hitler's British Girl*.

So, Hitler definitely associated with and perhaps had some sort of a relationship with a handful of women, but the circumstantial evidence could indicate that he was either bisexual or possibly homosexual, simply keeping women in the sidelines to head off questions regarding his real inclinations. According to some scholars, he was known to the Vienna police as a male prostitute between 1907 and 1912, and possibly pursued this living for the following two years in Munich as well. This shady part of his life is explored in both Desmond Seward's acclaimed *Napoleon and Hitler: A Comparative Biography* and by Walter Langer, the psychoanalyst commissioned by the Allies in 1943 to build a psychological profile of Hitler (the techniques developed by Langer to undertake this task would later found the basis for modern criminal profiling). Kept under wraps until Langer was free to publish *The Mind of Adolf Hitler* in 1972, the report brands Hitler a homosexual coprophile. Bearing in mind Hitler's later expressed hatred of homosexuality, it is hard to locate the truth of the matter, yet Hitler's own relations with women certainly indicate a confused attitude to his physical and emotional relations.

Contrary to general opinion, Hitler was neither the vegetarian nor the teetotaler touted by Joseph Goebbels, who wished to project the image of a revolutionary ascetic. It is true that his doctors put him on a low-meat diet from time to time, but this was to reduce his excessive flatulence and profuse sweating. Immediately after the death of his beloved Geli he frequently professed an abhorrence of meat, but Dione Lucas, a chef who used to prepare Hitler's meals when he dined in Hamburg in the 1930s, wrote in her *Gourmet Cooking School Book*: "I do not mean to spoil your appetite for stuffed squab, but you might be interested to know that it was a great favorite with Hitler, who dined at the hotel often. Let us not hold that against this fine recipe, though." Both Robert Payne's *Life and Death of Adolf Hitler* (1973) and J. H. Toland's *Adolf Hitler: The Definitive Biography* (1976) mention his fondness for Bavarian hams and sausage, and Albert Speer's memoirs mention Hitler's insistence on a well stocked meat locker in his bunker. As for alcohol, although Hitler preferred other recreational drugs, he was not averse to the odd drink or three, preferring sweet white wine with added sugar, according to Putzi Hanfstaengl, one-time member of Hitler's inner circle.

Also false is the notion that Hitler was out of his mind with syphilis. That he was less than balanced by the end of the war is beyond dispute, but whatever ailed him it does not seem to have been syphilis. A lot of his symptoms indicate for some the likelihood of Parkinson's disease. Toward the end of the war, concern for Hitler's general health prompted all sorts of tests, according to Himmler's files, including serological ones conducted by Dr. Walter Löhlein to determine the presence or not of syphilis. All results proved negative, and neurosyphilis can be ruled out as there was no dementia or loss of memory.

Whatever afflicted Hitler was not much improved by his addiction to methamphetamine; Hitler was a speed freak, thanks to his quack of a doctor Theo Morrell. Some of Morrell's treatments were as bizarre as the recipient. Hitler had dyspepsia, so Morrell prescribed special little red capsules containing the live bacteria extracted from Bulgarian peasants' stools. Morrell also gave Hitler an increasing number of daily injections containing 4.4 ml of vitamins laced with methamphetamine. Toward the end of the war, Hitler was taking six or seven injections a day and the effects of amphetamine addiction took their toll—he became wide-eyed and haunted and much given to summoning his generals in the middle of the night to harangue them for hours.

And finally, it seems that the old British ditty conjecturing the number and size of Hitler's testes is correct. Hitler really did "only have one ball." In 1923 he was languishing in Munich jail, where he was given a medical examination to assess his fitness to stand trial for treason. The extant notes state: "Urogenital system: Right testicle only present." This was to be confirmed by the autopsy conducted on his burnt remains by the head of the Autopsy Commission, Dr. Faust Shkaravski, who observed that Hitler's heart looked like boiled meat and that "only the right testicle was found." He was, it seems, unbalanced at both ends.

Spy's Turkish Delight

The tall, handsome and enigmatic character in flowing robes who wafted round the screen in *Lawrence of Arabia* (1965) is well wide of the mark. Thomas Edward Chapman, for that was his name before a family surname shift to Lawrence, was short and skinny with a disproportionately large head. He was a self-aggrandizing and pathological liar, a man with unusual sexual leanings, and who in battle could get so turned on by the death and violence that he shocked Arab and Turk alike.

Lawrence was the illegitimate son of Thomas Chapman (later Sir Thomas, 7th baronet of his line), a minor Irish peer who abandoned his wife, Edith, in Westmeath, Ireland, to run away to Oxford with the governess, Sarah Junner, herself the illegitimate issue of her mother's dalliance with a Norwegian sailor. Here, the couple lived under the assumed name of Lawrence and had five children, Thomas Edward included. Of all the children, only Tom was made aware of the regiment of skeletons in the family closet, perhaps causing him to take to a life of secrecy and fantasy from then on.

Before World War I he had spent quite a few years in Syria, where he worked on British Museum digs from 1910 until 1913, mainly on the excavation of the ancient Hittite city at Carchemish. Here, some scholars claim he began a rather disturbing relationship with an Arab boy who was perhaps twelve years old. Working as a donkey boy on the transport team servicing the site, Salim Achmed claimed he was fourteen in order to achieve a wage above that to which he was entitled, and the two soon became inseparable. Nicknamed "Dahoum" (Little Dark One), Salim moved in with Lawrence, to the unease of both the local community and that of the archaeological team; matters were hardly improved by Lawrence having the child pose nude for sculptures which he displayed on the roof of their quarters. When Lawrence had to return to England in 1913 he took Dahoum with him, and they returned to Syria the following year. In 1914, Lawrence left for England alone and Salim died of typhus during this absence. Lawrence later dedicated his *Seven Pillars of Wisdom* (1926) with a mawkish poem to "S.A." and his diaries refer to the lad as the "darling . . . after whom there can be no other."

Mainly through the international success of the aforementioned film, most imagine Lawrence to have been something of a maverick, so fiercely loyal to his beloved Bedouin that he was forever on the brink of open rebellion against his own superiors. This was never the case, however. Britain (and Lawrence) knew it was imperative to keep the Arabs pitted against the Ottomans instead of joined with them, and Lawrence's role in this strategy was crucial. Even after the Sykes-Picot agreement of 1916, by which France and Britain agreed how they would carve up Arabia between them, and the Balfour Declaration of 1917, which promised the Jews a homeland in Palestine, Lawrence still kept feeding the Arabs the same old stories of unity and self-determination. True, Lawrence was appalled by the Sykes-Picot Agreement and did his unsuccessful best to unsettle it, but this was not through any belief in the rights of the Arabs to independence. Apart from being devoutly anti-Semitic, Lawrence was also a Francophobe and the thought of the French getting their hands on lands he regarded as a British dominion was abhorrent to him. True, he was instrumental in promoting Faisal I of Iraq to power, but Lawrence privately thought him "a very weak man, an empty man. You were able to use Faisal to get what you wanted." The British just love to be loved, even by those they are selling down the river, so it fitted the pattern to have Lawrence painted a hero to the desert Arabs who were held in thrall by their beloved "Orence." In fact, he was then regarded by some Arabs as nothing but another interfering and imperialist foreigner, and by others as being the same but a useful tool nevertheless, and this is pretty much how he is remembered by Arab historians today.

While *Seven Pillars of Wisdom* may be a great work of literature, it is riddled with inconsistencies, exaggeration and untruths. When talking of his early life, Lawrence claims to have run away from home and lied about his age to get into the British Army, but he did no such thing.

After the Arab victory at Aqaba, he claims to have ridden across the Sinai Desert to Suez in 48 hours to carry news of the victory to the British, but Michael Asher, one of the world's most renowned desert explorers, put this down to impossible fantasy (and Asher is a great fan of Lawrence). On the subject of the attack on Aqaba of which both *Seven Pillars of Wisdom* and the aforementioned film make so much, there was no sweeping charge of Arab camelry bearing down on the town because the fighting was not focused there but at Abu el Lissal, the site of a Turkish blockhouse halfway between Aqaba and Maan. While here, there was some sort of charge culminating in the slaughter of every Turk in the garrison; Lawrence did not get the chance to join in the fun. Prior to the attack he had got overexcited and, firing his pistol erratically, shot his own camel in the head and had to wait for his men to come back after the carnage and drag the beast off him. Meanwhile, Aqaba itself was being shelled into submission by British warships, so by the time Lawrence had found himself another camel the place had surrendered and was wide open.

It is the incident at Dera that has attracted most attention. His account places him in Dera on a reconnaissance mission on the night of November 21–22, 1917. He was, he says, detained by Turkish soldiers who, miraculously at such close quarters, mistook him for an Arab. To cut a long story short, Lawrence claims that he was marched off to the bedroom of the commanding officer and local military governor, Hajim Muhittin Bey, who wanted to rape him. His resistance resulted in hours of beatings, stabbing with a bayonet and whippings until, having been held down for a protracted sexual assault, he was thrown out into the street again.

Lawrence says the troops who beat him spoke with a heavy Druze accent, but the Druze were exempt from military service and, once he was stripped off, it is hard to see how anyone could have failed to notice he was European. Given that the Turks were fully aware of Lawrence and his operations against them, if a garrison commander suddenly found himself holding a European masquerading as an Arab then the last thing he was going to do was have him tossed out into the street, assaulted or otherwise. In the first edition of the book, Lawrence says Bey was called "Naji," as he was fearful that someone might seek him out for verification so, ignorant of his infamy in the West, Hajim died peacefully in 1965 in Izmir. When confronted with the story, Hajim's family and those who had served under him were absolutely flabbergasted. Memories were of course a bit hazy, but no one remembers any such captive and there is serious doubt that Hajim was even in Dera at the time. He was a famed womanizer but also a dedicated officer and patriot, so the suggestion that he would capture the main thorn in the side of the Turkish forces and then let him go does not hold water. After the incident, Lawrence claims that, despite the violence of the assault and presumable resulting injuries, he leapt manfully onto a camel and completed the 250-mile journey back to Aqaba in three days. A couple of weeks later he was in Jerusalem for the liberation festivities, and all who saw him there on December 3 noted how well he looked.

Whether Hajim was in Dera on the night in question is immaterial. Lawrence himself was not there—he had no need to ride 250 miles to Aqaba, as he was there all the time. On November 21, 1917, he and Colonel Pierce Joyce are logged as having undertaken a motor reconnaissance together into the Wadi Yutm. They signed out one of the new cars delivered for the 10th Motor Section of the Royal Field Artillery for the trip, and Lieutenant Samuel Brodie remembers chatting with the two officers upon their return. Also, the Aqaba guard-ship HMS *Humber* has various entries in its log for the few days either side of the 21st, which confirm Lawrence's presence in the port.

After the war Lawrence returned to work in the Foreign Office, but by 1922 was depressed and sought anonymity in the ranks of the RAF as Leading Aircraftman John Ross, but he was soon exposed and left to join the Royal Tank Corps as T. E. Shaw, before returning to the RAF. On May 19, 1935, Lawrence was motorcycling back to Clouds Hill, his rented cottage in Bovington, Dorset, when he came up behind two schoolboys and swerved to avoid them, but crashed. Engineers' reports agreed that the bike was in second gear at the time of impact, so he could not have been doing much more than about 35 mph; had he been wearing his crash helmet he would have survived.

Villa Dolorosa

Whether he was the altruistic Robin Hood of Mexican ballads or the opportunistic, murdering rapist of more cynical appraisal, the legend of Pancho Villa rides on and is knocking on the White House door.

Born Doroteo Arango Arambula, he took to the hills in his teens to join a gang of cut-throats led by Ignacio Parra, otherwise known as Francisco "Pancho" Villa. By the time the real Villa died in an army ambush, Arambula was already recognized by the gang as the leader-in-waiting, so he not only assumed the dead man's crown but also his name. In the years leading up to the Mexican Revolutionary Wars (1910–21, with widespread killing until 1930), the all-new Pancho Villa and his gang had themselves a ball. They stole anything that wasn't nailed down, and any woman who took Villa's fancy but saw through his phony marriage scam (thirty-two of them at a conservative count) to get her into bed was subjected to brutal rape. When war came it was a tailor-made theater of operation for a thug like Villa.

Now parading himself as General Villa, Pancho was always on the lookout for a quick peso. He signed a contract with the Californian Mutual Film Company on January 3, 1914, grossing him $25,000 for the exclusive film rights to his campaigns, but with certain restrictions. All major battles would have to take place during daylight—preferably between the hours of nine and four when the light was most favorable—and only at times suitable to the schedule of Mutual film crews. (The contract is extant and currently on display in the Mexico City Museum, folio 3057 of the Federico Gonzalez Garza Archive.) Actually, this suited Villa down to the ground—regular hours, no night work and double pay; what more could a cut-throat ask? But you need a long spoon to sup with California lawyers.

Mutual supplied seven thousand old Confederate uniforms because Villa's men were thought too scruffy, and he had to wear face powder for close-ups as he was too swarthy for American audiences. He also had to travel with a personal attendant to keep him shaved and his hair trimmed. Certain charges and executions had to be reshot—no pun intended—and other footage, such as him shooting a woman in the head for daring to lunge at him after he killed her husband, ended up on the cutting-room floor. At Mutual's insistence, he delayed his attack on the city of Ojinaga, holding it under siege for three days until a film crew could get there to give the order to attack. (It was during this engagement that Villa is thought to have "disposed" of writer Ambrose Bierce.) And, according to El Paso historian Fred Morales, Villa also had to delay his attack on Juraz to avoid clashing with the World Series.

Farcical, perhaps, but this was the first real footage of war on the hoof. Previous attempts to film the Greco-Turkish War of 1897 did not amount to much, although the UK National Film Archive does hold some very poor-quality footage of the 5th Northumberland Fusiliers in action at Orange River on November 12, 1899, during the Boer War. Now united, the camera and conflict would never again part.

American audiences soon tire of losers, so when the fortunes of war ceased to favor Villa, Mutual packed up and went home at about the same time as the American government made public its support for Venustiano Carranza, a sworn enemy of Villa, whom they helped take the Mexican presidency. Missing the limelight and the money, and disgruntled at American support for Carranza, Villa got above himself, and on the night of March 9, 1916, he crossed into New Mexico to attack the town of Columbus. Reverting to type, he unleashed a fury of murder, rape and arson before running away to hide in the hills. Within days, President Woodrow Wilson had authorized General John "Black Jack" Pershing to go after Villa and bring him back dead or alive. Still grieving the recent loss of his wife and three daughters in a domestic fire, Pershing was not in any mood to pussyfoot around the Mexican troops sent to protest the sovereignty of Mexican soil and impede his progress. He crossed the border with 10,000 men on March 15 and, after the first face-off, the Mexicans wisely decided to ignore his presence on their turf and leave him to it. Overall, the Punitive Expedition, as it became known, was doomed to spend months in fruitless search of the arid hills and canyons, but there was the odd success. One of Pershing's young officers heard that Julio Cardenas was holed up in a villa at San Miguelito, just outside Rubio. One of the most senior Villistas, Cardenas was killed by a young officer, Lieutenant George Patton, later general Patton, who started his incredible collection of war loot with Cardenas's silver-studded saddle and side arms.

All good things come to an end, and so it was with Villa's war. He retired to Chihuahua where he married—legitimately for the first time—and settled down. But his many enemies had not forgotten him. On July 20, 1923, his car was ambushed in Parral where Villa, according to Mexican legend, met his end with arms outstretched and shouting "A great Hooray for my brothers of race." In reality, he stopped eighteen rounds with his body and four with his head, so he wasn't shouting anything at all. The assassins were neither sought nor caught as their puppet-masters were behind desks in the American and Mexican governments—Villa upset everyone. He was buried in Parral's Pantheon de los Dolores, but he would not rest for long. The Americans had put a price on his head and, some say, they got it in the end.

On the night of February 5, 1926, American mercenary Emil Holmdahl, who had variously fought for Villa and acted as a guide for Pershing's Punitive Expedition, looked up his old friend and cut off his head. Holmdahl was quickly arrested, but not before one of his associates, Al Jennings, was back across the border with Villa's head. Jennings allegedly passed the head on to one Frank Brophy for shipment to his close friend, Prescott Bush, George W.'s grandfather, who had allegedly funded the adventure. By February 9, the *El Paso Herald* (forerunner of the *Herald Post*) was carrying articles that clearly indicate American pressure for Holmdahl's release, and by the 11th was stating him to be on his way home. Diplomatic pressure had, it is said, been instigated by

Prescott Bush, Roland Harriman and Knight Woolley, ex-Yale men and members of Skull and Bones, the oldest students' society in America. There are more than a few who believe the Bonesmen are still in possession of Villa's skull.

Even within Mexico there is contention about where Villa's headless body ended up. After the initial desecration, the good citizens of Parral claim to have shifted what was left of Villa to another grave and dumped an unknown into the original grave to fox any future trophy hunters. Because of this action, the citizens of Parral maintain that when their government shifted what they thought was Villa's body to a more prominent marble home in Mexico City, they got the wrong man.

Who Stole Napoleon's Penis?

He was not French; he was not short; his marriage to "Joséphine" was not an affair of any enduring passion on either side; he was most certainly not killed by his wallpaper, or by anything else, for that matter.

Born in Ajaccio on Corsica, the year after the French invaded that island, Napoleon Bonaparte was essentially Italian, the son of minor Lombardy aristocracy and properly named Nabulione di Buonaparte. Although he was enrolled in a French military school in Troyes in 1779 on the condition that he learn French, this would be a language he never fully mastered, frequently lapsing back into his native Corsican whenever annoyed or frustrated. That he grew up hating the French and still hated them in his twenties is clear from the following, written in 1789 to Pasquale Paoli, leader of the Corsican revolt against the French: "I was born when my country was dying. Thirty thousand Frenchmen disgorged upon our shores, drowning the throne of liberty in a sea of blood; such was the hateful spectacle that offended my infant eyes."

As for the so-called Joséphine, she was in fact a semi-literate Creole from Martinique with sallow skin and a reluctance to smile in case she exposed her rotting teeth. Born Marie Josèphe Rose de Tascher, she was widely known as "Rose," a name that failed to please Napoleon, who insisted on calling her Joséphine. By his late twenties, Napoleon had resigned himself to his recurring bouts of impotence and seems to have directed his attentions to older women, whom he presumed to be less demanding in the boudoir, a misconception soon dispelled in no uncertain terms after marriage to the voracious Joséphine. (She was six years his senior and previously married to Alexandre de Beauharnais, guillotined during the French Revolution.) Having more important things on his mind on the day of their wedding, such as the imminent invasion of Italy, Napoleon kept her waiting at the altar for two hours, so it is safe to assume he was not in any romantic fervor to culminate his heart's desire. For her part, she later confided to friends that she had to overcome her revulsion at his physical appearance to go through with the wedding at all.

Their honeymoon was an equally businesslike two-day episode before he was off to war. Apparently the first night was a disaster, marked by the intervention of Joséphine's pet pug Fortune. Presuming his mistress to be under some sort of attack, Fortune hurled himself into the melee to deliver some rather nasty nips to the soon-to-be imperial buttocks. Fortune, a truculent creature at the best of times, met a sticky end in the jaws of Napoleon's chef's bulldog.

As soon as her husband had eased himself gingerly into the saddle, Joséphine, who later dismissed her husband's boudoir capabilities with "Bon-a-parte est Bon-a-rien" ("Bonaparte is good for nothing"), was hotfoot into the bed of a dashing young cavalry officer, Lieutenant Hippolyte Charles, the first in a long line of "comforters." Napoleon, too, had his share of dalliances before divorcing Joséphine in 1809 so he could marry the eighteen-year-old Marie-Louise of Austria, niece of the guillotined Marie Antoinette.

After Napoleon met his Waterloo in 1815 everyone, including most of the French, was glad to see the back of him. His campaigns had cost the lives of perhaps 1.5 million of his own men, so there can scarcely have been a single family in France without loss. Across Europe, another five million troops and civilians lay dead. Furthermore, the British pay income tax because of him. It was first imposed in 1799 with the piecrust promise that it was only a temporary measure to fund the Napoleonic Wars, but after he was safely exiled to St. Helena, Westminster thought it might as well stay in place.

There are many British paintings depicting Napoleon as a short and crestfallen figure aboard either HMS *Bellepheron*, to which he surrendered, or on HMS *Northumberland* for his transportation to St. Helena, but he was in fact of quite normal height for his time. French imperial measures of the day differed from the British in that the French inch equated to 2.71 cm while the British inch was, and still is, only 2.54 centimeters. So, French references to his being five feet two inches tall really relate to what we would now call five feet six and a half inches. Also, the English misunderstood the countless references to him as "Le Petit Caporal"—*petit* did not mean "small" but "beloved"; it was being employed in its affectionate sense.

As for the notion that he was killed by the arsenic in the wallpaper of his St. Helena home, or by a deliberate poisoning, these too are conspiracy theories that will not fade. Napoleon died at 5:49 p.m. on May 5, 1821, and the post-mortem was conducted at 2:30 p.m. the next day by Napoleon's surgeon, fellow Corsican Francesco Antommarchi, appointed by the deceased's mother. The examination was conducted in front of seven doctors and 10 other witnesses selected from Napoleon's own staff and British personnel. The official autopsy stated:

> *The left lung indicated healed pleurisy and both lungs exhibited clear fluid in the pleural sacs; the left side of the liver was abnormally adhered to the undersurface of the diaphragm, which separates the chest cavity from the abdomen, and was also stuck to the upper edge of the stomach at the lesser curvature; granules of digested blood filled the stomach which was severely ulcerated along its upper edge; the lining of that same organ was hardened and perforated toward the pylorus leading to the gut and at that perforating the stomach was "welded" to the liver, itself seriously enlarged. All other organs normal.*

Napoleon died of the stomach cancer that had claimed his father. He had himself demanded to be autopsied and for his son to be told if cancer was present, no doubt to allow him to prepare for his own medical heritage.

The accidental or deliberate arsenic poisoning theory has been around for quite some time, but the much-blamed wallpaper was not at fault. The heavy, Scheele's Green wallpaper was produced in Sweden and certainly did contain a great deal of copper arsenite which, when damp, would have leached arsenic trimethyl gas into the rooms. The conditions at Longwood House, as Napoleon's quarters were named, are known to have been so damp as to cause the wallpaper to fall off the walls in sheets. In 1980, a team from Glasgow University used an X-ray fluorescent spectroscope on samples of Scheele's Green allegedly taken from Longwood and identified arsenic levels of 0.12 g per square meter. To put this into perspective, the same team was not long after called to the country seat of Lord Armstrong of Northumberland, where men hired to strip a similar type of wallpaper all became ill. Although not Sheele's Green, this paper was shown to have levels of arsenic fifty times that of Napoleon's, but the Armstrongs had lived there quite happily for many a year without any ill effect.

Arsenic poisoning has been ruled out by every serious scientific body that has reassessed the evidence. Locks of Napoleon's hair are still plentiful and these reveal an arsenic level of 30.4 parts per million, 60 times today's norm. But this hardly backs up any claim of poisoning. Authenticated samples of hair from his sister, Pauline, and Joséphine herself indicate arsenic level 120 times higher than today's norm and no one has put this forward as proof that they succumbed to poison. In 2008, Padua University in Italy proceeded with the most sophisticated and conclusive study to date, employing a small nuclear reactor to irradiate the hairs. Next, the samples were subjected to a technique known as neutron activation, which allows highly accurate analysis without destroying the sample. Also in the study were samples taken from many of Napoleon's contemporaries, including both his wives and his son, and all presented arsenic levels on par with Napoleon's or even double. The tests also showed that, even as a boy, Napoleon presented what today would be considered suspiciously high levels of arsenic.

St. Helena's soil was high in arsenic, which would have been present in all the vegetables grown there, and arsenic would have been found in countless products including cosmetics and hair tonics. For example, Napoleon quaffed the island's wine in copious quantities; not only was arsenic present in the wine per se, but it was further used as a preservative in the storage barrels. Arsenic is also present in high levels in all fish and seafood, which would have been a staple on St. Helena, and many of the medicines of the day were also arsenic based. In short, everyone was up to the gunwales with the stuff. Yet chronic arsenic poisoning presents increased skin pigmentation, laryngitis, eczema, running eyes, numbness, wasting of the arms and legs and death from heart failure. Napoleon's heart was fine. Antommarchi could hardly have failed to notice such classic symptoms in his patient.

There are also Napoleon's last letters and his will, in which he most certainly did profess: "My death is premature. I have been assassinated by the English oligarchy and its hired murderers." This Parthian shot is invariably taken out of context to bolster conspiracy theories, whereas it was nothing more than a farewell goad to his numerous doctors, to whom he frequently opined that "medicine is the science of murderers." To put the cat firmly among the pigeons, he went on to make magnanimous bequests of lands and estates he did not own to the "people of France," and bequests to friends and relatives totaling a further six million non-existent francs. Napoleon died broke, but wanted to go in the sure knowledge that everyone in France would blame the English for stealing the money and lands as he lay helpless on his deathbed.

Blissfully unaware that no one was really bothered any more, he left instructions for his heart to be pickled and sent to Marie-Louise, from whom he had not received a single word during his exile. This lack of correspondence he attributed to his captors' blocking her mail, but she had in fact entered into a bigamous marriage with Graf Adam von Neipperg, the officer Napoleon had appointed as her guardian. As it happens, one of the English doctors present at the autopsy decided to keep the heart for himself, but left it in a sink overnight and the rats got at it. In the end, there were bits and pieces of Napoleon all over the place. His teeth were pulled out by the Irish doctor Barry O'Meara and if every tooth he subsequently sold for ten guineas was the real thing, then Napoleon must have had the teeth to rival a great white shark. Most of the organs were stolen by doctors present; one jar of imperial intestines turned up in the vaults of the British Royal College of Surgeons, but was destroyed in a German air raid in 1940.

The final indignity was that Napoleon's priest-confessor, the abbot Ange Paul Vignali, crept back into the post-mortem room to cut off the imperial penis—simply taking a lock of hair was just not enough for this turbulent priest. The good father proceeded to steal anything he could get his hands on—personal items, cutlery, stationery—before quitting the island with a train of trunks, each loaded with Napoleonic trophies and souvenirs. In 1916, Vignali's descendants sold the collection, including the "mummified tendon," which turned up in 1924 in the possession of Dr. Abraham Rosenbach, the celebrated Philadelphia collector whose legacy forms the core of the extant Rosenbach Museum and Library in that city. A few years later, Rosenbach took Napoleon's penis on tour, finally displaying it on a small velvet cushion in New York's Museum of French Art. The world-weary press of New York was less than impressed. *Time* magazine of February 14, 1927 said: "Napoleona went on exhibition last week at the Museum of French Art in Manhattan. Maudlin sympathizers sniffed; shallow women giggled, pointed. In a glass case they saw something looking like a maltreated strip of buckskin shoelace or a shriveled eel. It was a mummified tendon taken from Napoleon's body after the postmortem."

In 1971, suitably enshrined in a tasteful little casket and accompanied by an authentication certificate, the same item appeared on sale in Christie's Fine Art Auctioneers catalogue, in which it was tactfully listed as a withered "sinew," this being an accepted biblical euphemism for said appendage. Failing to raise its starting price of £13,000, the imperial penis was withdrawn only to resurface in a Paris auction in 1977, where it was snapped up for $3,000 by John Lattimer, professor emeritus and former chairman of Urology at the Columbia University College of Physicians and Surgeons. Lattimer was the senior medical officer with Patton at the famous crossing of the Rhine; he was selected to be doctor-in-attendance to the likes of Göring at the Nuremberg trials, and again came to public notice when the Kennedy family brought him in to go over the evidence from the JFK assassination. Throughout such a life, Lattimer had assembled an impressive collection of the weird and wonderful, including Göring's suicide capsule, Lincoln's bloodstained collar from the night of his assassination and bits and pieces of the car in which Kennedy was riding in Dallas. Obviously he thought Napoleon's penis belonged with such kindred items.

Perhaps it is to Napoleon's credit that there are few misconceptions attached to his military career. He neither torched Moscow before his retreat in 1812, nor ordered his men to shoot the nose off the Sphinx when in Egypt in 1798. While it is true he ordered the Kremlin and a few other prominent buildings to be destroyed before heading home on his trail of tears, it was the Russians themselves who burnt their capital to the ground on the orders of Fyodor Rostopchin, military governor of Moscow. With Napoleon on his doorstep, Rostopchin ordered the evacuation of the city and the destruction by fire of anything of use left behind—food stores, granaries, everything. On top of that, he left teams of arsonists who had instructions to lay low until the French Army had made itself at home, and then bring the town down around its ears. Three days later these teams went to work and, with the vast majority of Moscow then being of wooden construction, the whole place was soon an inferno.

As for the Sphinx, this was missing its nose long before Napoleon stood before it in 1798. Frederick Louis Norden, the Danish explorer, was there in 1737 and his sketches show the Sphinx to be without a nose. The figure is also missing its beard and cobra head-piece, all three hacked off on the orders of fundamentalist Muslim cleric Sayim al-Dahr, who rampaged through the area in 1378, defacing the symbol of "pagan idolatry."

Zig-Zag Wag

World War II came along just in time to save Eddie Chapman from being just another old inmate dying in some grimy prison on the island of Jersey.

Barely into his twenties when he deserted from military service in the Guards, Chapman disappeared into the underground of London's Soho, where he frolicked in the company of Noel Coward and Marlene Dietrich, who little suspected that he funded his lavish lifestyle by blowing open safes, and sleeping with bored society women and then blackmailing them for the return of incriminating snapshots. When things became too hot for him in London at the close of 1938 he shifted operations to Jersey, but his luck was running out. Undercover policemen from the mainland nearly caught him as he enjoyed afternoon tea with a young lady called Betty Farmer in the Hotel de la Plage. He spotted them as they crossed the forecourt and, biding his time, calmly waited for them to enter the tea room before making his own exit in a graceful commando roll through a closed window. The trouble with islands is that they are islands; he was caught and imprisoned in February 1939 and was still languishing in jail when the Germans took over the Channel Islands in July 1940. Chapman must have been the only person on Jersey pleased to see the Nazis arrive. Ever the opportunist, he saw this not as a worsening of circumstances but as an event to be turned to his advantage.

He eventually convinced his new jailors of the sincerity of his offer to spy for them on the British mainland, so they whisked him off to Nantes in France to train him up as a spy and saboteur. Kept "sweet" by a never-ending supply of wine and women, he was eventually deemed ready and parachuted into the Cambridgeshire countryside, just outside Ely on December 16, 1942, where all his machinations very nearly came to a sticky end on a pitchfork wielded expertly by a local farmer. Chapman convinced the man to take him to the nearest police station where he demanded to be handed on to MI5 who, as things turned out, were expecting him. They had just cracked some of the new German codes and picked up radio traffic relating to his return to the UK. He was taken to London's Latchmere House, a Military Intelligence Centre run by Lieutenant Colonel Robin Stephens, one of the best interrogators in the business. In Chapman's case, however, interrogation was not required—Stephens could hardly shut him up. Known as Fritz to his German handlers, Chapman had been sent home to blow up the De Havilland factory at Hatfield in Hertfordshire, the main production center of the Mosquito bomber.

Stephens saw the enormous potential of Chapman as a double agent, but what to do about the De Havilland mission? He could hardly have the place blown up to prove Chapman's credibility to the Nazis. So enter another bizarre character of World War II, Jasper Maskelyne, a professional illusionist and stage magician who, with the help of his so-called Magic Team, was variously required to make Alexandria and the Suez Canal "disappear" to enemy aircraft and convince Rommel that the assault on El Alamein would come from the south and not the north, where the real tanks stood disguised as trucks. He was just the chap to "blow up" a factory without damaging it. Maskelyne dressed the site with all sorts of debris and wooden replicas of damaged factory equipment, before covering the building with hand-painted tarpaulins presenting a picture of widespread destruction that could only be seen in proper perspective from the air. False stories of vile sabotage on the night of January 29, 1943, were fed to the press, and German reconnaissance aircraft were studiously ignored by the British when they came to take aerial shots of the "devastation."

Chapman not only agreed to return to Germany, but offered to bump off Hitler as a bonus; his German handler, Stephan von Groning, had promised him a seat near Hitler at the next Nuremberg rally if he was successful in his British mission. Stephens told him not to do any such thing. Hitler's erratic behavior was already working in the Allies' favor, so the last thing they wanted was Hitler dead and replaced by someone who knew what he was doing and in full command of his faculties. In March 1943, and now codenamed Zig-Zag by the British, Chapman was dropped off in neutral Portugal, from where he made his way back to a rapturous welcome in Berlin. On Hitler's instructions he was given his own house, a yacht, 110,000 reichsmarks and awarded the Iron Cross. Stephens recorded that the "Germans came to love Chapman . . . but he did not reciprocate. He loved himself, he loved adventure and he loved his country; probably in that order."

Within weeks, Chapman was moved to Oslo to teach at a German school for spies, where he met Dagmar Lahlum who, unbeknown to him at the time, was in the Norwegian resistance. She thought him an important German contact who should be cultivated and so began a touching affair in which each party thought the other to be someone else. In what could have been an extremely dangerous move for both, they revealed their double-agent identities to one another and became engaged. As he already had a fiancée called Freda Stevenson in England who was being supported for him by British Intelligence, he thought it only fair to get Groning to come up with a living allowance of 600 kroner a month for Dagmar to provide her with life's little luxuries. This situation backfired on her after the war when she was branded a "German whore" and prosecuted as a collaborator. Chapman must have had charm by the bucketful because, despite his having abandoned her, she kept her promise never to reveal his secret. Only after her death did her daughter find exonerating paperwork and clear her name.

Toward the close of the war, the Germans sent Chapman, now their most trusted agent, back to London to report on the accuracy of the V1 and V2 hits on the city. Unaware that their flying bombs were pretty much on target for central London, they fully accepted Chapman's reports that the missiles were overshooting and made unnecessary adjustments, leaving the bulk of the V1s and V2s falling south of the city where they did far less damage. With the war almost at a close, Chapman returned to Oslo and when peace broke out he abandoned

Dagmar, as he had Freda. He then nipped over to Tangiers to crack a few safes so he could buy a castle in Ireland and retire after marrying Betty Farmer, the young lady he had left in such spectacular style in Jersey's Hotel de la Plage. They had a daughter, Suzanne, and when it was her turn to marry, Stephan von Groning attended the wedding.

QUOTE MISQUOTE

"An Army Marches on Its Stomach"

Marching rations with a decent shelf-life were a major problem for erstwhile armies. The Romans, for example, sealed up minced ingredients in a sheep's stomach, which in its day was the closest thing to canned food. They brought this culinary delight with them when they invaded Britain, giving the Scots haggis. It was actually Frederick the Great who coined the above saying, and the erroneous accreditation to Napoleon arose because he used it as the rallying cry for his 1795 challenge to the French scientific community to produce long-life rations, as his armies were constantly hampered by retreating enemy adopting a scorched earth policy.

He offered a purse of twelve hundred francs to anyone who could supply the French Army with preserved rations and first up to the plate was Nicolas Appert, whose method involved the sealing of food in strong glass jars while it was still boiling. Napoleon hailed him a hero, demanded the process be declared a state secret and then defaulted on the prize money. Understandably annoyed, Appert published a book on the art of preserving food, a copy of which found its way into the hands of Englishman Peter Durance, who furnished the British Army with food in metal containers. (He patented the storage method in 1810.) Not long after that, Appert's factory went up in a sheet of flame—not a surprise—but he finally received his prize money in 1815, with the strongest possible hints that it might best be used to set up a canning factory. The first time that two armies marched to battle on canned food was at Waterloo in June of the same year.

"Come on You Sons of Bitches, Do You Want to Live Forever?"

This is attributed to marine Sergeant-Major Daniel Daly, but there was no mention of his so exhorting his men at any time in June 1918, when the Marines were under heavy pressure from the Germans in the battle of Belleau Wood in northern France. Ignoring the overwhelming odds, Daly led several offensives during the battle, but no one has managed to pin the quote to any one particular event. It just sounded like the sort of thing he might well have said. Awarded the Navy Cross for his outstanding valor throughout the entire engagement, it was likely that the military publicity machine put the quote out to the press, inspired by an earlier and less florid version. At the battle of Kolin on June 18, 1757, Frederick the Great employed the tamer: "Men, do you want to live eternally?"

"I Only Regret That I Have but One Life to Give for My Country"

These are supposedly the last words of Nathan Hale, a hero of the Revolutionary War hanged by the British for spying on Long Island.

Detailed to the execution squad was one Captain Frederick Mackenzie who recorded: "He behaved with great composure and resolution, saying [at the end] that he thought it the duty of every good Officer to obey any orders given him by his Commander-in-Chief; and desired the Spectators [at the gallows] to be at all times prepared to meet death in whatever shape it might appear." This statement was all a bit bland for a hero's farewell, so a few months later the Massachusetts press was claiming that Hale met his end berating his persecutors and sneering at death. The *Essex Journal* of February 13, 1777, claimed: "At the gallows he made a sensible and spirited speech; among other things, he told them they were shedding the blood of the innocent, and that if he had ten thousand lives, he would lay them all down, if called to it, in defense of his injured and bleeding country."

The more succinct version in the heading was conjured up by General William Hull, a childhood friend of Hale, who was aware of his fondness for Joseph Addison's *Cato* (1713), which includes the line: "What a pity it is that we can die but once in the service of our country."

"I Shall Return"

Just before his hurried departure from the Philippines in 1942, it is widely believed that "I shall return" was General Douglas MacArthur's reassurance to those he was leaving behind to face the Japanese, but he never said this.

He knew full well that at some point the advancing Japanese would force him to make a dash for Australia, and had thus prepared a statement to be released in his absence. The Office of War Information in Washington, D.C., insisted it should read "we shall return," but as President Roosevelt said: "Never underestimate a man who overestimates himself." MacArthur was convinced that the Philippines loved him more than America per se, and so stuck to the singular. As soon as he received word that MacArthur was safe in Australia, Colonel Carlos Romulo, a Filipino soldier and journalist who was then MacArthur's press officer, made a broadcast and issued the promise on MacArthur's behalf.

Few shared MacArthur's towering opinion of himself. When President Truman heard he was going to resign in 1951—MacArthur angered by disagreements over the escalation or limitation of the Korean War—Truman immediately ordered him sacked saying: "No way is that sonovabitch going to resign on me; fire him." He later explained: "I fired him because he would not respect the authority of the President. I did not fire him because he was a dumb sonovabitch, although he was, but that is not against the law in generals. If it was then half of them would be in jail."

"Ich Bin Ein Berliner"

Uttered near the Berlin Wall by John F. Kennedy on June 26, 1963, this most famous of all Cold War quotes is best described as the "gaffe that never was."

As *Berliner* in German can indeed denote a jam donut, the news services were soon buzzing with talk of a terrible translation error. Apparently, Kennedy's audience was falling about laughing as he passionately proclaimed himself to be such a delicacy. Pundits emerged to explain that if he wanted to proclaim himself to be a citizen of Berlin, then he should have said "Ich bin Berliner," and that the inclusion of *ein* left him looking like a donut. The speech, however, was professionally prepared and translated by Robert Lochner, the official translator for the visit, so such a gaffe would have been extremely unlikely. Also, Kennedy practiced the speech all afternoon in the office of the Berlin mayor and no one there started sniggering. (That mayor was Willy Brandt, whose real name was actually Herbert Frahm; he had escaped the Nazis and fled to Norway and thence to Sweden using false papers in the name of "Willy Brandt." When he went home after the war, he simply kept the assumed name.)

German linguist Jurgen Eichoff finally laid the matter to rest with an article in the German academic journal *Monatshefte*, in which he explained that "Ich bin ein Berliner" is not only correct but the one and only correct way of expressing in German what the President intended to say. Only a person who was born and raised in Berlin could say "Ich bin Berliner," while one expressing sympathy and solidarity with Berliners would have to use the Kennedy line. Eichoff makes his point clear by explaining that one could say of Kennedy "Er ist Politiker," he is a politician, while "Er ist ein Politiker," he is like a politician, would describe a private citizen who knew how to play the system and get his own way.

"In the Name of the Great Jehovah and the Continental Congress"

Ethan Allen is fondly remembered as a patriotic hero of the Revolutionary War—there is even a furniture and interiors company named after him. Yet he did not shout out the above words when calling on the British to surrender Fort Ticonderoga at dawn on May 10, 1775.

Some Internet sites and written sources describe Allen as crafty and a speculator, which is a bit like calling Hitler playful and unpredictable. Allen was a cheat and a swindler. As for his patriotic credentials, these are tarnished from his entering into secret negotiations with the British—he negotiated to take Vermont out of the war in return for vast tracts of land. Be that as it may, he and General Benedict Arnold did indeed capture Fort Ticonderoga on May 10, 1775, but there was no battle, and not a single shot was fired.

Despite its size, the fort was understrength and poorly guarded; Allen and Arnold simply marched their detachment of Green Mountain Boys into the parade ground to take up positions while the British slept. Instead of calling out the above, Allen strutted about shouting for the British commander, Captain William de la Place, to "Come out here, you old rat." The shouts succeeded only in rousing one Lieutenant Jocelyn Feltham who, trousers in hand, rushed off to rouse his senior. As Allen's force was fully positioned with muskets at the ready, de la Place told Feltham to go out and throw in the towel while he got dressed, and at this point they heard Allen's more pointed: "Come out, you sons of British whores, or I'll smoke you out." It was Allen, writing several years after the events, who invented the more lofty line, but as his critics pointed out at the time of publication, he did not hold commission from either of the authorities he invoked.

"Lafayette, We Are Here"

The Marquis de Lafayette rendered considerable service to the cause of American independence, so in World War I when the first American troops turned up in Paris on July 4, 1917, it was thought apropos to hold the welcoming ceremony at his tomb. Although most sources credit General John Pershing with the above statement, he was actually a somewhat cold and flinty character, definitely not given to such flowery outbursts. In fact, he did not speak at all on that occasion, having delegated the speech making to Colonel Charles Stanton, his chief disbursing officer.

Writing in 1930, Pershing himself acknowledged: "Many have attributed this striking utterance to me and I have often wished that it could have been mine. But I have no recollection of saying anything so splendid. I am sure that those words were spoken by Colonel Stanton and to him must go the credit for coining so happy and felicitous a phrase."

"Mother of All ..."

On January 6, 1991, Saddam Hussein made a speech in Baghdad in which he promised the *umm al-ma'arik* for the American and British forces coming to kick him out of Kuwait. This hollow vaunt, which barely managed a single echo in the shock and awe of Operation *Desert Storm*, was mistranslated by Western journalists as "the mother of all battles." Although the Arabic *umm* does indeed have a literal meaning of "mother (of)," in the context of the speech it carried a meaning of "the biggest" or "the best." The mistranslation is not understood by Arab-speaking people, but it is now entrenched in English usage. A simple Google search using the expression brought up 350,000,000 sites so it is safe to say that this will be Saddam's most enduring legacy to the West.

"Now I Am Become Death, the Destroyer of Worlds"

Pithy quotes encapsulating cardinal moments are rarely genuine because those to whom they are attributed were either wholly unprepared for the events in question or ignorant at the time of their significance. Later, profound and fitting lines have to be invented. And so it was with Robert Oppenheimer, who said nothing like the above after the first atomic test in the New Mexico desert on July 16, 1945. Even if he had waxed so lyrical, he would have been misquoting his *Bhagavad Gita* ("Song of God," a sacred Hindu scripture).

It was about twenty years later that the Hindu reverie came out in a somber American documentary of 1965 called *The Decision to Drop the Bomb*, which naturally included an interview with Oppenheimer. Throughout, he sat looking suitably awed by his brainchild, eyes averted from camera, even pausing to dab away an invisible tear (you can see the whole performance at www.atomicarchive.com/movies/movie8.shtml), and said:

> *We knew the world would not be the same. A few people laughed . . . a few people cried . . . most people were silent. I remembered the line from the Hindu scripture the* Bhagavad Gita; *Vishnu is trying to persuade the prince that he should do his duty, and to impress him takes on his multi-armed form, and says, "Now I am become Death, the destroyer of worlds." I suppose we all thought that, one way or another.*

Even though Oppenheimer is claiming only that the line ran through his mind at the time, Chapter 11, v. 31–33 of said poem runs differently. For a start, scholars argue over *kala*, which can mean either "time" or "dark" (the feminine *Kali* is the dark goddess, she with the skull-necklace and many arms). The lines, actually spoken by Krishna, are best rendered: "Time am I, shatterer of all things, and I have come to slay these men. Even if you do not fight all those warriors facing you, you shall die." An odd mistake for Oppenheimer to make, as he was heavily into literary allusions. (Some critics explain the translation on account of Oppenheimer being influenced by Sanskrit scholar Arthur Ryder, who preferred the unusual translation of "Death" instead of "Time.") He even named the test site "Trinity" after his late fiancée's favorite John Donne poem. All very lofty and literary, to be sure, but Frank Oppenheimer, also present at the test, only remembers his brother saying "It worked" and test director Kenneth Bainbridge's "Now we are all sons of bitches."

As the Italians would say, *se non e vero, e molto ben trovato* ("if it is not true, it is very well-invented") and the quip is extremely *ben trovato* for such an event. As soon as Oppenheimer "remembered" remembering it, a host of others leapt onto the Hindu bandwagon. American author and journalist William Laurence wrote effusively of the tremendous impact such words had had on him back in 1946 when he interviewed Oppenheimer but a few hours after the test, which is strange as his 1945 reportage makes no mention of the quote, nor does his *Dawn Over Zero: The Story of the Atomic Bomb* (1946).

"Nuts!"

This was the famous and likely bowdlerized reply made by General Anthony McAuliffe to a German request for his surrender during the Battle of the Bulge in December 1944. He and the 101st Airborne were having a tough time of it just outside the small Belgian town of Bastogne, which had been surrounded by the German Ardennes offensive. A German deputation of two officers and two sergeants approached the American lines under a white flag on December 22 to deliver the ultimatum of surrender or die. Major Jones and Colonel Harper took the message up the line to McAuliffe, who sent them back with the now famous, one-word response. The German officers did not understand, allowing Harper the pleasure of enlightening them before they stalked off back to their own lines in Prussian fury. The 101st held out.

While it is true that the typed reply did read: "To the German Commander: NUTS! The American Commander," McAuliffe always maintained that others had downgraded his reply from "SHIT!", which he intended as a tribute to one of his heroes, Count Cambronne, commander of the French Imperial Guard at Waterloo. Cambronne had been in much the same situation. The British offered him the option of surrender, only to receive the one-word reply of "Merde!" French historians cleaned this up to "The Guard dies but never surrenders!", which leaves both men cruelly robbed of their moment.

"Only Good Indian Is a Dead Indian"

General Philip Sheridan had no love for Native Americans, and would doubtless have had much sympathy with the above sentiment, but he never said any such thing. The usual story links the birth of the expression with a visit he made to Fort Cobb, in what is now Oklahoma, in January 1869. At some point he was confronted by Toch-a-way, chief of the Comanche, who, striking himself on the chest, announced, "Me, Toch-a-way; me good Indian." Sheridan's apparent response was: "The only good Indians I ever saw were dead." Not only does the alleged incident smack of theatrical apocrypha—who knows why a Comanche chief would demean himself before an enemy, acting and talking like a comic-book Indian—but Sheridan himself denied that any such exchange had occurred.

The link between the general sentiment and Sheridan was possibly forged by a speech made by Theodore Roosevelt who, according to his friend and biographer, Herman Hagedorn, made the following statement in New York in January 1886 (given in *Roosevelt in the Badlands*, 1921):

I suppose I should be ashamed to say that I take the Western view of the Indian. I don't go so far as to think that the only good Indians are dead Indians, but I believe nine out of every ten are, and I shouldn't like to inquire too closely into the case of the tenth. The most vicious cowboy has more moral principle than the average Indian. Turn three hundred low families of New York into New Jersey, support them for fifty years in vicious idleness, and you will have some idea of what the Indians are. Reckless, revengeful, fiendishly cruel, they rob and murder, not the cowboys, who can take care of themselves, but the defenseless, lone settlers on the plains. As for the soldiers, an Indian chief once asked Sheridan for a cannon. "What! Do you want to kill my soldiers with it?" asked the general. "No," replied the chief, "want to kill the cowboy; kill soldier with a club."

The mention of the "dead Indian" sentiment and Sheridan in the same breath by such a prominent person was likely enough to establish the erroneous link. By 1926, this link was strengthened by "The only good Indians I saw were dead" appearing in Gurney Benham's *Complete Book of Quotations*, wherein it was attributed to Sheridan; compilers of similar collections followed suit to perpetuate the myth.

"Peace in Our Time"

Neville Chamberlain is unfairly remembered as a silly old man bamboozled by Hitler over the Munich Agreement, by which Germany and Britain agreed to sort out any further dispute by diplomatic means rather than conflict. After the conference, Chamberlain's plane landed at Heston Aerodrome on September 30, 1938, and it was here that he held aloft the infamous "piece of paper" and spoke to the assembled crowd of "peace with honor" and "peace for our time." He later repeated these comments outside the prime minister's residence at 10 Downing Street. Although the PM spoke of peace for our time, this was misreported by the British Press and the BBC through confusion with "Give us peace in our time, O Lord," a popular line from the Book of Common Prayer.

Although determined to avoid a second European bloodbath if possible, Chamberlain did not see this as an objective to be achieved no matter the cost for he was not a deluded fool, nor was he blind to Hitler's ambitions. In his next formal address to Parliament, on October 5, 1938, Chamberlain made it clear he had no intention of scaling down arms production or placing too much faith in Hitler's promises:

> *I am told that the policy which I have tried to describe is inconsistent with the continuance, and much more inconsistent with the acceleration of our present program of arms. I am asked how I can reconcile an*

appeal to the country to support the continuance of this program with the words which I used when I came back from Munich the other day and spoke of my belief that we might have peace in our time. I hope honorable Members will not be disposed to read into words used in a moment of some emotion, after a long and exhausting day, after I had driven through miles of excited, enthusiastic, cheering people—I hope they will not read into those words more than they were intended to convey.

A forlorn hope, as it turned out.

"Peccavi!"

It is still widely believed that this was the punning message tele-grammed by General Sir Charles Napier after his celebrated capture of the Indian province of Sind in 1843—*peccavi* is the Latin for "I have sinned," hence providing the opportunity for some territorial wordplay. Sir Charles had no such turn of wit, and the jest was invented instead by Catherine Winkworth who later achieved fame as a noted translator of hymns. Just seventeen years old, she wrote to the still relatively new *Punch* magazine suggesting that it might have been fun had Napier sent such a message. Her letter appeared in the edition dated May 18, 1844 (Vol. 6, p. 209) and in next to no time everyone was saying that Napier *had* sent such a quip.

This is but one of many such inventions: Lord Clyde supposedly sent *Nunc fortunatus sum* ("I am in luck now") from China after he secured Lucknow; Lord Dalhousie is attributed with *vovi* ("I vowed"), after his 1855 securing of Oudh, an area of Uttar Pradesh; least likely of all as the supposed author was semi-literate, Drake sent Queen Elizabeth I the single word *Cantharide,* the proper name for "the Spanish fly," after dispersing the Armada in 1588.

"Rum, Sodomy, and the Lash"

This expression is still widely believed to have been Churchill's opinion of the three cornerstones of British naval might and tradition and, unusually for false attribution, credit for the coinage was laid at his door while he was still alive. His last private secretary, Anthony Montague-Browne, recalls in his memoirs that Churchill frequently lamented that he hadn't thought of the jibe, but whoever did was far from original. Expressions targeting three main failings, with the first being rum, are nothing new and seem to be of American invention not British. In 1884, the tub-thumping Republican, the Revered Dr. Samuel Dickinson Burchard, neatly scotched his own party's hopes for James G. Blaine in his run for the presidency against Grover Cleveland with a New York speech including the sentiment: "We are Republicans and don't propose to leave our party and identify ourselves with the party whose antecedents are rum, Romanism and rebellion." His comments were aimed at the Mugwumps, a Republican splinter group gone over to the Cleveland camp, but it was the inclusion of "Romanism" that lost Blaine the Catholic vote and the White House.

It seems to have been well before World War I that Burchard's gaffe was adapted to describe life before the mast in the British Navy, this transition likely through an existing British Army joke that the Royal Navy equivalent of wine, women and song was rum, bum and concertina. And neither expression shows any indication of fading from use. In 1977 the army tag was used by the British jazz musician George Melly as the title of his autobiography, and *Rum, Sodomy and the Lash* appeared as the title of a 1985 album issued by The Pogues, an Irish band originally named Pogue Mahone (Irish for "kiss my arse"). They apparently dropped the offensive element after the BBC made it clear that their records would not be played until they changed their name.

"Send More Japs"

When the tiny U.S. outpost of Wake Island came under a ferocious Japanese attack on December 8, 1941, right after the attack on Pearl Harbor, the Marines stationed there were under the command of Lieutenant Colonel James Devereaux and overall command lay with Commander Winfield Cunningham. Both men, but mainly Devereaux, have at various times had to endure the slander of being so stupid as to send the above reply when asked if they needed anything to facilitate their defense of Wake. The beleaguered forces received no help or backup and the island fell to the enemy on December 23, with Devereaux and Cunningham having to endure Japanese "hospitality" for the duration of the war.

How the silly story was started is unclear. Some say that there was indeed a specific communication from Wake that, according to procedure, the radio operator padded fore and aft with nonsensical phrases. Prior to the body of the text, the padding included: "Send us. Stop. Now is the time for all good men to come to the aid of the party. Stop," and the end padding included: "More Japs. Stop." Either way, some propagandist decided to inform the press that the defenders were doing so well that Devereaux was asking for more Japanese opponents, and the journalists included this in their pooled reports from Honolulu on December 16. Although this bit of folly went down well with the armchair commandos, both men, especially Devereaux, reacted quite violently when they got home after the war to find out the foolishness that had been hung about their necks. As Devereaux briskly informed the waiting press: "I did not send any such message. As far as I know it was not sent at all. None of us was that much of a damn fool. We already had more Japs than we could handle."

"Shoot If You Must, This Old Gray Head, but Spare Your Country's Flag"

This is the famously patriotic challenge supposedly issued by Barbara Fritchie to General "Stonewall" Jackson and his men as he led his column through the Maryland town of Frederick in September 1862, en route to the battle of Antietam (September 17), also known as the battle of Sharpsburg. As the column passed her home, some of Jackson's men supposedly took potshots at the Union flag flying defiantly from the side of her house, an act which, it is told, so incensed the old girl that she shoved her head out of the window to issue the above challenge. Impressed by this feisty display of elderly guts, Jackson is said to have saluted her personally before telling his men he would shoot out of hand any one of them who so much as insulted Fritchie, upon which his entire command turned to cheer the woman for her feisty display of grit.

The story circulated among Washington tea parties, and was enshrined in rhyme by John Greenleaf Whittier in his ever-popular poem "Barbara Frietchie" (as he spelled it), which first appeared in *Atlantic* magazine in October 1863. Winston Churchill visited Frederick in 1943 and stood outside the Fritchie house to recite the poem, and the Clyde Fitch play of the same title premiered in 1899 with the English actress Joan Stanwyck taking the title role.

This is all well and good, but the Jackson column never went anywhere near the Fritchie house; the men marched south on Bentz Street and turned west onto Patrick Street. In order to have passed Barbara Fritchie's house, they would have needed to turn east and march perhaps 500 yards off route. Anyone doing that would have been presumed to be dodging the column and thus at risk of being shot for desertion en route to battle. The memoirs of one man actually in that column are still in print. In his *War Reminiscences*, William Fulton, then of the 5th Alabama Infantry, records: "Whittier, I think, has written a poem about Barbara Fritchey [*sic*] waving a banner (and a whole lot of stuff), as we passed through the streets of Frederick, which is fiction, pure and simple. Nothing of the kind ever occurred."

It seems that when news of Jackson's impending arrival reached the Fritchie household, Barbara's immediate reaction was to order the flag to be taken down and anything of value to be hidden in case of looting. Furthermore, these orders were issued from her sickbed as she was at the time ninety-five years old and a few months from death; she was not in any fit state to be taking on a Confederate column. Future Supreme Court Justice Oliver Wendell Holmes was himself in Frederick shortly after the alleged incident, searching for news of his son who had fought at Antietam, and he makes no mention of any such incident in his subsequent *My Hunt for the Captain*. In June 1886 Colonel Henry Douglas, who had been at Jackson's side every second of his time in Frederick, presented an article to the *Century Magazine* stating that at no time was there any contact between Fritchie and Jackson, and that no wrangle over any flag with any person had occurred.

"Teufelshunden!"

No one can deny that the Marines fought like hounds from hell throughout the intense fighting in and around Belleau Woods in 1918, but at no time did any of their spirited assaults draw the cry of "Achtung! Teufelshunden!" ("Watch out; it's the devil-dogs!") from terrified Germans.

The myth first appeared on a 1918 Marines' recruiting poster commissioned from designer Charles Falls, who presented an image of a skinny black dog wearing a German spiked helmet running away from an aggressive-looking mastiff or bulldog cross type dog wearing a Marine helmet. Above the chase scene, the poster proclaimed: "Teufel Hunden—The German Nickname for the U.S. Marines."

The first problem with this slogan is the Germans would have got their own language right; the plural of *Hund* is *Hunde*, not *Hunden*, and the term would be presented as *Teufelshunde*. Secondly, in German *Teufelshunde* would not have conveyed grudging respect for tenacious and worthy adversaries, but would have been an insult for those who were careless, gung-ho and unprofessional. As soon as the story circulated, no less a person than the pre-eminent word-hound H. L. Mencken was on the scent to declare the term and the stories to be to be pure fiction in his *The American Language* (expanded 1921 edition). But, like the Marines themselves, this yarn is diehard; the Marine Corps Museum at Parris Island not only maintains the legend of the attribution, but also sticks stoically to the wrong spelling.

Another problem with the tale is the fact that the Marines were not the only Americans in the area. The Army's 26th Division was also fully deployed, so how would the Germans know which troops were *Teufelshunde* and which were not? It was indeed the Marines who took the woods, but the capture of Belleau itself was down to the 26th, nearly a month later, by which time the Marines were miles away at Soissons.

The tag appears to be the invention of *Chicago Tribune* correspondent Floyd Phillips Gibbons, who was attached to the Marines in that area and lost an eye to German fire during the battle for Belleau Woods. It would further appear that the inspiration for his invention was the unusual drinking fountain in the center of Belleau. This presents a massive gargoyle protruding from a wall and formed as the head of a rather vicious-looking hunting dog, prompting thoughts of *The Hound of the Baskervilles*.

"They Couldn't Hit an Elephant From . . ."

The highest-ranking Union casualty of the Civil War, Major-General John Sedgwick (1813–64), was killed at the battle of Spotsylvania Court House on May 9, 1864, taking a shot to the head while dismissing the threat of Confederate snipers with the above unfinished line. Perhaps.

Confederate snipers were nearly three-quarters of a mile away, but their shots were still causing artillery crews in Sedgwick's command to duck and scurry. Annoyed at such unmanly behavior, Sedgwick strode around in the open berating his men, "What? Men dodging this way for single bullets?

What will you do when they open fire along the whole line? I am ashamed of you." And it is after these well-attested words that the doubt creeps in. Some say that it was just after "I am ashamed of you" that the bullet struck him in the head, and that others added the bit about the elephant to mock him for berating them as cowards. If something sounds too good to be true it usually is, so we have to make up our own minds on this one.

"Up Guards and at 'Em"

Supposedly said by Wellington when ordering the Guards into action at the battle of Waterloo in 1815, immediately after the battle the man himself disowned the line accredited to him by the British press. In an interview with the English writer and politician John Crocker on June 22, just four days after the victory, Wellington stated: "What I must have said, and possibly did say was 'Stand up, Guards!' And then gave the commanding officers the orders to attack." Nor did Wellington, on reviewing his new recruits sent him in Spain in 1810 say: "I don't know what effect these men will have on the enemy, but by God they frighten me." What he did write in the August of that same year when talking of his officers was: "As Lord Chesterfield said of the generals of his day, "I only hope that when the enemy reads the list of their names, he trembles as do I." Lastly, Wellington never instructed the commanding officer of any Highland regiment to "Get your drunken bastards up that hill"; Wellington was not so crass.

"Veni! Vidi! Vici!"

Julius Caesar never said any such thing—there is no trace of the saying during his lifetime, only attributions made by those writing centuries after his death. That said, the attributions are uniform in pegging the line to his rapid victories in 47 BC over Pharnaces of Pontus, in what is now modern Turkey, and most say this was the three-word message sent back to the Senate. Suetonius, at his most prolific throughout the reigns of Trajan and Hadrian, does not attribute such words to Caesar, but in his *Life of Julius Caesar* (37:2) says instead that the words appeared as a caption on a placard carried at his subsequent triumph through Rome: "In his Pontic triumph he [Caesar] displayed among the showpieces of the procession an inscription of but three words, 'I came, I saw, I conquered,' not indicating the events of the war, as the others [the other triumphs] did, but the speed with which it was finished."

"We Will Bury You"

This is the best-remembered of all Cold War blunders by Nikita Khrushchev, but in this case he did not intend his words to be taken by the West as a threat of attack.

Of Ukrainian peasant stock and not fully literate until in his thirties, Khrushchev was nothing if not outspoken. When hosting a diplomatic gathering in Moscow in November 1956, he proclaimed pride in the Bolshevik ethos and, turning to the assembled Western ambassadors and representatives, he bluntly informed them: "If you don't like us don't accept our invitations and don't invite us to come to see you. Whether you like it or not history is on our side. We will bury you." There was a lot more of the same and by the time he ran out of steam only a few red-faced Poles were left in the auditorium, studiously examining their footwear.

The Western press kicked into hyperdrive, wholly unaware that the expression used, *my vas pokhoronim*, was a Russian idiom meaning "we will outlast you." In effect it implied "we will still be around to dance on your grave," and did not mean "we will kill you." The Soviet machine tried to smooth things over, but the phrase was already embedded in English. It still crops up as a title for books, films, rock songs and even occurred as the leitmotiv of a classic episode of *Spongebob Squarepants* entitled "Rock-a-Bye Bivalve," which would no doubt amuse Khrushchev to no end.

Of course, Khrushchev is best "remembered" in the West for banging his shoe on the desk to mark the time of his words when holding forth in anger at the UN on October 13, 1960, after a Filipino delegate accused the USSR of devouring Eastern Europe and stripping it of all freedoms. Many people of a certain age can conjure up images of Khrushchev doing this, and would swear blind they had seen TV coverage of the incident, so it is somewhat disappointing that the whole shoe-bang likely belongs to the realms of false memory. Everyone, including Khrushchev's son and daughter Sergi and Lena, has searched for footage of the event and come up empty handed.

The first thing against the tale is the layout of the UN desks of the day and Khrushchev's short and portly stature; his belly would have presented an insurmountable obstacle to his reaching down to remove a shoe in the first place. This fact caused the myth to be modified to his having brought in a spare shoe for the purpose and, grinning maliciously at friendly delegates, brandishing it as though a gavel. But there is not a single photo or piece of footage showing Khrushchev engaging in any shenanigans with a shoe and, given the significant media presence, had he done so then no one, but no one, would have failed to capture it on film—who would have missed a shot like that? According to former picture editor of *Life* magazine John Leongard, who was in the General Assembly press booth at the time, Khrushchev did not indulge in any desk-beating or boot-brandishing theatricals. Sergi asked NBC and CBC to trawl their archives but they, and CBS Moscow, found nothing.

"Whenever I Hear the Word 'Culture,' I Reach for My Browning/Revolver/Pistol"

Frequently misattributed to Nazi Party authorities Goebbels or Göring, this quip is still as popular as it is parodied. The line is in fact taken from Act 1, Scene 1 of Hanns Johst's *Schlageter*, a celebration of Nazi ideology first performed on Hitler's birthday in 1933. Taking its title from Albert Schlageter, a Nazi martyr, after his execution by the French for espionage and sabotage, the line features in a discussion between the eponymous hero and another character, Friedrich Thiemann, debating the value of studying for their exams when their nation is not free. The original form was: "Whenever I hear of culture . . . I release the safety catch of my Browning." So popular was the play in Germany that variants immediately sprang up. Göring's personal favorite seems to have had him reaching "for my Parabellum," the proper name of the German pistol more widely but incorrectly called the Luger. (Georg Luger only imposed improvements on the Parabellum, which had been named from the old Roman maxim *si vis pacem, para bellum* — "if you want peace, prepare for war.")

The success of the play secured Johst the role of Hitler's pet playwright, a pedestal from which he oversaw the elimination of countless writers and artists considered degenerate. After the war he was held by the Allies until 1949, when he was turned over to his compatriots who banged him up for another three-and-a-half years, after which he never worked again.

THE JUST AIN'T

Aces High

The first problem with the Battle of Britain is identifying when it happened. The British Air Ministry had no doubts, as shown in its publication of late 1940 entitled *The Battle of Britain: An account of the great days from 8th August to 31st October 1940*. The official commemorative dagger commissioned from Wilkinson Sword Ltd. is dated August 8–December 15; Wikipedia says July 10–October 31; the History Learning Site says August 1–October 12, while the air warfare historian, Francis Mason, gets even more precise in his *Battle Over Britain* (1969) which states 00:01 hrs., July 1 to 23:59 hrs. on October 31. Most German historians, on the other hand, cite August 13 as the starting point and reckon it dragged on until May 1941.

Then there are the fighter pilots themselves. The film industry has done nothing to stifle the notion that the Luftwaffe faced squadrons of phlegmatic upper-crustonians who, with a cheery "Chocks away!" took to the air to hold back the Germans. In reality, a scant 180 fighter pilots were public school (i.e. privately) educated and the overwhelming majority were blue-collar. Furthermore, over 20 percent were other nationalities—Canadian, Czech, French, North African, Dutch, American and, most significantly, Polish.

The still-quoted Nazi propaganda claiming that the Polish Air Force had been destroyed on the ground in the opening hours of the invasion is just not true. The Germans did bomb the airbases, but enough planes had already been deployed to cost the Luftwaffe nearly 200 aircraft before the surrender. The Polish pilots arrived in Britain battle hardened, as borne out by the fact that the Polish 303 Kosciuszko Squadron took down more enemy planes than any other squadron during the Battle of Britain and throughout the entire war in general. They were also too savvy to allow their planes to be armed according to RAF conventions, which seeded the last twenty-five rounds in every gun with tracers to tip off the pilot he was about to run out of ammunition. This, of course gave the enemy the same message, which the Poles thought just too sporting. When they ran out of ammunition they would *taran*, their word for ramming or trying to use the propeller to chop up the enemy from behind. So extensively did the Poles resort to such risky tactics that *taran* is now the accepted term for such tricks in flying-speak.

Mention the Battle of Britain and everyone thinks of the Spitfire—still foremost in all anniversary fly-pasts—but it was the Hurricane that did the most damage to the Luftwaffe, despite that throughout the whole war only 14,231 Hurricanes were produced as against 20,343 Spitfires. Although the Spitfire was all metal and the Hurricane constructed of frame and fabric, the latter was far more robust and easier to fix up after battle damage. More importantly, the turnaround time to refuel and re-arm a Spitfire was over twenty-six minutes, while the Hurricane's pit-stop lasted a mere nine. The Spitfire, which only narrowly escaped being called the Shrew or the Shrike, may have been faster, more maneuverable and capped with a higher ceiling, but the Hurricane was an extremely stable gun platform. It was the Hurricane that, throughout the Battle of Britain, accounted for almost two-thirds of enemy kills: 1,593 out of the total 2,739, and the lion's share of kills up until close of play in 1945.

And what of the notion so dear to the British heart—that the so-called "Few" stymied Hitler's invasion despite their being hopelessly outnumbered and outgunned. The usual figures show the RAF as outnumbered 3:1, but this also is not so. The great irony was that the British grossly overestimated the size of the Luftwaffe and the Germans suffered from the opposite illusion. While it is true that as a result of the fiasco in France and the debacle at Dunkirk the RAF had lost some 450 fighters, there were still over 700 left to face the coming combat instead of the 300 the Germans thought, hence Hitler later wryly congratulated Göring, "You have apparently shot down more aircraft than the British ever possessed." In fact, German intelligence was abysmal across the board. They initially dismissed the relevance of British radar, discounting the sites as worthwhile targets. They were also unaware that their much vaunted Enigma codes had been cracked, allowing the British to know the precise details of deployment orders within minutes of their being sent out to German airfields. Also, the major weakness of the German Me 109s (the principal single-seat fighter of the battle) was their limited range—by the time they got into British airspace, the German fighters had a scant fifteen minutes' flying time before they had to head for home or risk not getting back at all. By August 9 the Germans had 1,011 fighters and the RAF 1,456. Nor was German backup and production as efficient as their enemy's; by mid-September 1940 British aircraft production exceeded losses, which could not be said for the Germans.

It is precarious to bandy loss figures, however, because everybody exaggerated. Many German and British pilots spun lines worthy of fishermen with long arms, and their optimistic reports were further inflated by a web of claim and counterclaim from both sides. For example, after a particularly hard-fought August 18 engagement, the British claimed to have downed 144 German planes instead of the true figure of 69, against which the Germans admitted only 23. This creative accounting was pretty typical of the general pattern, so it is perhaps more accurate to look at the casualties. Between July 10 and October 31, the RAF lost 1,535 aircrew against the Luftwaffe's 2,662; between mid-August and mid-September alone the Germans lost 1,132 aircrew and 862 planes against Fighter Command's loss of 201 pilots and 493 planes across the same period. The Stukas, with their infamous screaming sirens christened *Jericho-Trompeten* (Trumpets of Jericho) by the manufacturers, suffered such disproportionate losses that they were withdrawn from combat. If the Battle of Britain taught the Luftwaffe anything, it was that slow, ground-attack planes should not be pitted against fighters. After 1940, the Stuka was deployed only in areas where there was little or no enemy fighter cover.

All said and done, there was a no-holds-barred struggle for aerial supremacy which the RAF won hands down, sending the Luftwaffe packing and putting a dent in Göring's image from which he would never quite recover. But that still leaves the big issue—did that victory alone stymie Operation *Sealion*, which aimed to land some 160,000 troops along forty miles of Britain's southern coast, or was it the specter of the British Navy that more concerned the Germans? Aerial supremacy was desirable for many reasons, but the Germans knew only too well that their command of the skies would not seriously impede the ability of the Royal Navy to scupper any invasion force before it was halfway across the Channel. Even the wash from a fast-passing destroyer would swamp the small German invasion barges, whose crews would have been mad even to contemplate a Channel crossing in September or October; it is doubted that 30 percent would have made it across if left to their own devices.

Even a superficial trawl of German sources reveals that the German Navy was never keen on *Sealion,* and its abandonment at the time of the Battle of Britain was more a matter of coincidence than direct cause. The following is an extract from *A Brief Statement of Reasons for the Cancellation of the Invasion of England*, as prepared by the German Navy Historical Staff in 1944:

> *As the preliminary work and preparations proceeded, the exceptional difficulties became more and more obvious. The more forcibly the risks were brought home, the dimmer grew faith in success; just as in Napoleon's invasion plans in 1805, the fundamental requirement of success was lacking, that is, command of the sea. This lack of superiority at sea was to be compensated for by air superiority but it would never have been possible to destroy enemy sea superiority by use of our own air superiority. The sea area in which we were to operate was dominated by a well prepared opponent who was determined to fight to the utmost of his ability. The greatest difficulty was bound to be maintaining the flow of supplies and food. The enemy's fleet and other means of naval defense had to be considered as a decisive factor. Owing to the weakness of our naval forces there could be no effective guarantee against the enemy breaking into our area of transports, despite our mine barges on the flanks and despite our air superiority.*

This statement pretty much sums up the attitude of Grand Admiral Raeder, head of the Kriegsmarine in 1940, who had been brave enough to tell Hitler that *Sealion* was "stillborn" from the beginning. This opinion was given long before the Battle of Britain and Adolf Galland, head of Luftwaffe fighter arm, reckoned there was never any serious intent to invade in the first place. (Galland narrowly escaped trial for treason for his pivotal role in the little-documented Luftwaffe fighter pilot mutiny of 1944, when the leading lights of German fighter command collared Göring with effectively a list of demands and ultimatums.) According to Werner Pfiffer, one of the senior Kriegsmarine officers on Raeder's staff, all serious interest in *Sealion* was abandoned during the Berghof (one of Hitler's HQs in the Bavarian Alps) meeting of early July 1940: "It was the opinion of all the higher navy staff that the whole thing could not be carried out, even if the Luftwaffe gained supremacy in the air and the English Channel was mined, because the British Navy could not be prevented from breaking into invasion lines." Although no historian, there is also the recollection of Herbert Döhring who ran the Berghof: "*Sealion* was completely sidelined after the conference, he didn't mention it at all in the following months; he was only preoccupied with Russia, not with England at all." Even Goebbels' diary of August 7, 1940, records, "Invasion not planned. But we have to talk about it in our propaganda in a hidden way to confuse the enemy."

As Dr. Andrew Gordon, maritime warfare historian at the Joint Services Command and Staff College, states: "the link between the air battle and the non-event of *Sealion* is much less direct and exclusive than commonly wished by Battle of Britain celebrants. Certainly, the RAF added daytime command of the air to the indisputable command of the sea which Britain already possessed, but the airspace over southern England did not thereby become the last court of appeal against invasion."

Angels of Mons

That the vast majority of the British public was prepared to believe God sent heavenly reinforcements to lend a hand at the battle of Mons is remarkable enough, but it beggars belief that such a notion still has legs in the twenty-first century.

Under the command of General Smith-Dorrian, the 3rd and 4th divisions of The Old Contemptibles (a name adopted by the British troops for themselves) were taking a hammering at Mons on August 23, 1914, and had to retreat under heavy fire. Their somewhat miraculous survival inspired an obscure Welsh writer from Monmouthshire to dash off a short story entitled *The Bowmen*, which attributed said survival to the intervention of St. George and a celestial army of archers who cut down the pursuing Germans. This was Arthur Llewellyn Jones, who wrote under the pen name of Arthur Machen, and the London *Evening News* carried his story on September 29, 1914. Specializing in tales of the supernatural and those of gothic horror, Machen had not an inkling of the hysteria he was about to unleash; fiction was about to become "fact" as the readers, in their droves, took his yarn as reportage.

Although Machen's tale actually spoke of St. George leading the ghosts of the archers from Agincourt, who shot dead the Germans with invisible arrows, countless "eyewitnesses" at the Front began embellishing this to include brigades of angels with flaming swords — God was indeed an Englishman. Increasingly alarmed, Machen published a reminder that the story was pure fiction, but this only produced a few street attacks on his person, rebukes from the Church admonishing him to "walk humbly and give thanks for having been made the vessel and channel of this new revelation" and demands from the press that any attack on the veracity of the story be treated as treason.

Not only is there still an Angels of Mons Truth Society, but the respected historian A. J. P. Taylor obviously believed something uncanny had gone on. In his acclaimed *The First World War* (1963) he states: "The battle of Mons was a small affair by later standards, no bigger than some of the engagements in the Boer War. Still, it was the first British battle; and also the only one where supernatural intervention was observed, more or less reliably, on the British side. Indeed the 'angels of Mons' were the only recognition of the war vouchsafed by the Higher Powers."

Those who are determined to believe in angels frequently invoke a letter supposedly dated September 5, 1914 (before the first publication of Machen's story in the *Evening News*) and written by Brigadier-General John Charteris to his wife: "then there is the story of the Angels of Mons going strong through the 2nd Corps, of how the Angel of the Lord on the traditional white horse, and all clad in white with flaming sword, faced the advancing Germans at Mons and forbade their further progress." But this text did not see publication until 1931 in Charteris' memoirs, *At GHQ*, in which the dates of all original letters had all been altered for reasons best known to the author. During World War I he had been responsible for propaganda and misinformation, and perhaps he simply could not break old habits of secrecy.

As for Machen, he bitterly regretted his monstrous angels who, like Frankenstein, long outlived their creator. In the reissue of *The Bowmen and Other Legends of War* (1915) he wrote: "It began to dawn on me that if I had failed in the art of letters, I had succeeded, unwittingly, in the art of deceit; the snowball of rumor that was then set rolling has been rolling ever since, growing bigger and bigger, till it is now swollen to monstrous size."

Beef, Birds, and a Walk Around the Block

The so-called Beefeaters at the Tower of London are the subject of much confusion, most thinking them properly titled Yeomen of the Guard, whereas they were formed in 1485 as the Yeomen Warders of Her Majesty's Palace and Fortress the Tower of London. The wholly separate Yeomen of the Guard still function as the royal bodyguard. The mix-up was started by Gilbert and Sullivan and the popularity of their *The Yeomen of the Guard* (1888), which in spite of its title recounts the lives and loves of the custodians of the Tower. The nickname dates back to the seventeenth-century expression "beef eater," which was a sneer at a fat and contented servant living high on the hog in a noble household, and was first applied by other regiments jealous of the Beefeaters' status.

Every visitor to the Tower is regaled with tales of the antiquity of the site's famous ravens, who for centuries fed off the countless victims of the axe and whose abandonment of the Tower would presage invasion or some other terrible military disaster. But the Tower historian, Geoffrey Parnell, cannot trace reference to any ravens prior to 1895, when the Royal Society for the Prevention of Cruelty to Animals (RSPCA) journal, *the Animal World*, carried an article about two of the Tower's ravens terrorizing the cat of a young resident, Edith Hawthorn. The 1845 publication of Poe's *The Raven* started a craze in England for pet ravens, and it seems likely that the first such birds in the Tower were those kept by the warders themselves. Those held there now have their wings clipped so they cannot fly away and bring down the country.

Despite the singular nature of the name, the Tower of London is actually a massive complex comprising no less than twenty-one towers, the one seen on all the postcards being the White Tower that stands central to the still fully functioning military installation. Outside of legend and invention, the Tower has never been the place of bloody execution. Within the Tower itself, only seven faced the axe and one the firing squad in 458 years: William, 1st baron of Hastings in 1483; Anne Boleyn in 1536; Margaret Pole, countess of Salisbury, in 1541; Katherine Howard in 1542, along with the viscountess of Rochford, who colluded in the Queen's adultery; Lady Jane Grey in 1553; Robert Devereaux, earl of Essex in 1601; and Josef Jakobs, shot as a German spy in 1941. The list is hardly the roll call of a dark and bloody ground, although far more faced execution on nearby Tower Hill or Tower Green.

Arguably the Tower's most famous prisoner is Adolf Hitler's deputy Rudolf Hess, who was held there after he crash-landed in Scotland on March 10, 1941, to conduct secretive peace negotiations with the British. British Army officer Norman Baillie-Stewart served five years in the Tower from 1933 to 1937 for selling military secrets to the Germans, and upon his release went to Germany to become Lord Haw-Haw (see "Lord and Lady Haw-Haw," page 32). The last prisoners were a couple of conscripts actually stationed at the Tower with the Royal Fusiliers, who absconded in 1952 after beating up their sergeant. Caught and returned for a quiet chat in a cell with five other sergeants, the London gangsters Ronnie and Reggie Kray served their time there before going on to greater infamy.

Bunkum Hill

The battle of Bunker Hill is sometimes hailed as the first armed clash of the Revolutionary War, but it was in fact well down the line of other armed confrontations. The first happened at Lexington on April 19, 1775, when British regulars returned fire from a group of militia trying to block their progress to Concord to impound munitions that had already been spirited away. After armed confrontation in Concord itself, the British march home turned into a running battle with snipers and small but highly mobile groups of local militia who took full advantage of their superior knowledge of the immediate terrain. Things having thus started, there were plenty of other skirmishes and minor engagements in the six weeks leading up to the so-called battle of Bunker Hill, fought on the wrong hill on June 17, 1775.

As things heated up, Colonel William Prescott and a force of about 1,200 men set out on June 16, with orders to fortify Bunker's Hill (the original and proper name), to prevent the British gaining control of Boston harbor and the surrounding area. With geography perhaps not his strongest point, Prescott marched straight past Bunker's Hill and up Breed's Hill, where he had his men dig in. At first light, the captain of HMS *Lively*, down in the harbor, spotted the new fortifications and ordered them fired on, but the guns could not achieve sufficient elevation to do anything other than scare the raw militia. Eventually, the British force under General Howe arrived; he was puzzled to find Bunker's Hill unoccupied, while Prescott sat wondering when the enemy was going to bother to turn up. Howe sent out riders, who returned with more up-to-date information, so it was about 2:00 p.m. before the British moved on and redeployed around Breed's Hill. Howe ordered a bit of cannon fire to keep the Americans busy, while he took stock of the situation. There was the first American fatality—one Asa Pollard, whom Prescott ordered to be quickly buried as his corpse was bad for morale. An inordinately large number of volunteers stepped forward for the burial detail and, having planted their comrade, downed shovels and sprinted off. Quite how many desertions there were from the American side is hard to determine, as estimates of the original force vary from 2,500 to over 4,000, but by the time the action started in earnest there were 1,400 defenders facing 2,600 British regulars.

The day may have started in farce, but this was no half-hearted affair. Those who stayed with Prescott fought like wildcats, right down to hand-to-hand combat after running out of ammunition. We remember the day as a victory, and perhaps it was. The British eventually drove them off the hill and into full retreat, but the victory was pyrrhic. British general Henry Clinton noted in his diary: "A few more such victories would have shortly put an end to British dominion in America." British deaths and casualties ran to 1,054 compared with the Americans' 450 but the Americans took courage from their new knowledge that the British regulars could be beaten in a full-on fight. There is a popular myth telling how the Americans used guerrilla tactics, while the British lined up in red coats to be shot down like ninepins, but this was not the case. Both sides fought partisan and formal array battles in equal part.

Funded by subscription, there now stands a 221 foot-high obelisk atop Breed's Hill, completed in 1843 out of solid granite. With the burgeoning tourist industry, guides at the memorial tired of smart-aleck visitors pointing out the folly of the site being called the Bunker Hill Memorial when it was in fact on Breed's Hill. To simplify matters, Bunker's Hill was flattened and Breed's Hill was renamed Bunker Hill.

Come Friendly Bombs...

That Guernica was subjected to aerial bombardment in the April of 1937 during the Spanish Civil War is not in dispute, but the who, what, and why are matters of claim and counterclaim.

The standard version of events blames the raid on the German Luftwaffe's Condor Legion (they have never denied it), who supposedly wanted to test out the effectiveness of the pattern bombing of civilians in preparation for World War II. In accordance with this supposed hidden agenda, they selected an innocent town at random and attacked on the busy Monday market day to allow the bean counters to come up with a clinical scale of civilian kills per ton of high-explosive dropped. Yet there is nothing to support this highly colorful version of the events. The Republicans were in full flight and, given the direction they were heading, any idiot could see they were going to bottleneck at Guernica in the Basque province of Vizcaya. Even those living in the surrounding area had figured this out for themselves and, market day or not, stayed well clear of the "innocent" place that had an arms factory. In short, it would have been a miracle had the place not been bombed.

That said, it was not until 1970 that Franco finally acknowledged the raid, even then claiming the Germans had done it without his knowledge. The Germans, who had never made any secret of their involvement, immediately responded with damning evidence of the paperwork that had shuffled between Franco and the Luftwaffe, proving conclusively that they had acted at his behest. The Germans also reiterated their claim that the destruction of the town had not been the objective. The Condor Legion sent out two Heinkel 111s, one Dornier 17, 18 Junkers 52s, and three Italian SM79s carrying 250kg (550lb) and 50kg (110lb) bombs and 1kg (2.2lb) incendiaries; the planes attacked in small waves; there was no carpet-bombing. Guernica is still a small place, but back then it was even smaller, with a population of about five thousand. Depending on who is telling the story, accounts of the extent of the devastation range from a little cosmetic damage to obliteration, but it is fair to say that about 50 percent of the town was either leveled or seriously damaged, so if the Germans or Franco had intended to wipe the place off the map, then another bombing run of the same manner would have done the job. Still, thankfully, some early architecture survives; the nineteenth-century parliament buildings are still there, as is the Tribunales, the fifteenth-century Church of Santa Maria la Antigua and the thirteenth-century church of St. Thomas.

No one can deny, however, that the town took a hammering; three of the four quadrangles of the old town were destroyed. It is the significance of the untouched quadrangle that raises major questions. Guernica has long been a spiritual focus for the Basques, and in that fourth quadrangle stands the sacred oak, or *Guernikako Arbola*, under which the ancient Council of Vizcaya received their royal charters of privileges in the Middle Ages. If the Nationalists' intention was to eradicate the city and demoralize the Basques, then surely this quadrangle would have been the prime target. Many foreign correspondents arriving shortly after the raid recorded their deep skepticism of the story the Republicans were trying to feed them. It should also be remembered that while the Basques today remember their involvement in the war as a cohesive ethnic group fighting fascism, over half of them were in fact allied with Franco and the Germans.

Cold War spy Kim Philby, whose left-wing sympathies for Russian-backed Republicans can hardly be questioned in the light of later revelations, was then a correspondent for the *Times* and on April 28 wrote:

> *It is feared that the conflagration destroyed much of the evidence of its origin, but it is felt here that enough remains to support the Nationalist contention that incendiaries on the Basque side had more to do with the razing of Guernica than General Franco's aircraft . . . Few fragments of bombs have been recovered, the facades of buildings still standing are unmarked, and the few craters I inspected were larger than anything hitherto made by a bomb in Spain. From their positions it is a fair inference that these craters were caused by exploding mines which*

were unscientifically laid to cut roads. In view of these circumstances it is difficult to believe that Guernica was the target of bombardment of exceptional intensity by the Nationalists or an experiment with incendiary bombs, as it is alleged by the Basques.

Others took photographs of buildings that had obviously been torched from the inside, with the abandoned petrol cans still scattered about in evidence.

As one might expect, the Basques get hostile at any suggestion that they finished the place off themselves to discredit the Nationalists. However, contemporary observers with knowledge of 1930s bombing capability point out that the level of destruction inflicted on the three razed quadrangles could not have been achieved with the payload the Condor Legion was known to be carrying.

So, was the Nationalist attack a relentless three-hour air bombardment of Basque tradition, or a single run dropping thirty-six tons of bombs on specific objectives? If it was the latter, then the Germans did not do a very good job. Blaming poor visibility resulting from cloud, smoke and dust, they missed the bridge, the railhead and the Unceta arms factory. Nor do things get any clearer when it comes to the death toll. The Basques talked of 1,700 dead and 800 wounded, while others estimate the number of fatalities as low as 250 or even 150. During the 1970s the Spanish academic, Ramon Salas Larrazabal, tiring of all the wild guesses and contradictions, painstakingly trawled records of local births and deaths and came up with a figure of about 500 to cover all the deaths and missing persons from Guernica and its environs at the time of the raid. Larrazabal does, however, point out that this figure would include a goodly number of people who simply thought it was high time to up and move to a safer part of the country. Whoever was telling the truth, the Republicans won the propaganda battle by commissioning Picasso to run up a massive daubing for the Spanish Pavilion at the 1937 World's Fair. *Guernica*, with its gored horse, screaming mothers and dead babies, ensured Guernica's toponymous fame as a byword for callous brutality. Picasso's picture was indeed worth a thousand words and whipped up a lot of anti-Franco feeling, particularly from America, which walked the fine line of condemnation while remaining strangely silent about the American pilots involved in the first ever full-on bombing of civilians in the Moroccan town of Chechaouene, when helping the Spanish put down the 1925 Berber uprising. Here, the casualties were extremely high and, to quote an expression local to that town, "everyone in Chechaouene has heard of Guernica, but no one in Guernica has heard of Chechaouene."

It is difficult, too, to think offhand of any book or film that does not depict Franco's forces as cardboard cut-out bad guys and the Republicans as noble and even-handed idealists struggling to stem the tide of murderous fascism. Even today there is little mention of the perhaps 50,000 civilian murders committed by these noble idealists, who were every bit as enthusiastic in their atrocities as the fascists. Like all good Communists, they had a particular hatred for the Church, and in all some seven thousand clerics and nuns were variously raped, crucified, thrown to the bulls in the local arena, burned or buried alive or castrated and thrown down wells. The most ardent cleric-killer was a woman known only as *La Pecosa* (the "fickle one"), who seems to have taken particular delight in organizing the gang-rape and execution of nuns. On the night of July 19, 1936 alone, the Republicans went on a drunken killing spree through Barcelona and torched fifty of the city's churches, leaving only eight others and the cathedral untouched. In the city of Barbastro in Aragon, over 90 percent of the clergy were murdered, about 70 percent in the Castilian city of Lerida, and Tortosa in Taragon; Segorbe in Valencia, Malaga, Minorca and Toledo escaped with a mere 50 percent cull of their clerics. No one came out of that war with hands clean.

Crockett's Last Cringe

The ill-advised defense of the Alamo, ending on the evening of March 6, 1836, occurred during the Texan War of Independence (1835–36), Texas's attempt to cede from Mexico, which had outlawed slavery. Basically it was a fight for the freedom to enslave others, not such a noble cause. The famous John Wayne movie depicts a valiant little band of Texans determined to defend the Alamo to the death, trying to buy time for General Sam Houston to rally and train his raw recruits in sufficient numbers to crush the advance of the opposition commander Santa Anna. Actually, Houston had ordered the dilapidated old mission to be abandoned and had sent Jim Bowie with a detachment of perhaps thirty men down to San Antonio to remove or spike the guns and trash the place. As explained in "Kentucky 'Fraid Chicken," page 28, the less-than-savory Bowie was in Texas at the time only to avoid awkward questions about land fraud in other states he had graced with his presence. Other groups, led by the likes of David Crockett and William Travis, drifted in to "help" with the destruction and the unkind have said that, far from some noble act of self-sacrifice, they all embarked on some serious partying only to wake up with a fearsome hangover and half the Mexican Army on their doorstep.

Only recently vindicated as authentic, one of the most objective contemporary accounts is that written by Lieutenant-Colonel Jose de la Pena of the Mexican Army and nothing he says lies at odds with accounts given by the twenty or so surviving women, children and slaves granted safe passage. De la Pena is critical of both sides. He notes that on arrival at the Alamo the guards were all drunk or slumped at their posts and the other occupants out for the count; Santa Anna could have just walked in and taken the place over. But that is not what he wanted. The initial and much-disputed offer of surrender was turned down flat by Santa Anna, who knew he could steamroller the place and he was keen for a quick victory to boost the morale of his troops, who were vexed after a long march over the desert and the "absent-mindedness" of their paymasters. It was for this reason that no Mexican bugler sounded out a haunting *El Deguello* as made much of in films of the events. Translating as the "Throat-Cutting Song," this was an ancient Moorish ruse adopted by the Spanish, and was not played on any instrument but howled as a wordless dirge calling on the enemy to surrender or die. Santa Anna would not have ordered it howled or played as he wanted no surrender.

The actual number of the defenders is unknown, certainly less than 200, and when push came to shove they did put up a spirited defense. Their long-guns far outranged those carried by the opposition because Santa Anna had tooled up his army on the cheap with a batch of weapons bought from the British, who had in turn taken them off Napoleon's collapsed Grand Army after the battle of Waterloo. Further confusion in the Mexican ranks was caused by most of the men being non-Spanish speaking Mayans, who did not fully understand their orders.

At no time did the "noble and upright" Travis (a perjured philanderer who had long since abandoned his wife and child to their fate) draw a line in the sand and invite those willing to die to cross over it. This embellishment was the invention of one Moses Rose, AKA Louis Rose, who slipped over the wall the night before the final assault. Because of this, he is still invoked as the embodiment of cowardice. In fact, Rose was a decorated veteran of Napoleon's army, so it was a twist of fate that he would, nearly twenty years later, find himself being shot at by the very weapons last carried by his old comrades-in-arms. Having emigrated to Nacogdoches in Texas, he found himself embroiled in this new conflict and, having seen and inflicted so much slaughter in his time, said he felt no shame in his reluctance to throw away his life in such a pointless action.

When the final assault came, at least fifty of the defenders fled over the low east wall, where they fell prey to Mexican lancers. The majority of the rest perished inside the Alamo and in his *Alamo Traces: New Evidence and New Conclusions* (2003), American historian Thomas Ricks Lindle puts a well-documented case for the defenders' score to have been 145 dead and 442 wounded. Crockett and a few others were rounded up and given promise of protection by General Manuel Castrillon, but this was overridden by Santa Anna who had the prisoners hacked down by saber on the spot; Castrillon was nearly killed trying to intervene. Crockett, a bit of a wishy-washy character by all accounts, apparently tried to talk his way out of the situation claiming to be a non-combatant civilian in the wrong place at the wrong time—all a terrible misunderstanding. In all, wrote de la Pena, it was not a heroic affair for anyone.

When news of the Alamo debacle reached Sam Houston, he immediately embarked on what became known as the Runaway Scrape, which ended when he had secure intelligence regarding the Mexicans' location and dispersal. At 3:30 p.m. on April 21, 1836, Houston and perhaps nine hundred men burst out of the brush screaming "Remember the Alamo!" and attacked Santa Anna's camp on the San Jacinto River while the Mexicans were enjoying an afternoon nap. Santa Anna himself was in an opium-induced fog after raping a quadroon woman named Emily West. (The myth developed that she had been sent by Houston to seduce Santa Anna to make the attack all the easier, resulting in Emily, whose complexion was known at the time as "high-yellow," emerging as the heroine celebrated in *The Yellow Rose of Texas*.) Infuriated by the massacre at the Alamo and other atrocities inflicted by Santa Anna, the Texans paid in kind in a vicious twenty-minute purge resulting in 630 killed and 730 captured, including Santa Anna, which brought the war to a close.

As for Santa Anna, he was a born survivor and eventually returned to Mexico to exact his revenge. In 1869 he started shipping chicle to the American Thomas Adams, who flavored it and marketed it as Chiclets, thus initiating the chewing-gum industry.

Curragh on Camping

The UK has given the Irish plenty of reasons for resentment, but it is completely false that Eire conspired, colluded or in any way gave support to the German military during World War II. The most often heard calumny claims that U-boats were routinely refueled in Eire, but this never happened; it was in Vigo and Cadiz, in pro-Nazi Spain, where German subs were routinely refueled and provisioned. The IRA most certainly did play footsie with the Nazis and were falling over themselves to facilitate the invasion of their own country, but that is another matter. Although Eire trod the uneasy path of neutrality, her leanings were most definitely pro-Allied and she wanted no truck at all with the Nazi regime. Those who persist with this myth would do well to remember the seventy thousand Irish citizens who made their way to the UK to enlist in the British Army—proportional to their respective population figures, this was a higher enlistment rate than the English managed to rack up. Furthermore, there never was an Irish Brigade in the Waffen-SS, as there was a British Free Corps formed under John Amery, the son of Churchill's cabinet minister, Leo Amery.

It is true that the German and Japanese embassies continued to function in Dublin throughout World War II, but then so too did the British and American embassies, toward whom there was a very definite bias in the way that downed airmen of those nations were favored. The Irish government under Éamon de Valera decreed that only airmen on non-combatant missions would be repatriated, which meant that in practice British fliers could trot out any old story and get shipped home, but Luftwaffe bomber crews could hardly expect the same privilege by claiming to be out on an instrument test, or similar. Allied airmen who were quite obviously returning from active runs were often given the old "The border's just up the road there; turn left at the junction, but don't you dare make a run for it while I go home for my supper" routine. Also, any Irish plane spotting a U-boat or other hostile vessel would radio its location back to base on a frequency they knew damn well was being monitored by the British. That said, some Allied airmen were detained and ended up in the delightfully "Irish" camp at Curragh.

Located in County Kildare, this POW camp was straight out of *The Chronicles of Ruritania*. Determined to maintain her stance of neutrality, Ireland classified all German and Allied combatants as "guests of the nation" and held them in the same camp with a token fence between the two sides. The guards were under orders never to shoot directly at escapees, only to fire warning shots over their heads in order not to alert them that the guards had only blank ammunition. But few prisoners ever felt the urge to escape. They all had pleasant quarters with their own mess bars; they were allowed out of the camp any time they liked to take part-time jobs in the area or simply nip down to the local pub, where there would be Luftwaffe in one room and Allies in the other, although in practice they frequently mixed and threw each other parties. All in all, it was a very pleasant place to while away the war. The only "restriction" imposed on inmates required them to sign a pledge promising to return before dark each time they left the camp. How civilized.

On one occasion, two Canadian airmen crashed near the camp, their malfunctioning instruments leading them to believe themselves in Scotland. Tramping across the moors, their initial delight at spotting the pub turned to stunned horror when they walked into the wrong room to be greeted by hordes of drunken Luftwaffe pilots; they immediately fled through the adjoining door to find hordes of equally drunken Allied airmen who finally managed to convince them of the "normality" of the situation. The only man to make a determined escape was an American pilot who, trying to play the game, signed his exit pledge, walked out a few yards and then ran back in claiming to have forgotten his gloves. Thus, in his mind, when he left camp the second time without re-signing the pledge he was free to make a run for it. He made his way swiftly to the border with Northern Ireland and walked into the nearest military camp to demand transport back to the UK mainland.

To his surprise and anger, he was immediately arrested and taken back to Curragh under armed guard and handed back to the camp, where he was roughed up by his fellow inmates whose privileges had been suspended because of his escape. One British pilot received a severe reprimand in the mail after writing back home reporting that his golf swing had improved no end since his stay in Ireland.

When the war ended everyone was rostered for repatriation, but only after settling their bar bills. Having tasted the Irish approach to life and forged links with the community some elected to stay—and who can blame them?

De Sade Whips Up a Storm

Amusingly, the diary of King Louis XVI carries a single word entry for July 14, 1789 — "Nothing!" — so he obviously did not consider the loss of the Bastille to be of any significance. The French make much of the incident (it is still celebrated as a national holiday), claiming the noble citizenry regarded the place as a symbol of royal tyranny and marched on it to free the downtrodden. But, as French prisons went, the Bastille was one of the best. Never holding more than forty prisoners, each inmate had a fifteen square foot room with basic items of furniture and any little luxuries their friends cared to bring. All in all, life was quite tolerable. The only thing the mob wanted from the Bastille was the thirty thousand pounds of gunpowder and the barrels of shot stored in the old fortress. They did not give two hoots about the prisoners, who actually numbered only six: four forgers and a couple of lunatics. Had the mob struck a few days before, they would also have liberated the Marquis de Sade who seems to have instigated the entire affair by spending his time yelling out to the crowds about all the munitions stored in the prison, how undermanned the garrison was and how the place would be a pushover for even a small force. Fortunately or unfortunately for him, his friends and relatives drummed up enough cash to buy him out of the Bastille on July 4 and have him transferred to a "rest home" in the country.

Earlier the same day, the mob had ransacked Les Invalides in Paris and "liberated" over thirty thousand muskets, but no powder or shot, hence the attack on the Bastille (it is hard to go looting with empty guns). Far from half the population of Paris turned up at the gates, as is invariably shown in films, contemporary paintings and etchings, only some five hundred or so drunks arrived about mid-day to mill around aimlessly, wondering what to do. Prison governor Bernard-René de Launay was more puzzled than alarmed. The place was all but empty and scheduled for demolition. There were over thirty cannon atop the thick walls, so he did not feel he had anything to worry about. He invited the crowd to send a couple of representatives so things could be smoothed over, but while this was going on the mob gained access to the undefended outer courtyard and, thinking the lack of defense some sort of cunning trap, began firing wildly in all directions depleting their own numbers by about sixty. Some of the garrison went to watch the fun before opening fire themselves with little effect. Everytime a ceasefire was agreed, some idiot in the crowd fired a shot and it all kicked off again. Toward evening, the scales were tipped by the arrival of mutinied troops from the Garde Française to help the mob and, come 5:00 p.m., de Launay—rather foolishly as things turned out—thought it best to open the gates to avoid further bloodshed. The mob sawed his head off and started lynching the garrison until their new allies from the army turned their muskets on the mob to ensure safe escort of all surviving soldiers.

Basically it was a pointless mess that left the main movers and shakers of the Revolution no choice but to turn the day into one of glorious destiny. They commissioned Marie Grasholtz to make wax busts of the released prisoners; they were perhaps unaware that she spent most of her time at Versailles teaching the female members of the royal family the art of wax modeling. Marie later married an engineer called Tussaud and moved to London, where she established the famous museum that bears her name.

Departing of the Red Seer

The lurid account of the death of Gregori Rasputin is well known—he was a charismatic devil who, despite being poisoned, clubbed, stabbed and shot countless times, refused to die. The usual sources of such received wisdom are cheap films with titles like *Rasputin the Mad Monk*. But die he did, not at the hands of Russian nobles concerned about his influence over the Russian royal family, but shot by British Military Intelligence (BMI) concerned about the progress of World War I.

Rasputin was an opportunistic charlatan whose claims to be able to control the Tsarevich Alexei's apparent hemophilia gave him a grip on the Russian royals. In fact, he could do nothing to improve the prince's condition or ease his sporadic attacks, relying instead on verbal sleight of hand—"think how much worse it would have been had I not been here." In the autumn of 1912, the royals were on holiday in Spala, Poland, when the boy had his worst attack of all, including severe abdominal bleeding as the result of a fall. It is this Spala Incident, as it is known, that gives the strongest indication that the child's condition was not the hemophilia of general legend, but aplastic anaemia. The abdominal bleeding at Spala did not assert itself until perhaps three weeks after the fall, which is not in keeping with hemophilia but fits aplastic anaemia, as indeed do the bouts of remission that are never present in hemophilia. Either way, a cable was sent to Rasputin, who had more sense than to rush to the sickbed and carry the can if the lad died, so he simply cabled back "God has seen your tears and heard your prayers. The Little One will not die" and then stood ready to decamp if he did. But Rasputin was lucky and the boy made a miraculous recovery the next day.

After that Rasputin could do no wrong; Tsarina Alexandra and to a certain extent Tsar Nicholas II, thought that Rasputin had some sort of hot-line to heaven. That they were so easily impressed, and subsequently swayed in many matters, by a disheveled peasant trickster is perhaps unsurprising when the frequency with which the pair took drugs is taken into consideration. They were, by any reasonable definition of the term, addicts. The tsarina, a neurotic hypochondriac, used morphine, cocaine and Veronal, a powerful barbiturate, to "treat" her various psychosomatic aches and pains, which accentuated her frequent bouts of hysteria and paranoia, while her husband was dosing himself with cocaine and smoking marijuana laced with psychotropic henbane. Much of the extant correspondence between the pair is littered with reference to such usage, and the French representative to the Russian court, Maurice Paleologue, recorded in his diary for November 6, 1916 his concerns over the amount of drugs the tsar was taking and their effects on his judgment as he became increasingly indifferent to the gathering storms.

As 1916 drew to a close, a lot of people were keen to see the back of Rasputin by any means necessary, and close contact began between Prince Felix Yusupov and Captain Oswald Rayner of BMI. These two had been friends since their days at Oxford University, and reports from St. Petersburg to London indicate the depth of British concern over Rasputin's badgering the Tsar to withdraw all Russian troops from World War I. Doing so would free up some 350,000 German troops to reinforce the German effort at the Western Front, making life even more uncomfortable for the already beleaguered Allied forces. In short, if Rasputin sustained his campaign and was successful, it could well have lost Britain the war. Rasputin had to go. Rayner's chauffeur, William Crompton, kept a transport log that shows numerous meetings between the pair, the last on the day before the assassination on the night of December 16–17, 1916. The victim was lured to Yusupov's Moika Palace, where Rayner shot him straight through the forehead. No mystery; no satanic protection from the effects of bullets; just bang you're dead. The devil-refusing-to-die legend was invented later by Yusupov at the famous libel trial against Hollywood film studio MGM.

Quite unforeseen, Rasputin proved more trouble dead than alive. His death was the first domino to fall in the chain leading up to the Russian Revolution in March the next year. Calling in favors from the British, the Yusupovs grabbed whatever gems they could carry and headed down to the Crimea to board HMS *Marlborough*, which took them from Yalta to Malta, from where they made their own way to London to live in reduced circumstances until MGM released *Rasputin and the Empress* (1932). A great box-office success, this was a film in which the Yusupovs were thinly disguised as Prince Paul Chegodieff and his wife Natasha, the latter being raped by the character of Rasputin. The Yusupovs sued over this aspect of the film alone, yet far from denying his role in the killing of Rasputin, the prince reveled in his part and fed the court and journalists a lurid and highly purple account of the events. He and his co-conspirators baked cyanide scones and likewise laced the Madeira wine in readiness for Rasputin's visit, but the devil ate all the cakes and became roaring drunk on the wine before suggesting they pay a visit to a nearby gypsy camp in search of carnal delights. At this, Yusupov claimed, he bid Rasputin turn and look at some newly acquired religious icon and, turning up the volume on the gramophone playing *Yankee Doodle* to cover the noise, shot him twice, point-blank, through the heart from behind. Instead of dying, Rasputin launched a terrifying attack, forcing Yusupov to flee the room to seek help. Other conspirators returned and battered Rasputin with heavy knouts until "dead." Turning off the record player, they left to find a carpet to wrap up the body, but found their victim gone when they returned. They next heard him running across the yard shouting that he was going to tell the Tsarina everything so, biting on his hand to steady his nerve, Yusupov claims that he brought the devil down again with more shots, but found him still snarling when approached. Reluctant for any more shooting out in the open, he and a couple of others kept stamping on Rasputin's head with their heavy winter boots before wrapping him in the carpet and dumping him into the frozen river. Just to cap it all, Yusupov claimed that when he was discovered Rasputin had clawed his way out of the carpet to die of drowning.

Yusupov's highly colorful account is flawed to say the least. First, had he mixed the cyanide into the cake mix prior to baking as he claimed, it would have vaporized in the oven and killed everyone in the kitchen. Second, Rasputin had a serious intolerance of anything sweet, such as cakes and Madeira, which would have had him crawling on the floor in agony. On June 29, 1914, he had been attacked by a demented prostitute called Khionia Guseva, who sliced open his abdomen and ran around shrieking that she had killed the Anti-Christ. The damage left him with hyper-acidosis, making the ingestion of any sugar an extremely painful experience. Besides, the original autopsy by Professor Kossorotov found no evidence of any poison in the system and only three gunshot wounds: two from small-caliber jacketed rounds and the fatal shot to the forehead from a very heavy-caliber round. This autopsy was reviewed in 1993 by Dr. Vladimir Zharov, and again in 2005 by the pre-eminent forensic pathologist Dr. Derrick Pounder, and neither found any fault with the original. The Firearms Department of the Imperial War Museum in London further stated that, when it came to the kill shot, "the size and prominence of the abraded margin of the entry point indicated a large lead unjacketed bullet," their best guess being a Webley .455 British officer's service pistol. At the time of the shooting, Britain was unique in that its service pistols still used the old-style heavy lead slug.

Yusupov had to lie; he could hardly now announce to his fellow émigrés that he had colluded with agents of a foreign power to undertake an act that precipitated the very revolution that had reduced them all to working for a living in any country that would take them in. He won his case, along with the staggering amount of £25,000, which prompted Hollywood lawyers to demand that every film from then on carry the now-standard: "Any resemblance to actual persons, living or dead, is purely coincidental." Hearing of Yusupov's windfall, Rasputin's daughter Maria tried to sue him for her father's death, but the French court to which she presented her case ruled against her, as it had no jurisdiction over crimes committed in another country. Disillusioned, she joined the Ringling Brothers' Circus as a lion tamer, but quit the circus in Miami to work as a riveter in a naval dockyard. She later met and befriended the Yusupovs' daughter. Rayner made it back to England and, before he died in 1961, confessed his part in the killing to his cousin, Rose Jones. The afternoon of that confession he burned all his papers in the back garden of his house in Botley, near Oxford.

Ducats and Drakes

Although dear to the English heart, the image of Sir Francis Drake (c. 1541–96) and the Plymouth Hoe Bowling Club calmly finishing their game before crushing the Spanish Armada of 1588 is an eighteenth-century invention, careless of the facts that bowling greens were unheard of until the 1640s, and Drake is known to have been embayed with his fleet.

The advancing Spanish fleet was under the command of the duke of Medina Sidonia, who had no naval experience whatsoever. Philip II had put him in charge of the venture on account of the prominence of his family, not his competence. Even Sidonia could see the folly, and wrote to the King pointing out that: "The undertaking is so important that it would not be right for a person like myself, possessing no experience of seafaring or of war, to take charge of it." Nor were the English above the same stupidity. Their fleet was under the command of Lord Howard of Effingham who, although Lord High Admiral, knew little of naval engagement and suffered from seasickness. However, he danced a nifty gavotte and was a great favorite of the queen.

The Armada comprised 40 ships-of-the-line and 100 or so smaller craft; the English had about 200 ships, 100 deployed in the Channel and the rest in reserve—60 of those deployed were fully equipped men-of-war and all the lesser craft were heavily armed, so any talk of the English being outnumbered is sheer nonsense and, at the end of the day, there was no great battle. The two fleets danced aloof like a couple of schoolboys waiting for the other to throw the first punch, and only at Gravelines did they engage. Yet even here the English managed to sink only one ship and force two others to run aground in the unfamiliar waters.

After this, the Spanish headed for home and it was at this point that their real problems began. Harried by assorted privateers and driven before increasingly bad weather, the Armada decided to take the scenic route home by heading up the east coast of the UK, with the intention of hanging a left around Scotland and Ireland before seeking friendly harbor back in Europe. Throughout this trip they lost thousands to disease, as well as dozens of ships that were driven into rocky coastlines inhabited by welcoming Scots and Irishmen, who cheerfully slaughtered all who made it ashore. To put things in perspective, during the so-called battle the Spanish lost 5 ships and 600 men, with another 800 wounded, but on the trek home they lost 62 ships and over 20,000 men.

Only on Fair Isle did the Spanish make it ashore in sufficient numbers, pro rata the locals, to establish a stand-off. The flagship of the supply fleet, *El Grand Grifon*, ran aground there on August 20, 1588, remaining for about six weeks to effect repairs, and debate has raged ever since about whether it was contact with these Spanish and their Moorish influence that produced the distinctive Fair Isle knitting patterns.

The Spanish Armada's objective is also misunderstood. Invasion to take control was never in the cards; the purpose of the venture was to inhibit the activity of Drake's pirate fleet, and to reduce the ability of the English crown to support Dutch insurgents in the Netherlands. To this end, one of the main aims of the Armada was to clear the way for the landing of a force under the Duke of Palma from Flanders, whose job it would be to give the English such a pain in their own backyard that they would be forced to withdraw their forces from mainland Europe to defend the homeland.

The English fondly remember this "battle" as the breaking of Spanish naval supremacy and the setting in ascendance of their own naval star, but this cozy, fireside myth is refuted by the three other Armadas sent against England in the 1590s and the undisputed Spanish supremacy in most naval and land battles between 1585 and 1604.

The Dune Conspiracy

The evacuation of Dunkirk, named for the church on the dune, from May 26 to June 4, 1940, spawned so many myths it is hard to know where to begin.

Some of the more fanciful British and American newspapers told of British troops' prayers being answered by the Channel becoming as still as a millpond, and by the descent of a divine fog to shroud them from the evil Stuka bombers determined to annihilate them. There were "eyewitness" accounts of the Guards drilling on the beach, oblivious to enemy fire, and then refusing to embark until they all had regulation haircuts.

Dispatch riders put on displays of acrobatic riding skills to entertain the mass of troops who stood quietly in ordered lines awaiting their turn to board a ship to freedom. Remarkable accounts indeed, but remember that there were no correspondents at Dunkirk.

Many of the writers who acted as willing cogs in the propaganda machine lived to regret their reports, most notably the British Alexander Werth. In 1960 he issued an apology after it became clear that his fantasies of military order ran in stark contrast to the reality of panic, cowardice, desertion and the shooting of officers by drunken troops who prowled the nearby streets, looting and raping. This was pretty much the picture painted by the dispatches of Lord Gort, commander of the British Expeditionary Force (BEF). Such was much to the chagrin of the authorities back home, who also told the Kent police to keep their collective mouths shut about the behavior and mental state of the returning troops, many of whom had thrown away their weapons and equipment.

As early as 1960, General Sir Harold Franklyn, a divisional commander at Dunkirk, made public statements complaining that the whole affair had been glamorized out of all proportion. All the yarns concerning relentless bombing and shelling were sheer nonsense: "I walked along the beaches on several occasions and I never saw a corpse . . . there was very little shelling." (The weather was atrocious and not suited to flying; the Luftwaffe sent only a few planes to harass the evacuees on May 27 and the afternoons of May 29 and June 1.) Five years later, British war historian Sir Basil Liddell Hart hammered the final nail into the Dunkirk coffin with his revelations that, although the German breakthrough was reported at the time as being due to their vastly superior numbers, it was the BEF that enjoyed superiority of numbers and equipment. Even a quarter of a century later no one wanted to hear the truth, leaving Sir Basil subjected to howls of indignation from the public and the sound of ear-covered humming from the corridors of power. Not until the last piece of paperwork had been wrested from Whitehall's gnarled fist was the full extent of the British shame and betrayal at Dunkirk revealed. For years the British had maintained that the invasion's failure was down to a lack of commitment or downright betrayal by the French and Belgians, but it was the other way round.

Despite having fielded a superior force, it soon became apparent to the War Office that the Germans out-thought them at every turn, so an exit was planned by Churchill behind closed doors on May 22, 1940. General Gort was given orders from Churchill, via Anthony Eden, that he, Gort, was to be conservative with the truth to his opposite numbers in the French and Belgian forces, while Churchill did the same to the French president Paul Reynaud. With everybody assured of British commitment to victory, and no possibility of retreat, the British started edging toward the back door after sucker-punching the Belgians into remaining in the field to delay the advancing German Army Group B while the British made a run for the beach. Unaware they were being thrown to the wolves, the much-maligned Belgians held up the German advance for five days, unaware they were simply covering the fast retreating British.

Codenamed *Operation Dynamo*, the evacuation began on May 26 and managed to bring home some 340,000 men. Even when the evacuation was under way, Gort was kept under orders not to tell the French and Belgian commanders the truth, but to leave them facing the Germans alone. When the French finally figured out what was going on, they too headed for the beaches where they would be evacuated in equal numbers. Yet over 40,000 of them were left to the Germans.

And what of evacuation itself? Dear to the British heart is the image of hundreds of tweed-clad civilian stoics heading across the Channel in their weekend pleasure craft with a Thermos flask and a cheery "Back in time for tea, dear." Unfortunately for that particular myth, the public was not informed that the evacuation was under way until June 1. Some civilian craft were pressed into service, but almost all were crewed by navy personnel, and the owners, instead of indulging in impromptu heroism, often asked for payment or compensation for vessels lost. Some have-a-go types did make the crossing, however, and in the main these smaller craft were restricted to running like shuttles from the beaches to the transport ships standing off.

The reason for the halt of the German advance at Dunkirk is often debated, but it was neither divine intervention nor a loony decision by Hitler, thinking he would leave the British forces intact in case they wished to join him instead of fighting him. The order to halt did not come from Hitler but from General Karl von Rundstedt. Panzer general Heinz Guderian visited his leading units on the approaches to Dunkirk, and concluded that von Rundstedt had been right: less than half the tanks were still in battle condition, supply lines were stretched to breaking point and any further advance across the reclaimed but still-treacherous wetlands would be foolhardy. In his post-war memoirs and discussions with Sir Basil Liddell Hart, Guderian did indeed try to shift the blame to Hitler, but without any real conviction. The order to halt the Panzers had been issued by von Rundstedt as early as May 24, and by the time the tanks were battle-ready again the German focus was on Paris, not Dunkirk.

Enemy at the Roof

Just as the British cleave to the fabrication that they stand uninvaded since 1066, Americans like to claim the same status since the War of 1812, when the British crossed the Canadian border to burn a few buildings in Washington. Although a brief encounter, Pancho Villa entered American territory in 1916 to devastate the town of Columbus, New Mexico. Furthermore, in World War II the Japanese invaded and held parts of Alaska.

Alaska is big. Its Aleutian Islands chain extends so far into the ocean that the farthest flung is only seven hundred miles short of Japan, which makes Alaska the most northern, western and eastern of the American states. This quirk of American geography was not missed by the Japanese, who began their assault on U.S. territory on June 3, 1942, when they attacked the Dutch Harbor installations on Unalaska Island, right up near the mainland, and two days later invaded Kiska and Attu islands at the tip of the chain. Rightly fearing this development to be detrimental to national morale, the American government issued a D-Notice to keep from the public the fact that the enemy was dripping in through a hole in the roof. Alaskans who found themselves in Japanese hands were interned on the Alaskan Panhandle or shipped back to equally dire camps outside Otaru, Hokkaido. Either way, most succumbed to starvation or disease while the Japanese formed a thin one-thousand-mile front across American territory.

Prior to any counter-invasion, there were several offshore battles as the U.S. Navy struggled to prevent the arrival of Japanese reinforcements and provisions. The heaviest of these engagements was the battle of Komandorski Islands of March 26–27, 1943, which left the USS *Salt Lake City* and USS *Baily* badly damaged and the Japanese presence on Attu alone risen to something in excess of 2,500. On May 11, 1943, the relief of Attu began, but as none of the landed vehicles would run in the tundra-like temperatures most of the supplies stayed stranded on the beach. In all, the retaking of Attu cost 3,829 U.S. casualties: 549 killed, 1,148 wounded, 1,814 laid low by frostbite, exposure and disease, and 318 victims to accident or friendly fire in the fog. The Japanese death toll numbered 2,351 and 28 taken prisoner after what was the second biggest battlefield banzai charge of the war. (The biggest ever was the massed break-out attempt at Cowra POW camp in Australia in 1944.) The Japanese forces on Attu, under Colonel Yasuyo Yamazaki, did not even try to contest the landings, opting instead to dig in on the higher and more central land and make the Americans come to them. The ploy failed; despite all sorts of booby traps and sporadic suicide attacks, the Americans overwhelmed the enemy in what became known as Massacre Valley. Thinking their job done, the Americans established camp at Massacre Bay, unaware that Yamazaki was far from finished. He consolidated what forces he had left to mount a suicide attack on the sleeping Americans, which U.S. troops finally crushed with enormous firepower.

The next U.S. objective was Kiska, with a Japanese garrison twice the size. In the lead-up to the actual invasion on August 17, 1943, the

Americans bombed Kiska and shelled it from offshore, an action which led to the infamous "battle of the Pips" on July 27. A task force led by Rear-Admiral Robert Griffin, and grouped round the battleships *Mississippi* and *Idaho*, was fog-bound and about eighty miles to the west of Kiska when it picked up an alarming pattern of blips on the radar. The battleships fired off over five hundred shells before pausing in puzzlement at the resilience of the holding pattern of the pips and the lack of return fire. They had in fact been bombarding a ridge of peaks on a tiny and unnamed nearby isle. As it turned out, there were Japanese ships in the area at the time, but they were on the other side of Kiska where they too were busy making a strikingly similar but more fatal faux pas.

When time came to send in the bailiffs to evict the fifty-five hundred squatters, the Americans were taking no chances. No more Attu — the invasion force numbered just short of thirty-five thousand men and was backed up by ninety-five ships and nearly two hundred aircraft. But there was no one home. Realizing the hopelessness of their position in the islands, the Japanese had used those same July fogs to evacuate the entire garrison. While *Mississippi* and *Idaho* were merrily shelling rocks they mistook for Japanese warships, the Japanese were on the other side of Kiska shelling and firing torpedoes at the island of Little Kiska, which they had mistaken for an American fleet. The only ones not to see the funny side of it were the Japanese troops waiting on Little Kiska for their time to embark. Of course, when the Americans landed they were unaware of this and lost nearly two hundred of their own to friendly fire in the fog and the odd booby trap; the USS *Abner Read* hit a mine, resulting in a further eighty-seven casualties.

'Tis an ill wind that blows no good, and this particular gust brought in the Alaskan Highway. Concern over a Japanese invasion of Alaska had prompted a start on the project in March 1942, but the reality of the Japanese arrival imparted a new sense of urgency that made the highway the fastest completed road in history. With an on-site force of up to seventeen thousand U.S. Army engineers, the fourteen-hundred-odd miles from Dawson Creek in British Columbia to Delta Junction was completed in less than ten months which, if watched from the air, must have looked like time-lapse photography. It was military restricted until 1948, when it was opened up to civilian traffic.

Exit Stage Left, Pursued by the Bear

As with the storming of the Bastille, the so-called storming of the Winter Palace in St. Petersburg was far more important in its symbolism to the people than it was in any military or practical sense. Russia abounds with vast and brooding canvasses showing the noble peasants, dying in great numbers as they march resolutely to their destiny at the Winter Palace. There was no last-ditch shootout between the Bolsheviks and Alexander Kerensky's government however, and if anything the night of November 7, 1917, was ruled by farce and confusion.

Tired of sitting around waiting for something to happen, the Bolsheviks decided to send an ultimatum to Kerensky (then the prime minister of the Russian Provisional Government) at the palace, demanding his unconditional surrender and the transfer of power. By the time someone had been found to deliver the message, and he in turn had made his way there on a bicycle, there was only about five minutes of the allotted time left. Since the note told Kerensky that the guns of the cruiser *Aurora* and those of the Peter and Paul Fortress were trained on the palace, and that these would open up before any infantry attack, Kerensky decided quite sensibly to agree to the terms. He told the palace's defenders—some teenage cadets and a women's battalion (later gang-raped by the noble peasantry)—that the game had been played and they had better make themselves scarce.

Clasping Kerensky's acceptance of the ultimatum, the messenger left the palace to find his bike had been stolen, leaving him with a long trudge back to those awaiting the reply. Unaware of the time it had taken their messenger to complete his mission, the revolutionaries assumed the lack of a reply to be a refusal of their terms, and decided to send out the pre-arranged signal to the guns to open fire. The only trouble was that the signal involved a red lantern, which no one could find. When they did, the night sky was lit by a fearful barrage as the ship and fort discharged round after round of blanks, the only ammunition they had. Undeterred, the Bolsheviks marched on the Winter Palace, where there was some sporadic gunfire in the grounds that resulted in the deaths of six invaders, all shot by their own side in the confusion. At a loss for anything more constructive to do, Kerensky simply wandered out of his office, got into a car he had the foresight to "borrow" from the American Embassy and, despite the protestation of the American ambassador, David Francis, kept the diplomatic flags on the front to ensure his safe passage into history. He later wrote that the Bolshevik guards on the gates of the palace saluted him as he left.

Behind him, the mob was milling around the corridors and two thousand rooms of the palace, stealing anything they could get their hands on. And then they found the wine cellars. Every last pretense at discipline and military order went out the window as the now-drunken mob set on the aforementioned women's battalion. Less sybaritic commanders arrived and tried to take control, but the mob simply shot at them when they tried to block access to the rapidly dwindling stock of what had been the largest single wine cellar in Europe. As the bulk of the revelers lapsed into stupor, the new commanders had the cellar doorways walled up, but when the mob woke up again they blasted their way in with grenades and carried on drinking. Eventually, martial law was declared and the "noble" peasants reeling round the Winter Palace found themselves under attack from sober troops who quickly flushed them out and took possession of the buildings.

Five-Bob Hero

Had it not been for Longfellow's wildly inaccurate *Paul Revere's Ride* (1860), this Bostonian silversmith of the title would not be remembered at all. Prior to the publication of Longfellow's ditty, there was no mention of Revere in any account of the war nor in any biographical dictionary of American worthies. Yet within a few years of Longfellow's poem going into print, he had a sizeable entry in Samuel Drake's *Dictionary of American Biography*, magnate J. P. Morgan was offering $1 million (at today's value) for one of Revere's punchbowls, and the Daughters of the American Revolution ran round slapping plaques on any building boasting the remotest connection with the man. Of course, he might have been airbrushed out of Revolutionary history owing to the fact that four years after his overrated ride he was facing charges of cowardice and insubordination in the face of the enemy after the American navy raid into Penobscot Bay, in present day Maine, to capture the British fort. It seems that it was largely due to Revere's masterly inactivity as artillery commander that the American ships ended up being scuttled to preclude their capture, before the crews made an ignominious trek back to Massachusetts. But now to the night of April 18, 1775.

For months Revere had been riding messenger for the Revolutionary Committee, but the image of him as a lone-wolf patriot, selflessly riding through the night is a bit wide of the mark. He was always trying to overcharge his time and needed reminding, quite pointedly, that the going rate per trip was four shillings, not the five he always demanded on extant invoices. On the night in question, it became known that the British Army intended to march into Lexington to arrest prominent patriots John Hancock and Samuel Adams before moving on to Concord to confiscate the cache of weapons and powder stored there. With strict instructions to move as quietly as possible, as the countryside was teeming with British patrols, Revere was hired to ride to Lexington to warn the two revolutionaries of their peril and then to proceed to Concord. Thus he did not scorch through the night yelling "The British are coming!"; most Bostonians regarded themselves as British at the time, so such a warning would have made no sense to anyone. Any farm he passed en route was woken to the news that "The regulars are out!" Just to make sure the message got through, a second rider, a cordwainer called William Dawes, was dispatched along a different route but with identical instructions. Both arrived in Lexington at about the same time. Revere's route was shorter, but he had stopped in Medford to warn Captain Isaac Hall, leader of the local Minutemen and acclaimed distiller of a potent rum for which the town is still famed; opinion is divided regarding the state of Revere when he arrived in Lexington.

It was agreed that the two would team up for the last leg of the journey, and they had not long been on the road when they met a local doctor Samuel Prescott, who, sneaking home from a lady's house at one in the morning, thought it might be a good idea to join them as a sort of blanket alibi for the entire night. The three had gone but a few miles when they ran into a British patrol. Revere was captured, but Dawes and Prescott escaped by jumping their horses over a nearby wall. Dawes, however, got hopelessly lost in the dark, leaving it up to Prescott to complete the ride to Concord, for which the captive Revere would get the credit. Held for some hours, Revere finally managed to convince his captors that the whole countryside was raised against them and they had best make themselves scarce. The British troops obviously concurred, because they stole Revere's horse and made off into the night, leaving him with a twenty-mile walk home.

Even Dawes's and Prescott's legacies overshadow Revere's. Dawes's great-great-grandson was Charles Gates Dawes, vice-president to Calvin Coolidge from 1925 to 1929 and the architect of the Dawes Plan, by which the post-World War I reparations were to be extracted from a crumpled Germany, this gaining him the 1925 Nobel Peace Prize. The good doctor did even better; the marriage line started by his sister eventually produced Samuel Prescott Bush and the two presidents Bush.

At the end of the day there were dozens of riders abroad that night and it seems that Longfellow singled out Paul Revere for no other reason than his having a fancy and romantic name that lent itself to rhyme. That's fine, but the trouble with such ill-deserved fame is that it marginalizes the real hero riders of the Revolution such as Israel (perhaps Isaac) Bissell who set out on April 19, 1775, to ride the 350 miles from

Watertown, Massachusetts, to Philadelphia to warn everyone along the way that the war had begun. Or Sybil, the sixteen-year-old daughter of Colonel Henry Ludington of Fredericksburg (now Ludingtonville), New York, who, on the night of April 26, 1777, rode forty miles—twice as far as Revere—to raise the reinforcements needed to force the British out of Danbury, Connecticut, which they had attacked.

Goldfinch's Wig

The so-called Boston Massacre of March 1770 is a much misremembered affair. Five deaths do not a massacre make; it was not the first clash with the British authorities; it was not the match that lit the fuse of revolution; it was not a dignified and peaceful gathering of sober and respectable citizens gunned down by guffawing troops and a sadistic officer—the troops involved were largely cleared of any misdeed, having been defended by one of the leading Revolutionaries.

On the evening of March 5, 1770, Private Hugh White stood sole guard on the King Street Customs House and noticed a fracas developing nearby as Edward Gerrish, a local wigmaker's apprentice, mocked and taunted a British captain, John Goldfinch, for not paying for his account. As Goldfinch had in fact paid the wigmaker in full, he tried to ignore the insults and goads, but Gerrish raised the stakes by prodding and shoving. White went to intervene and, when Gerrish turned on him White gave him the butt of his musket to the side of his head.

That should have been the end of the matter but Gerrish, emboldened by further drink, returned with a group of riff-raff and began to taunt White with insults and snowballs. As the mob grew in size and became more threatening, White moved into the customs house and bolted the door. Aware of his predicament, Captain Thomas Preston mustered a small detail of the 29th Foot who, with fixed bayonets, marched across to White's aid and formed a semicircular line in front of the building as the mob continued to grow. The snowballs were now impacted down to ice and, either stupidly or cynically, voices from within the crowd gave calls for the troops to open fire. Out of the dark, an ice ball or a club struck down Private Montgomery who, on recovering his feet, fired into the crowd. In the following confusion, with cries of "Open fire!" from provocateurs within the mob, the other troops also fired, much to the dismay of Preston, who at no time gave any such order. In any event, the troops did not open up in volley, but unevenly, as if unsure what to do. Eleven of the crowd were hit; three died on the spot and two others later from their wounds. The troops did not reload and fire again.

Bostonian artist Henry Pelham churned out a painting showing Preston, saber raised, barking for yet another volley to be fired into the crowd of soberly dressed men in frock coats and tricorn hats while the victims of the first shots lay bleeding at their feet. Paul Revere plagiarized this image to produce an etching for mass production, thus stealing Pelham's credit. As mentioned before, this was not the first violent clash of the American Revolution—it was preceded by other incidents of greater magnitude. There had been the Stamp Act Riots of 1765, followed in 1766 by running battles between gangs of patriots and British troops in New York. Further riots flared in the opening months of 1770, when a mob attacked the homes of leading Boston Tories, so the mob-inspired debacle outside the Boston Customs House was but one in a long line of clashes.

No matter; the Revolutionaries were so determined to make political capital out of the incident that the authorities had little option but to put Preston and his eight men on trial. Despite shadier Revolutionaries threatening the judges, court officials, witness and jurors, John Adams (Washington's successor to the presidency) stepped forward to defend the British soldiers. Adams was well aware of the facts of the incident and, desperate to avoid sullying his cause with hollow victories. When summing up, he urged the jury to cast aside the propagandized image of the perpetrators and see them for the ugly mob they were: "The plain English is, gentlemen, they are a motley rabble of saucy boys. Negroes and mulattoes, Irish teagues and outlandish jack-tars. And why should we scruple to call such a set of people a mob? I cannot conceive, unless the name is too respectable for them." Adam's diary entry for March 5, 1773, the third anniversary, records the trepidation with which he accepted the brief for the defense, knowing there were those who would kill him for doing so:

> *I devoted myself to endless labor and Anxiety if not to infamy and death, and that for nothing, except, what was indeed was and ought to be in all, sense of duty. In the Evening expressed to Mrs. Adams all my Apprehensions: That excellent Lady, who has always encouraged me, burst into a flood of Tears, but said she was very sensible of all the Danger to her and to our Children as well as to me, but she thought I had done as I ought, she was very willing to share in all that was to come and place her trust in Providence.*
>
> *Before or after the Trial, Preston sent me ten Guineas and at the Tryal of the Soldiers afterwards Eight Guineas more, which were . . . all the pecuniary Reward I ever had for fourteen or fifteen days labor, in the most exhausting and fatiguing Causes I ever tried: for hazarding a Popularity very general and very hardly earned: and for incurring a Clamor and popular Suspicions and prejudices, which are not yet worn out and never will be forgotten as long as History of this Period is read . . . It was immediately bruited abroad that I had engaged for Preston and the Soldiers, and occasioned a great clamor . . .*
>
> *The Part I took in Defense of Cptn. Preston and the Soldiers, procured me Anxiety, and Obloquy enough. It was, however, one of the most gallant, generous, manly and disinterested Actions of my whole Life, and one of the best Pieces of Service I ever rendered my Country. Judgment of Death against those Soldiers would have been as foul a Stain upon this Country as the Executions of the Quakers or Witches, anciently. As the Evidence was, the Verdict of the Jury was exactly right.*

With the Revolutionaries' determination to generate what political heat they could from the event, it is perhaps little wonder that a veritable host of "witnesses" stood ready to testify that Preston gave the order to fire on an orderly crowd that was not abusive, violent nor provocative. Given the known location of most of these men at the time of the shootings, they must have had the ability to see round corners and through buildings, but they were wasting their time. More reliable and measured witnesses were also in abundance, and prepared to testify in support of the statements made by Preston and the other six men on trial for murder. Several men who had been close enough to Preston to hear what he said swore that he only ordered his men to make a great show of loading their weapons, but at no time told them to fire. One Richard Paines stated that he had actually asked Prescott if he intended to give such an order, and was given a firm "no." Many saw a club being thrown at the line to strike Private Montgomery and affirmed that he was indeed the first to fire. Benjamin Frizell, who had been observing the events from the corner of the customs house, said that there was at first just the one shot, then two and then perhaps three or four, but at no time was there volley fire as if from troops under a direct command. Countless others affirmed that the only "orders" to open fire came from provocateurs in the crowd. Witnesses William Wyatt and Edward Hill told that Preston had actually rebuked his men for opening fire without orders and prohibited reloading.

Preston's trial ran from October 24–30 in Boston's Suffolk County Courthouse, where the jury acquitted him on all charges. The trial of the other soldiers opened on November 27, with Adams arguing that if the men were endangered by the mob then they had a legal right to fight back. If only provoked but not endangered, then they were at worst guilty of manslaughter. The jury was swift to agree and acquitted six of the men straightaway. The other two were found guilty, as they had been seen to fire aimed shots into the crown instead of the panicked firing unleashed by the others. But all had been assured that even these two would not hang, but be given benefit of clergy. This referred to a bizarre loophole in English law, exploitable by anyone who could prove they were literate by reading the first verse of Psalm 51, still known as the "neck verse." Intended to remove clergy from the jurisdiction of secular courts, this was first enacted in 1350 when literacy was mainly the province of the clergy. Increasing literacy rates, however, turned the act into an anachronistic shield used by so many non-clerics that thumb branding was introduced by Henry VII to stop recidivists saving their neck a second time. Benefit of clergy persisted until 1841 in the UK, and 1869 in America.

Gordon of Elephant's Trunk

Charlton Heston has been instrumental in creating more historical myths than any other actor. He showed us El Cid as a noble and Christian knight despite his having spent most of his time fighting in the pay of Muslim warlords, and his *Khartoum* (1966) showed a stoic General Charles Gordon, abandoned by perfidious politicians, defending a doomed Khartoum against a Muslim army under the Mahdi Muhammed Ahmad. In fact, Gordon was the author of his own downfall.

The Gladstone administration was resolved to evacuate the Sudan and, given Gordon's previous experience of the area, decided with some reluctance that he was the best man to oversee such an operation. Gordon set out for Egypt in January 1844 and arrived in Khartoum on February 18. Although his brief was to report and evacuate, Gordon had plans of his own and accepted the appointment as governor-general of the Sudan from the khedive, which placed him in direct conflict with his orders from London. Wrongly assessing the Mahdi as some petty rabble-rouser of ephemeral popularity, Gordon evacuated perhaps twenty-five hundred women, children and wounded before digging in to defend Khartoum against attack. He also started sending deliberately misleading and ambiguous reports back to London, which did not further endear the government to Gladstone. His own surviving papers and diary entries make it clear that he never had any intention of following orders.

The siege of the city began on March 18, and Gordon soon learned that his opponent was not some one-trick pony who would be quickly cowed. Khartoum stands at the confluence of the Blue and White Niles, both rivers still easily navigable in March, so London repeated its orders for Gordon to pull out using every boat available. Again, Gordon chose to ignore the orders and stayed to defend the city. He was deliberately putting Gladstone in an impossible position. Gordon knew there would be public pressure to send a relief column, which is what he had wanted all along. Unfortunately for Gordon and everyone else in Khartoum, Gladstone was not a flexible pragmatist; he resisted the public pressure and even that of Queen Victoria when she threw her hat into Gordon's ring. Eventually he had no choice and, through gritted teeth, ordered General Sir Garnet Wolseley to make preparations for the relief of Gordon. Realizing time was now very much of the essence, the British government took an unusual step that has left us with one of the most prominent names in the travel business.

In 1841 a temperance-preaching cabinetmaker had the idea of transporting several temperance groups together to hear speakers at other meetings. He approached the railways to arrange for special trains at a fixed price on which he could sell tickets. His first venture transported five hundred day-trippers from Leicester to enjoy a day out in Loughborough and made him a tidy profit. From this auspicious start, Thomas Cook expanded his field of operations at home and abroad, and of prime interest to the British government was the fact that the company had by then organized educational tours up the Niles and had "agreements" with local chieftains to guarantee safe passage. The government handed the company the logistical problem of the swift shipment of eighteen hundred troops with supplies to Khartoum. The bill for this staggering feat of organization was £500,000 which, in conjunction with the prestige of the job itself, left Thomas Cook in an unassailable position in the burgeoning travel business.

Wolseley elected to take the Nile route to avoid the quicker but more arduous trek overland and, since this got him there two days too late, he did come in for a bit of flak from those who maintained that the overland route would have got him there in plenty of time. On the night of January 25, 1885, the Mahdi and his "ephemeral rabble" of fifty thousand men overran the city to kill or enslave all within. Accounts of Gordon's death vary from the Victorian romance of his strolling among the flabbergasted enemy with a fly-swatter until killed, to the darker version of his being taken captive for ransom, which was declined by the British who wanted rid of him. Either way, his head ended up on a pike and the Mahdi's forces were free to rampage through what is now Darfur, committing breathtaking atrocities.

Great Sprawl of China

Although the greatest military structure of all time, the so-called Great Wall has generated it own coterie of myths over the years, most notably that it is the only man-made structure visible with the naked eye from the moon. This piece of nonsense was started by Robert Ripley's infamously unreliable "Believe It or Not" which, somewhat remarkably, made the claim in May 1932, nearly forty years before the first lunar landing of 1969. Since then, countless astronauts, including the Chinese Yang Liwei in 2003, have made a point of stating that no structure, including the wall, is visible from even one thousand miles out, much less from the moon. No matter how long the wall is, it is not particularly wide, so at whatever point an outward-bound astronaut loses sight definition of, say, a motorway network, that will also be the point at which the Great Wall of China disappears from view.

It is confusing to talk of *the* Great Wall of China, as no such single structure has ever existed; no Chinese ruler ever demanded the building of a wall that for all its length looked like the pictures in the travel brochures. Different dynasties built different walls in different places to ward off invaders from the north, but there were just as many other walls built between the feuding Chinese provinces of the Warring

Period, which lasted from the middle of the fifth century BC to the year 221 BC. In 214 BC, Shih Huang-ti, the first to rule over a united China, decided it might be a good idea if all these walls were joined up to present a defensive line well to the north of the line of any extant sections of the wall today. In all there have been five major walls: the Quin Wall of 208 BC; the Han Wall of the first century BC; the Sui Wall of the seventh century; the twelfth-century Wall of the Ten Kingdoms and the Hongwu/Wanli/Ming endeavors undertaken across the four-teenth to the seventeenth centuries. It is this many-hands approach to the project that accounts for the meandering path of the wall, which on many occasions doubles or even trebles back on itself, something that engineers would never have allowed to happen had the job been one continuous project.

The sections of the wall closest to Beijing, so popular with tourists, are not yet even five hundred years old and once the wall disappears into the distance it is a very different story. Much of the "Great Wall" is nothing but earth mounds, and never in its entire history did the wall stop an invasion. (What wall ever has?) It is also a misconception to perceive any part or era of the wall as a barrier against the Mongols; Shih Huang-ti died in 210 BC, about a thousand years before the ninth-century rise of the Mongol hordes who persistently plagued China, wall or no wall. Huang-ti's main concern was the Xiongnu of northern China and beyond, a troublesome lot who would evolve into the Huns and later move west. Essentially the wall was a frontier marker; at no time did Chinese military strategy revolve around holding the wall or any part of it. As with most other civilizations at the time, the cities were the fortified strongholds.

The section that the tourists visit is the new build of the seven-teenth century, with work largely completed by 1640, but to no great purpose. In 1644 the Kokes Manchu Army out of north-east Asia arrived en masse at the wall, leaving the Chinese general Wu Sangui no option but to open up the gates at the Shanhai Pass, letting them in to take over the whole country. Once in charge, the Manchu dynasty extended its influence so far north of the wall that it lost any significance that it may have once held.

Hancock's Half-Hour

Although hailed as the Rubicon crossed to set America on the road to war with Britain, nothing much happened on July 4, 1776. The events of this date were instead a rather unimportant link in a chain of events set in motion by what is still known as Lee's Resolution:

> *That these United Colonies are, and of right ought to be, free and independent States, that they are absolved from all allegiance to the British Crown, and that all political connection between them and the State of Great Britain is, and ought to be, totally dissolved. That it is expedient forthwith to take the most effectual measures for forming foreign Alliances. That a plan of confederation be prepared and transmitted to the respective Colonies for their consideration and approbation.*

The Resolution was the motion calling for a declaration of independence, which was put before the Continental Congress in Philadelphia on June 7, 1776 by Richard Lee, later the eleventh president of America. (George Washington was the first elected under the present Constitution; before his tenure there were fourteen presidents.) Congress appointed a committee of five to draw up the first draft, which was produced by Thomas Jefferson, and revised by Benjamin Franklin and John Adams before being presented to Congress. Once again, Congress made a number of amendments—the famous "life, liberty and the pursuit of happiness" had originally appeared in the draft as the far less inspiring "life, liberty and the pursuit of property."

The formal Declaration of Independence was issued on July 2. The Pennsylvania *Evening Post* of that date proclaimed: "This day the Continental Congress declared the United Colonies Free and Independent

States," and in a letter to his wife dated July 3, 1776, John Adams informs her that:

> *The second day of July, 1776, will be the most memorable epoch in the history of America. I am apt to believe that it will be celebrated by succeeding generations as the great anniversary festival. It ought to be commemorated as the day of deliverance, by solemn acts of devotion to God Almighty. It ought to be solemnized with pomp and parade, with shows, games, sports, guns, bells, bonfires, and illuminations, from one end of this continent to the other, from this time forward forever more.*

As American historian Richard Shenkman points out in his *Legends, Lies and Cherished Myths of American History* (1988), myths die hard. When this letter surfaced in the nineteenth century, those into whose hands it fell thought it their duty to alter the date and content of the letter to fit the popular myth of July 4 to avoid upsetting people.

Though the statement had been issued on July 2, there remained bones of contention to sort out in the written form of the Unanimous Declaration of the Thirteen United States of America—it was never called the Declaration of Independence. July 4 was only the date of the vote on the final draft, which did not meet with anything like unanimous approval. Some individuals missed the vote, for reasons ranging from complacency to opposition, and quite a few delegates were openly hostile to the move—in the penultimate vote both Pennsylvania and South Carolina voted "nay," Delaware was divided and New York abstained. After the "ayes" eventually carried the vote, John Hancock, president of Congress, and its secretary, Charles Thomson, took the draft away to a private room where, after a brief meeting of about half an hour, they, and only they, signed that draft. There never was any solemn signing ceremony involving a steady procession of somber statesmen of grey-haired sagacity; most of the fifty-six signatories were in their twenties or early thirties, and signatures were added in a gradual, when-you-have-the-time process that ran through into late August. Some did not get round to signing it for years, with Thomas McKean not adding his name until 1781. Then there was Robert Livingstone, one of the original committee of five detailed to draw up the first draft. He drafted it, voted for it and even sat down and framed it but, standing back to admire his handiwork, realized he had forgotten to sign it.

Heavy Knight?

The most common myth relating to suits of armor maintains that the garments were so heavy that wearers had to be lifted onto their horses by crane. This is a silly notion that seems to have evolved from the popularity of Mark Twain's *A Connecticut Yankee in King Arthur's Court* (1889). Later, the fallacy was immortalized by Sir Lawrence Olivier's film version of *Henry V* (1944), despite the howls of protest from the production's historical advisor, Sir James Mann, master of the armories at the Tower of London.

At the time of the battle of Agincourt (1415), the average suit weighed around thirty-five pounds, this increasing in the next century to something around the fifty-pound mark. The heaviest suit on record is that made in 1570 by the royal workshop at Greenwich for the 3rd earl of Worcester. Without the optional musket-ball-proof plates (about twenty pounds), this entire get-up weighed just over eighty-one pounds, which is about ten pounds lighter than the full marching gear of a World War II British infantryman. Knights had to be able to mount and dismount with speed, as well as run, crawl under defenses and scale siege ladders, so armor had to strike the optimum balance between protection and maneuverability. It is also worth mentioning that the horses favored by knights were not the sleek steeds of Hollywood epics, but sturdy punches and shires trained to bite and kick all in their path. One good kick from a rough-shod shire horse could easily be fatal, to even a man in armor, so it was not unknown for a knight's mount to kill and maim as many as its rider.

Suits of armor on display are also partly responsible for the notion that medieval people were much shorter than modern humans. The various sections of a suit were joined by strong leather panels to allow for vigorous movement and, when on display, these are always "relaxed" to avoid stress. A display suit in a museum that may appear as tailored for a wearer of, say, five feet, two to three inches will in fact accommodate a man of five feet, seven to eight inches. True, some doorways and access points in medieval buildings are so small that one has to stoop to pass through, but this was more to do with building methods and defense: the smaller the hole, the stronger the door and the easier to hold out. According to Margaret Cox and Charlotte Roberts, both forensic archaeologists of international reputation, the adult height in both sexes has remained pretty much constant since the Neolithic era.

Armor was not the sole province of the knight, nor were all such men of noble birth. Knights were made not born. Anyone who distinguished himself on the field was eligible for elevation, not just by the crown but by other knights, feudal lords or even the clergy. Anyone who could afford a suit of armor could wear it without accusations of pretensions to the peerage. In the fourteenth century a made to measure suit would have cost about £16 (three years' wages for a skilled worker), but there were plenty of second-hand suits available or the cheap-and-cheerful option of suits cobbled together from bits and pieces salvaged from the battlefield.

Discussions of armor are often replete with debate over terminology. One should not, for example, use the expression "chain mail" to refer generically to armor made from interlinked strips or rings of metal. The matter is complicated and best explained by the following statement from the Arms and Armor Department at New York's prestigious Metropolitan Museum of Art:

> As with so many misconceptions, the origins of this misnomer are to be found in the nineteenth century. When early scholars of armor looked at medieval artworks, they noticed what they thought to be depictions

of many different forms of armor: rings, chains, bands of rings, scales, small plates, etc. With poetic license, all early armor was referred to as "mail," distinguished only by its appearance, hence the terms "ring-mail," "chain-mail," "banded mail," "scale-mail," "plate-mail," and so forth. It is today commonly accepted, however, that most of these different depictions are actually various attempts by artists to efficiently show the surface of a type of armor that is difficult to render both in paint or sculpture. Rather than showing each interlinking ring, the small links were stylized by dots, slashes, S-shapes, circles, and the like, which readily lent themselves to misinterpretation.

In short, armor buffs will tell you that such armor should indeed be referred to purely as "mail," rather than chain mail, to avoid any error. Chain mail is, in fact, linguistic overkill, as the word "chain" adds nothing to the meaning of the definition.

"Lance-rest" is another misnomer. The short section hinging out to the horizontal from the torso armor is actually called the "lance-arrest" and was designed to lock into the hand-protecting cup to prevent the lance being rammed backwards on impact. Given that the combined weight and kinetic energy of rider and mount was transferred to the tip of the lance on contact, the lance-arrest was designed to act as a kind of shock absorber to disperse impact that would otherwise do serious damage to the holder's right arm. Without this, Newton's "every action has an equal and opposite re-action" would come into play; if the force of impact was sufficient to unseat the opposing rider, then the man on the other end of the lance would likewise be lifted out of his saddle.

The prevailing trend for men's clothes to button left over right is a direct result of the structure and fixings of early armor. All plates and sections secured left over right as a defense against the majority of weapon strikes, which would typically be delivered by a right-handed opponent, raking across the recipient's body from the left to the right. The left-over-right armor configuration meant that the blows would thus be less likely to get under any of the joins. When this trend invaded civilian fashion, it had the added advantage that any man would find it easy to reach in under any heavy outer garment to gain swift access to a sword, typically carried on the left. Women's clothes had no need of such considerations and favored the reverse, as ladies of station had dressers for whom such buttoning was more convenient.

Hide and Sikh

The first Indian Mutiny is misunderstood, but there was another during World War I and a third during World War II, when Subhas Chandra Bose raised not one but two armies of his compatriots to fight for Germany and Japan. Details of this were kept firmly under wraps until quite some time after the war and it is only in recent decades that the full extent of Indian National Army (INA) activities and atrocities became free knowledge. In the case of the first mutiny, in 1857–58, it is commonly said that the single cause was the new-issue British musket cartridge, which the native troops believed greased with a mixture of cow and pig fat, making it taboo to Hindu and Muslim alike, especially as the user had to bite off the tip to render it operable. Their issue was certainly picked on as a handy catalyst by the mutineers, but trouble had been brewing for quite some time and the ammunition was just a flashpoint.

There were general suspicions among the Indian population that the British were determined to unravel the very fabric of Indian social structure, including the abolition of the caste system. Legislation was afoot to allow Hindu widows to remarry; the admittedly repugnant customs of child marriages and suttee (the act of a widow burning herself to death on her husband's funeral pyre) had been outlawed; laws had been passed to enforce equal treatment and inheritance rights of converts to Christianity; militant missionaries conducted aggressive proselytizing campaigns; everywhere saw the systematic replacement of the native aristocracy by British officials with regional powers. In short, the invaders were rightly perceived as having embarked on a program of subjugation through insidious anglicization. Unrest was therefore pandemic long before Sepoy Mangal Pandy took the first open step of revolt on March 29, 1857, at the military enclosure at Barrakpore in West Bengal.

As for the cartridges, there was unfortunately a grain of truth in the rumors. The first experimental batch of cartridges were indeed greased with cow and pig fat before being shipped to India in 1853 to see how they stood up to the climate. Never issued, these were simply held in secure storage at Dum Dum (home of another infamous cartridge) and then shipped back to London's Enfield arsenal for examination in 1855. Not until New Year's Day 1857 was the new round issued, along with instructions on how the tip should be bitten off to expose the powder, but by this time it had been decided that a mixture of beeswax and sheep tallow was more suitable. To be fair, the fact that the British Army had even considered the use of blended cow and pig tallow highlights their complete insensitivity and the lofty disregard for native recruits' mores.

Garrisons were soon buzzing with talk of taboo tallow and no amount of assurance assuaged the situation. Eventually waking from their imperial torpor, the British suggested that native troops be allowed to snip the tip with small scissors or to grease their own rounds with ghee or vegetable oil. It was too little, too late. British Intelligence knew something was afoot—the provinces teemed with native runners carrying a simple chapatti from village to village, this acting as a coded general alert that something big was about to happen. Everything was set to boil over when, on March 29, 1857, Sepoy Pandy took to the parade ground to denounce the cartridges as a ploy to destroy their religious integrity and called on his fellow soldiers to rise up and slaughter all Europeans. Lieutenant Baugh, adjutant of the 34th Native Infantry, tried to arrest him but was cut down by a sword carried by Pandy, who then shot himself, inflicting a non-fatal chest wound. He was executed a few days later. Matters lulled until April 24, when about eighty sepoys of the East India Company's 3rd Native Cavalry, stationed at Meerut, refused to even touch the new issue cartridges and were immediately sentenced to ten years' hard labor. This sensitive response unleashed the rebellion. Proof that no one actually believed the rumors about the cartridges is furnished by the fact that none of the natives showed the slightest reluctance to use the ammunition against the British after the rebellion got under way.

But the mutiny was doomed. There was no coordination and little support from the general population. The Sikhs, enemies of the Hindus, zealously aided the suppression and it is perhaps fair to say that many of the retaliatory excesses inflicted on the mutineers were inflicted by indigenous peoples. After the suppression, however, the British also disgraced themselves. Prisoners were used for pig-sticking practice on the polo fields, while others were strapped across the muzzles of cannon and blown to pieces. It was a sad and sorry affair from which no one emerged untarnished. The only positive outcome saw the autocratic East India Company stripped of its powers and a new British resolve to discuss matters with native committees before taking decisions impacting on local culture. Unsurprisingly, denizens of the Indian Subcontinent prefer to call the event the First War of Independence and hail the instigator as Shaheed (Martyr) Pandy. The Second Indian Mutiny was a short-lived affair of little consequence in 1915, but the third was both extensive and embarrassing to the British.

Bose had long been a thorn in the British side. He took a far more aggressive approach to the cause of independence than Gandhi and, like the IRA, saw alliance with Hitler as a means to rid his country of the British once and for all. Aware of his plans, British Intelligence canceled his passport and kept him under surveillance, but he gave them the slip on January 19, 1941, and, with the Special Operations Executive hot on his heels with orders to kill him on sight, he led his would-be assassins on a merry dance through the Khyber Pass. He made his way into Afghanistan, through Russia and into Germany, where he was welcomed by Hitler himself. With his pitch angled to Indian independence, Bose toured the POW camps holding Indians taken prisoner in North Africa and other theaters of war, raising a considerable army that swore allegiance to Hitler and Bose, in that order. In addition to Indian soldiers who had deserted from the British Army, thousands of civilian Indians from occupied Europe flocked to his banner and, with his similar force raised under the Japanese, the INA numbered at least 85,000 troops, including the Rani of Jhansi Women's Regiment.

With his first regiments attached to the Waffen-SS, Bose came to realize that Hitler's interest with the cause of Indian independence was next to zero. So, he took himself off to Japan where he was given a brief to replicate his venture with many of the Indian troops taken prisoner after the fall of Singapore (scene of the Second Indian Mutiny of 1915, when Indian troops killed their British officers and went on the rampage). Bose couldn't believe his luck. The Japanese had fallen heir to forty-five thousand Indian troops with their capture of Singapore. All but a couple of thousand turned coats to join the INA and fight the Allied forces for the rest of the war throughout the Malay Peninsula and Burma, their numbers constantly swelled by ex-pat Indians living throughout those areas.

As the Allied victory came nigh, however, the Indian SS brigades were in full retreat through France, where they are remembered as some of the most vicious rapists and looters. With the BBC forbidden to make any broadcast on the matter, and the press likewise muzzled, many of the INA's leading lights and senior officers were taken back to India, where the British had to back down from their planned trials and retribution after the population rose as one to defend men they viewed as patriots and heroes. It was a bitter blow for the British, who now had to face the reality that the Indian Army could never again be relied on, and this realization was a major impetus behind the 1947 withdrawal of the British from India.

Bose, knowing that he was one person the British were determined to have dangling from a rope, resolved to disappear. On August 18, 1945, he supposedly died when his plane, bound for Tokyo out of Taiwan, dropped out of the sky. There were two post-war investigations, one in the mid-1950s and another in the opening years of the new millennium, the second revealing that no plane with Bose had even taken off, let alone crashed. In 1985, attention focused on a reclusive Indian monk known as Bhagwanji or Gumnami Baba and living in Faizabad, Uttar Pradesh. Prior to his death in the September of that year, the monk had admitted his true identity and handwriting experts confirmed that letters written by the monk were a perfect match to known samples of Bose's hand.

Highland History Out of Kilter

Among the many things wrong with films like *Braveheart* is the way the Highland warriors wear kilts and the notion that each Highland clan army had its own distinctive tartan, worn as some sort of uniform by which all could tell friend from foe. The belted kilt was in fact designed by a mid-eighteenth-century Lancashire Quaker called Thomas Rawlinson, who established iron works and brick factories in the Highlands at Glengarie and Lochaber. The furnace heat proved too much for the labor force then wearing the cumbersome philamor, best described as a sort of heavy-duty toga that could be gathered up between the legs when required, and Rawlinson's belted kilt proved far more convenient and comfortable. As for the tartan, the origins of this are far more complex.

The Scots did not become the major power in what is now called Scotland until perhaps the sixth century, and by then had not developed the skills required to produce a complicated cloth such as tartan. On the other hand, graves of Tocharian warriors excavated in China and dated to 800 BC have revealed the occupants to have been wearing such clothing and, even more surprising, 3000 BC mummified corpses unearthed in the Takla Makan Desert in Xinjiang Province were found with red hair and likewise clad. Indeed, some see *tartan* deriving from *Tartary*, the old name for China, as early mention of such cloth indicates its importation from that country into England before being shipped north.

Roman military records do tell of brightly colored and striped clothing worn by their enemies of the UK's northern reaches, but these records are not detailed enough for the reader to discern precise patterns. Another fifteen hundred years passed before any meaningful references to tartan emerged, but even these are unclear as the term used is *breacan*, the Gaelic for "checkered," so this cloth might more have resembled gingham than any tartan. In the first couple of decades of the 1600s, tartan denoted a kind of woolen cloth rather than any particular patterning. The first proof of the existence of what we now call tartan appears in a German woodcut of the early 1630s, which shows philamor-clad Highland mercenaries in the army of Gustavus Adolphus, king of Sweden.

By the 1730s, tartan weave was indeed widespread in the Scottish Highlands but without any clan differentiation. No one clan has ever been uniform in its tartan and no one individual, be he a common soldier or a Highland warlord, has ever been identifiable by the pattern of his clothing. All extant portraiture of lairds and warlords of stated identity are dressed in various weaves bearing no resemblance to any present pattern purporting to be that of a Campbell, a MacDonald etc. Furthermore, in battle the custom was to cast aside the cumbersome philamor and fight in just a shirt with an agreed color of ribbon in the hair. The local weavers and dyers set the colors, dictated by nothing more partisan than the dyes they could extract from local vegetation. Inland weavers discovered that heather, variously treated, would provide yellows, dark greens and orangey browns, and they could also distill purples and blues from berries, the availability of which might vary from glen to glen. West coast weavers used gypsywort and seaweeds to produce a variety of greens, and weavers with wealthy clients augmented local dyes with woad, cochineal, madder and indigo, imported from England or Europe. In short, it was the manufacturers who dictated the choice of colors within any one region.

If tartan was common by the 1730s, its day was soon to end. After the battle of Culloden in 1745, and because the English even then believed the tartan to be some sort of battledress, King George II sanctioned the Act of Proscription of the Highland Garb of 1746, which also outlawed the bagpipe, thought to be an instrument used to summon the clans to war. The weavers went out of business overnight; all the pattern sticks lay to rot, leaving no clue as to who made which pattern and where.

The revival of "traditional" tartan came with George IV's grand visit to Edinburgh in 1822, a royal razzamatazz overseen by the novelist and poet Sir Walter Scott, the leader of the Gothic Revival in Scotland and a man with a stirringly romantic world view. Scott passed on to the guests the expressed desire of the king that it would be jolly good fun if all turned up in their "clan tartan." Not having a clue what that was, the various lairds rushed to their tailors and told them to come up with something, and fast. So, just as it had been before, that which is today recognized as a tartan exclusive to a particular "name" was invented by the design departments of assorted tailors across the land. The next boost to the tartan myth arrived with Victoria's love of Balmoral (the royal private residence in Scotland), which prompted her husband Prince Albert to design the now famous Balmoral tartan. (There are at present over two thousand recognized tartans and only about a hundred clans.) And just to please the queen, the Scots hurriedly invented "traditional" Highland games to boot.

Before you could say "Bonnie Prince Charlie," everyone was wearing kilts, tossing cabers and eating shortbread out of Balmoral tartan biscuit tins.

Spotting an economic opportunity, a couple of con-men called John and Charles Allen decided it was time to cash in on the tartan revolution. The English brothers reinvented themselves as the Versailles-born brothers Sobieski-Stuart, issue of a secret marriage between a princess of the Polish royal family and Bonnie Prince Charlie. The claim was completely improbable, but the brothers Sobieski-Stuart became celebrities throughout Scotland and published their fantastic *Vestiarium Scoticum* in 1842 to resounding acclaim. Purporting to be an accurate and detailed register of traditional tartans and clan variations, the book became the bible of all cloth makers and the first point of reference for anyone wanting to find out about their "official" tartan.

How Now, Mau-Mau?

There was no organization called the "Mau-Mau"—this was a name invented in 1948 by the white colonial police in Kenya for a burgeoning movement reacting to a life of virtual slave labor under British rule. The origin and meaning of the term is unknown, but it was perhaps intended to mimic the muted vocalization of jackals on the prowl, or inspired by the Kikuyu *mumumumumu*, a term used to mock secretive whispering. Either way, to its members the movement was only ever referred to as *Muingi* (the "Movement"), *Muigwithania* (the "Understanding") or *Muma wa Uiguano* (the "Oath of Unity").

Call the rebels what you will, by 1949 the Kenyan Press was awash with lurid imaginings reflecting whites' paranoia: the Mau-Mau held voodoo-like rites in the bush before setting out to disembowel a white family and feast on their bodies and there were "special action squads" being trained on goats to learn how to rape white women to death. But behind all the hype, the "White Mischief" society was waking up to the fact that "Toby and Missie" were not, and never had been, toe-curlingly grateful for being allowed to sleep in a hut at the bottom of the garden after a 16-hour day of run-fetch-clean. To quote Professor David Maughn-Brown, expert in African Affairs:

> The causes of the revolt were socio-economic and political and amounted, to put it crudely, to the economic exploitation and administrative oppression of the Kikuyu by the white settlers and the colonial state. [It was a response] to years of frustration at the refusal of the colonial government to redress grievances over land or to listen to demands for constitutional reform . . . it was a peasants revolt triggered off by the declaration of the state of emergency [1952] and the

eviction of the squatters from the farms on the White Highlands, the best arable land in Kenya.

This situation, Maughn-Brown explains, presented the colonial authorities with a public relations problem: they could not denounce the Mau-Mau as yet another communist-backed uprising, nor could they admit that the uprising sprang from the fact that the whole colonial enterprise had been exploiting and most shamefully abusing—to the point of unpunished rape and murder—the Kikuyu people for years and that now they were fighting back. With the truth an unacceptable path for the authorities to tread, they had to paint the "enemy" as gangs of base thugs who had crossed over to the dark side of satanic ritual and voodoo-crazed sex orgies. Only thus could they "justify" the unbelievably savage backlash they unleashed on people who just wanted a fair day's pay, the right to some of their own land and a course of redress against white aggression.

The only remarkable thing about the Mau-Mau rebellion is that it was so long in coming. Whites, who accounted for perhaps 0.5 percent of the population, owned or controlled up to 40 percent of the prime arable land, leaving about three-quarters of the Kikuyu labor pool living below the basic requirements line. In all, over 90 percent of the total workforce received less than 40 percent of the total wage bill, and this was the reward for a people who had willingly furnished over 100,000 fighting men for World War II. What began as a civil disobedience, strikes and non-cooperation was met with such a vicious backlash that the situation soon spiraled down to widespread violence, with the vast majority of the atrocities perpetrated by the authorities and the gun-happy Kenyan Farmers Association. The Mau-Mau had no guns or external support, so throughout the "war" the government forces killed over 11,000 Mau-Mau and brought about the deaths of perhaps 100,000 others by beatings, starvation and disease in "fortified villages," which was the favored euphemism for what were essentially concentration camps. By contrast, the Mau-Mau killed 592 members of the security forces and 32 European civilians—half the number that died drunk at the wheels of their cars in Nairobi over the same period.

Countless "free-fire" zones were established in cities and urban areas to allow whites to gun down any black on sight, and most British Army units ran a "lottery" for the man with the most confirmed kills per month. Rape, castration, amputation and burning alive were common, as was the attitude of the only officer to be brought to book as a sop to international outrage when the reality of what was happening leaked out. Captain Gerald Griffiths of the Durham Light Infantry told all his men they could shoot anyone they liked so long as they were black, and they could do as they pleased with the women and children. Griffiths himself frequently murdered for fun, his favorite "jape" being to allow innocent blacks with the appropriate paperwork to pass through checkpoints and then turn the Bren gun on them. He got five years' imprisonment in 1954 and the next year Baroness Barbara Castle visited Kenya to report back on "a Nazi attitude toward the Africans," commenting that, "In the heart of the British empire there is a police state where the rule of law has broken down, where murders and tortures of Africans go unpunished and where the authorities pledged to enforce justice regularly connive at its violation."

The distinguished historian, Victor Kiernan, wrote that conditions in the "protected" or "fortified villages" were "probably as bad as any similar Nazi or Japanese establishments" with "Japanese methods of torture" common. But the massed beatings and killings at Hola concentration camp on March 3, 1959, proved an atrocity too far. Survivor John Maina Kahihu recalls that eighty-five detainees refused to join the labor details that morning and were thus singled out for "inducement to productive work." This ominous intention involved two hundred guards and troops being brought into the compound and divided up into those who would hold machine guns on the scene and those who would conduct the exercise in "inducement." This was to be no quick lesson. When all the men were in position, the beatings began at 8:00 a.m. on the blow of a whistle and did not cease until 11:30 a.m. Given the climate, the inducers had to keep taking breaks for drinks and showers before returning to duty and, by the time it was all over, there was just a bloody heap of bodies. Kahihu admits he was lucky: "They beat us like dogs. I was covered by other bodies—just my arms and legs were exposed. I was very lucky to survive. But the others were still being beaten. There was no escape for them." The authorities tried to cover their tracks by blaming the deaths on contaminated water, but the truth erupted onto the international scene and, within weeks, all the Kenyan concentration camps and labor camps had been shut down by a colonial system in tatters and full retreat.

Prominent activist Jomo Kenyatta was released from prison to become the first president of an independent Kenya in 1963, and wealthy Africans from other nations flooded in to replace the white elite. The Kikuyu stayed at the bottom of the pile, having exchanged one bunch of parasites for another. By the 1970s the new top 20 percent were enjoying 70 percent of the nation's wealth, with Kenyatta himself the country's biggest landowner while his fellow Kikuyu enjoyed the same old poverty. But that is what revolution typically means: everything goes through one complete cycle to return to the starting point. In January 2008, old rivalries were again at large, with Kikuyus being burnt alive in their churches and hacked to death in the street by gangs of thugs from the rival Kalenjin, Luhya and Luo tribes, mainly because Kenyatta and his successors had done nothing to address the iniquities of Kenyan society.

Juden—Troopers

It is perhaps commonly known that the Waffen-SS comprised brigades of many nations—even some 800 Swiss joined up—but little is voiced today of the levels of Jewish support (practical, if not ideological) for Hitler. While it is true that countless Jews already in the grip of the Nazis in the camps were given the unforgivable choice of collaborating as Kapos to brutalize their own or die themselves, the actions of others, discussed here, sometimes transcend the comprehensible.

Although it is not possible to put a definite number to them, an estimated 150,000 Jews were active in the German war effort and not just in the lower ranks: there were Jewish admirals and generals, with about twenty known Jews being awarded the Knight's Cross, Germany's highest military honor. There was Commander Paul Asher, who served aboard the *Bismarck*, and Admiral Bernhard Rogge; generals Johannes Kukerfort and Helmut Wilberg, even Helmut Schmidt, chancellor of Germany from 1974–1982, did his stint in Hitler's army. Highest ranking of all was Field Marshal Erhard Milch, who stood trial at Nuremberg for his role in the deportation of Jews to the concentration camps, and the allocation of Jewish slave labor to be worked to death in the factories of many a company that today gets defensively hostile when questioned about its enthusiastic applications for such resources. Most disturbing of all were the Jews in the Gestapo, and those who were involved on the darkest side of all—Lenta-Kaiserwald Concentration Camp was run by the Jewish doctor Eleke Scherwitz; at Westerbork, the staging camp for Auschwitz, Arthur Pisk was head of the Ordnungsdienst ("Order Police") that policed the camp while the head of administration was Kurt Schlesinger; and Dr. Hans Eppinger took poison in his cell at Nuremberg to avoid hanging for the horrendous experiments he had conducted on his fellow Jews in Dachau.

The most bizarre case was the offer from Zionists such as Yitzak Shamir, later the Israeli prime minister, and Avraham Stern—he of the Stern Gang (Jewish anti-British insurgents)—to throw their lot in with Hitler to help defeat the British, whom they hated for blocking Jewish settlement of Palestine. In January 1941, Shamir, Stern, a group of other leading Zionists and prominent members of their associated National Military Organization (NMO) made a formal representation to German diplomats in Beirut to suggest a military-political alliance "for the solution of the Jewish Question in Europe and the active participation of the NMO in the war on the side of Germany." The original document is held in German Auswertiges Amt Archiv, Bestand 47–59, E224152 and E234155-58; the original text is replicated in *The Palestinian Problem in*

German Politics 1889–1945 (Israel: 1947, pp. 315–17) by David Yisraeli and opens its address as follows:

> *The NMO which is very familiar with the goodwill of the German Reich government and its officials toward Zionist activities within Germany and the Zionist emigration program takes the view that: 1. Common interests can exist between a European New Order based on the German concept and the true national aspirations of the Jewish people as embodied by the NMO. 2. Cooperation is possible between the New Germany and a renewed, folkish-national Jewry. 3. The establishment of the Jewish state on a national and totalitarian basis, and bound by treaty, with the German Reich, would be in the interest of maintaining and strengthening the future German position of power in the Near East. On the basis of these considerations, and upon the condition that the German Reich government recognize the national aspirations of the Israel Freedom Movement mentioned above, the NMO in Palestine offers to actively take part in the war on the side of Germany.*

This offer by the NMO could include military, political and informational activity within Palestine and, after certain organizational measures, outside as well. Along with this, the "Jewish" men of Europe would be militarily trained and organized in military units under the leadership and command of the NMO. They would take part in combat operations for the purpose of conquering Palestine, should such a front be formed.

Among the many non-combatant Jewish supporters of Hitler was Erik Jan Hanussen, the son of a synagogue caretaker who became Hitler's tutor for speech making and crowd manipulation; a major party fund-raiser, for a time he was also one of the largest individual financial supporters. On the night of March 25, 1933, Hanussen was shot and dumped in a shallow grave outside Berlin. He had overplayed his hand by trying to capitalize on inside information from Hitler's circle and "prophesying," in highly paid private sittings, the Reichstag fire, days before it actually happened. Then there was the poet Gertrude Stein and her lover, Alice B. Toklas, who both saw out the war quite happily in France under Nazi occupation. In 1938, Stein had actually approached Gustav Hendrikksen of the Nobel Committee to suggest Hitler for the Peace Prize "because he is removing all the elements of contest and of struggle from Germany. By driving out the Jews and the democratic and Left element, he is driving out everything that conduces to activity. That means peace . . . By suppressing Jews . . . he was ending struggle in Germany." The girls' best friends in Nazi France were the senior Vichy official, Bernard Fay, responsible for the deportation of thousands of French Jews to the camps, and his Gestapo boyfriend with whom the girls spent many a happy night discussing "the Führer's qualities of greatness." After the war Stein campaigned tirelessly for Fay's release from prison.

Ninja Turtles and the Ironclads

So famous is the 1862 clash between the USS *Monitor* and CSS *Merrimack* that most assume these to have been the first of the ironclads per se, whereas they were only the first to do battle in anger. The first of the true ironclads saw action in Korean waters in the sixteenth century.

In 1592, Toyotomi Hideoshi of Japan struck a deal with Portugal for the supply of three hundred thousand muskets for his invasion of Korea, where the highly innovative warlord, Yi-Suns(h)in, was preparing a welcome for him that he would not forget in a hurry. Realizing that the invaders would be almost entirely reliant on their shipping, Yi designed and built a small fleet of galleys he christened "turtle ships" on account of their extremely shallow draft and convex cap of spiked iron cladding. When the Japanese first arrived in Pusan harbor, they were joined by perhaps a dozen or so turtle ships which, well protected against musket and cannon, proceeded to sink over 60 Japanese craft. Later, in Chinhae Bay, Yi and his flotilla took their time to sink another 240 Japanese ships, a loss that completely scuppered Hideoshi's plans. When they went into action this time, the turtle crews took the precaution of sealing up their ears with wax, as they had learned from the first engagement that while cannonballs might bounce off the metal cladding, the noise inside was something to experience.

Typically dismissive of Eastern history when it comes to recording who was first past the post with any particular innovation, Western sources are fairly unanimous in naming the French *Gloire*, launched in 1859, and the British *Warrior*, launched the following year, as the first viable ironclads. Furthermore, the first ironclads in action were not *Monitor* and *Merrimack* but the CSS *Mississippi*, the CSS *Louisiana* and the CSS *Manassas*. These three Confederate ships can claim to be the first ironclads in action after engaging Union ships on the Mississippi River on October 12, 1861. The Union ships were not ironclad and so took some serious punishment while watching their best shots bounce off the enemy's armor.

Which takes us to the first ironclads to go head to head, but it was not the USS *Monitor* and the CSS *Merrimack* that engaged on March 9, 1862, in Hampton Roads Harbor, Virginia—it was the USS *Monitor* and the CSS *Virginia*. When Virginia ceded from the Union at the beginning of the Civil War in 1861, the Northern steam frigate, USS *Merrimack*, was still in Gosport Harbor, so the order was given to destroy her rather than let her fall into enemy hands. Unfortunately, the job was hurried and incompetent, allowing the Confederates to raise and convert her to an ironclad, commissioned as the CSS *Virginia*. The confusion is caused by the Union winning the war and writing the history books in which they constantly referred to the ship under the name by which she had been known to them which, rather confusingly, reads like two Union ships slugging it out to a draw, as the event turned out.

Occult Reich

Spawned in the 1940s, the industry built on the myth that the Nazi regime emerged from the occult shows no sign of slowing down. Apart from films of the *Indiana Jones* genre, showing Nazis hunting down the Ark of the Covenant or the Spear of Destiny, there are countless serious books trying to impart occult "spin" to every sign and symbol used, especially the swastika.

Like the Star of David, the swastika first rose to significance in ancient India among the Hindus (the word comes from the Sanskrit *svástika*), but it is also noted in other early cultures, from Japan to the Native Americans, and has even been found carved into mammoth tusks unearthed in Ukraine and dated to some time around 10,000 BC. It was frequently used to decorate synagogues and early English churches—in the latter it was also used at the base of stained glass windows, and was called a fylfot. Until the rise of Hitler, it was even used as the marketing symbol and company logo of the Danish brewery. But, despite all that antiquity, ubiquity and the fact that the original Sanskrit means nothing more sinister than "well-being" or "good fortune," the symbol will now and forever be associated with Nazi Germany and its fate is accordingly sealed. The Hitler-was-a-warlock mob claim the Nazis always presented their swastika rotating anticlockwise to announce the evil of their intent, but this is not so. The Nazi swastika presented the standard clockwise spin and Hitler was not some kind of satanic messiah.

Those with axes to grind have theories a-plenty to explain why Hitler adopted the swastika. The seriously challenged Unity Mitford never tired of telling anyone dumb enough to listen that Hitler had done so in her honor. Her family did indeed own the Ontario gold-mining town of Swastika, where she was allegedly conceived, but this had nothing to do with it. The selection of the symbol was for reasons anti-Semitic, not anti-Christian, and there is no reason to look further than the writings of the man himself.

According to Hitler's turgid ramblings in *Mein Kampf*: "I myself, after innumerable attempts, had laid down a final form; a flag with a red background, a white disk, and a black swastika in the middle. After long trials I also found a definite proportion between the size of the flag and the size of the white disk, as well as the shape and thickness of the swastika." To be fair, Hitler only lays claim to formatting the flag; the adoption of the swastika was due to its ancient use by the medieval German *Vehmic* (punishment) Courts, which capriciously incinerated anyone Jewish who stepped out of line. These courts spawned a network of anti-Semitic societies that still permeated the Austrian and German establishments of the early 1900s, particularly the dark and dangerous Thule Society, with its numerous connections to the formative Nazi Party. Between 1919 and 1921, Hitler virtually lived in the National Socialist library run by Dr. Friedrich Krohn, a prominent Thulian acknowledged by Hitler as the designer of a strikingly similar banner that had inspired his own. Krohn in turn acknowledged his inspiration for such a banner to have been the 1907 Christmas hate-fest of the Order of the New Templars, held at Werfenstein Castle, which had been decked out with swastika banners for the occasion.

So, Hitler's selection of the symbol was purely political, a move to strike a note with other like-minded organizations, and his own variation on the theme was first hoisted at Nuremberg on March 14, 1933, after his appointment as chancellor.

One Lump or Two?

The Boston Tea Party on the night of December 16, 1773, is remembered on both sides of the Atlantic as a blow struck by American patriots against taxation without representation. But the riot was instigated by a British bid to *lower* the tax on tea to undermine the smugglers, and patriotism had nothing to do with it.

Most of the tea consumed in America was smuggled in from Holland by rapacious merchants, such as John Hancock, who faced ruin if the impending Tea Act allowed the masses to buy tea from legal sources that was cheaper than their bootlegged beverage. Puppet-mastered by Hancock and other interested parties, a sixty-strong mob stormed Griffin's Wharf and, dressed up as Indians, boarded three East India Company merchant ships, *Dartmouth, Eleanor* and *Beaver*, to throw the cargo over-board. As with so many pivotal events in history, the element of farce raised its frivolous head. Cheered on by a drunken mob, the equally drunken "Mohawks" on the ships had to abandon their task when enveloped in a pall of tea dust that threatened to choke them to death.

Leading Bostonian radical Samuel Adams tried to spin the incident into a blow struck by the common man against British tyranny, whereas the average colonial Joe did pretty well; he was a great deal less taxed and oppressed than his UK counterpart. It was the well-heeled colonial gentry who saw their comfortable lifestyle threatened. Adams, Hancock and other disaffected colonials constantly lamented their lack of representation in London's Parliament; "Taxation without Representation is Tyranny" was their battle cry. But this cry for representation in Westminster was a smoke-screen. They knew they could never acquire enough seats to influence voting, but the cry made a good cloak of honorable motive to dignify an undignified scramble for power and money. Those who set America on the course to independence did so for their own gain, without a thought for the common man upon whom they immediately imposed oppressive taxation without representation. In Massachusetts, only 16 percent of white males owned enough land to qualify for a vote and in the Virginias this figure fell to six percent. It was not until the nineteenth century that the majority of adult white males were enfranchised. Women and blacks, of course, were another matter. The final irony is that residents of Washington, D.C., took to calling their city "the Last Colony," as it was not until 1961 that they gained the right to vote in presidential elections, and a further nine years before the district was allowed to elect a non-voting delegate to the House of Representatives.

Pearl's Before Swine

Before examining some misconceptions that still surround the attack on Pearl Harbor (just before 8:00 a.m. on December 7, 1941), it is best to dismiss the myth that Churchill and Roosevelt knew all about its coming but did nothing, just to give the American public and administration the appetite to enter World War II. Apart from the fact that polls showed 70 percent of Americans to be in favor of entering World War II against both Germany and Japan, the most obvious nail in that particular coffin is the fact that if Roosevelt did know the details of the attack in advance, he could have arranged an ambush on the high seas, become a hero and had his war as well. As things turned out, without considerable help from Britain, official and unofficial, the Japanese would not have had the capability to launch such an attack in 1941, but more of that later.

The major flaw in the conspiracy theory, as with so many others, is the numbers game. Intelligence flows upward, through a chain of command to the chief executive, not from that point down. Before Churchill or Roosevelt could be made aware of any single fact, it would have to be common knowledge throughout that chain. The notion that either men had his own spy bunker where they sat alone, hunched over radio consoles and cracking codes on their own, is laughable. Of course they, and everybody else in the loop, knew something was going to happen and happen soon, but no one knew what form the attack would take and where it would strike. American Admiral Stark thought it would most likely be "against either the Philippines, the Thai or Kra Peninsula or possibly Borneo." Others thought the Malay Peninsula or Singapore. With little time to organize anything, Roosevelt did indeed become aware of the date of the attack; messages from Tokyo to Japanese diplomats in America were decoded in the early hours of December 7, revealing instructions for them to stand by to deliver a certain message to the U.S. government later on that day, and to then destroy all cipher machines and sensitive documents. Only a fool could fail to figure out the likely significance of those instructions.

The message in question was not delivered until a couple of hours after the attack, apologists for the Japanese maintaining that this was due to the ambassador's inability to find someone to decode and type it. Not only is this idea an invention, but nowhere in that fourteen-page ramble was there mention of any declaration of war, not even the breaking off of diplomatic relationships. It was a protracted Japanese rant at the way they felt they had been treated by America and other nations. The meeting in Tokyo to draft the declaration of war had not yet taken place, and the fruit of their labors was not put into American hands until December 8.

At dawn of the day in question, two privates, Joseph Lockard and George Elliot, had been detailed to the Opana Hill radar station to babysit the tracker screen until 7:00 a.m. Neither was trained but both had been told to watch for blips. At 7:02 a.m. they noticed a very large blip indeed, at a range of about 130 miles, but when they phoned the Information Center at Fort Shafter the duty officer, Lieutenant Kermit Tyler, told them: "Don't worry about it, just shut down and get back for breakfast." Tyler wrongly assumed it was a delivery of new B-17 bombers due in from California, but Lockard and Elliot kept monitoring until 7:40 a.m., by which time the blip filled the screen. Presuming this to be some sort of malfunction, they shut down the radar equipment on one of history's great what-if moments because at 7:49 a.m. Mitsuo Fuchida, responsible for coordinating the Japanese air offensive, broke the hitherto complete radio silence with "To! To! To!—Attack! Attack! Attack!" As this was the first Japanese radio transmission of the operation, it dismisses assorted charlatans claiming to have picked up radio traffic from the Japanese task force en route to Pearl Harbor while making no secret of its destination. It also highlights the misconception about any famous but non-existent attack cry of "Tora! Tora! Tora!" While tora in Japanese means "tiger," it was only pilots *leaving* the scene who radioed out "To ra," meaning successful attack.

But was it? Not only did the Japanese have the advantage of surprise to attack a harbor filled with ships at berth, but they also had a massive task force clustered round 6 carriers that dispatched 414 attack planes, 23 submarines, and 5 midget submarines to do the dirty work. Yet they managed to only sink 6 of the 95 ships riding at anchor: 5 battleships and 1 destroyer. True, others were damaged, but these were all repaired and returned to very active service against the Japanese. Had the fleet been at sea and attacked in deep water, many more ships would have been lost for good with horrendous fatalities. As it was, the death toll was 2,345 military and 57 civilians, which is why the sinking of the battleship USS *Arizona* is the most remembered—1,777 of the day's tally died when she blew up and sank. The myth persists that she took one down the stack, hence the violence of her sinking, but this is not true. Of the ten bombs aimed at her only two hit home, the first causing minimal damage but the second, a modified 16.1 inch naval shell, struck beside Number 2 turret to ignite the magazine of black powder used to power the catapults for launching reconnaissance planes. This in turn blew the forward magazine, and that was the end of her. Her remains form the core of a memorial park at Pearl Harbor and it is believed that, as a mark of respect, she is still in commission and will always remain so. It would have been a nice touch had the Navy taken that step, but she was in fact decommissioned on December 29 that year.

In the two main feature films of the disaster, the ill-named *Tora! Tora! Tora!* (1970) and the more recent and fanciful *Pearl Harbor* (2001), somber brooding is the order of the day for the actor having to deliver the falsely attributed "I fear all we have done is to awaken a sleeping giant and fill him with a terrible resolve." Admiral Isoroku Yamamoto, the commander of the Japanese Combined Fleet, also never said the more succinct "Gentlemen, we have just kicked a rabid dog." Privately furious at his own government's tardiness with any notice of war, these inventions were possibly inspired by his letter of January 9, 1942, to Minister Ogata Taketora, which lamented: "A military man can scarcely pride himself on having smitten a sleeping enemy; it is more a matter of shame, simply, for the one smitten. I would rather you made your appraisal [of the success of the attack] after seeing what the enemy does, since it is certain that, angered and outraged, he will soon launch a determined counter-attack." And so to the British connection.

That murky story starts back in 1920 when the Japanese ambassador in London asked for help to build up Japanese naval air strength. In particular, they wanted the technology to build aircraft carriers and to learn the techniques of deck landings and take-offs, and how to drop torpedoes from the air. The British admiralty were firmly against such assistance, as "Japanese incompetency in the air is very significant and on the whole satisfactory." The Foreign Office and the Ministry of Trade, however, thinking of the possible orders for aircraft and maybe even carriers, decided to lend a helping hand. Aware they could hardly send an official delegation, the Foreign Office recruited Colonel William Forbes-Sempill, 10th baronet of Craigievar, to go out to Tokyo and do it on the sly. Then employed by the Air Ministry, Forbes-Sempill and his team were outfitted in quasi-Japanese uniforms, so they did not "look British," and by the end of 1921 had established the first naval air base in Japan. The Japanese pilots were quick and fearless learners, so by the time Forbes-Sempill returned to London in 1923 the Japanese Navy Air Corps was a reality; the rest of his team stayed on to oversee the building of the first Japanese carrier, *Hosho*.

Whitehall, now aware of just how well things had gone in Japan and that they should never have embarked on such a lunatic venture in the first place (especially as no orders for planes or anything else were forthcoming), told Forbes-Sempill he should have no more dealings with Tokyo and forget he had ever been there. Yet by 1930 Japan had three more carriers, all more advanced than *Hosho*, and conducted a mock land-base attack that served as the blueprint for the attack on Pearl Harbor.

Back in 1922, Squadron Leader Frederick Rutland, an expert in carriers, had also been approached by the Japanese, who convinced him with a wad of cash to resign his commission and pop over to Tokyo to tell all he knew. Codenamed "Shinkawa" (New River), he was there in the background all the time that Forbes-Sempill and his team were working for the Japanese Navy. After the acknowledged success of the 1930 maneuvers, he was given £100,000 (about $5 million at today's values) and a salary of £3,750 (about $170,000 today) to set up businesses in London, near the U.S. Navy installations in California and the last, crucially, in Honolulu so he could report on the comings and goings from Pearl Harbor. As the FBI arrested an increasing number of Japanese spies, Rutland, rightly fearing he was next on the list, escaped back to England in the spring of 1941, by which time it is anyone's guess how much he was responsible for what would happen at the close of that year. He bought an expensive house in the desirable community of Marlow, Buckinghamshire, but was arrested and interned. The documents condemned him as "a paid agent of the Japanese," signed by MI5 officer A. F. Blunt.

Having no evidence that they were willing to expose in a public trial and risk compromising their top-secret, code-breaking operations, British Intelligence released Rutland in 1944 after which he "disappeared." Forbes-Sempill became a director of the upmarket British preserves manufacturer Tiptree; the MI5 officer who exposed Rutland became Sir Anthony Blunt, and looked after the Queen's paintings before being exposed as a Soviet agent in 1979; and Mitsuo Fuchida, the man who gave the order to attack Pearl Harbor, became a Christian and in 1952 toured the United States with the Christian Missionary Army of Sky Pilots.

Pillage Idiots?

No one could accuse the Vikings of being a pushover when it came to a fight, but they most certainly were not the bunch of mindless raiders English history has painted them. The average English peasant was more at risk of rape and pillage from the next village than from any visiting Viking. Those northern peoples who did take to the seas were predominantly traders who established bases as far afield as America, Russia and the Far East, but they were still enough of a military might to invade and occupy England in 1066.

First, a line of distinction: all Vikings were Norsemen, but not all Norsemen were Vikings. The vast majority of Norse were placid farmers, with "Viking" applying only to those who abandoned the plow to go a-roving; be they Danish, Icelandic or another race, the term more described the activity rather than any ethnic origin. This being the case, Viking, or *Vikingir*, was used until the Middle Ages for raiders of any nationality, which confuses the issue to no end. In fact, the word fell from use about that time and did not resurface in general usage until the mid-nineteenth-century revival of Romanticism, which just loved the notion of rune-reading rogues carrying off meekly protesting maidens and so invented the modern concept. Opera producers thought the male leads in Scandinavian romps might look more imposing with horned helmets and, of course, everybody had to have blond hair. It was poor translation of the circa twelfth-century poem *Krakumal* that gave rise to the skull cup nonsense. The line talking of men drinking "from the branches of skulls" (cattle horns) was rendered "from the skulls of those whom they had slain."

As for their personal hygiene, the Vikings were second to none in their day. In fact, everyone who had anything to do with Norse traders or raiders noted their "unhealthy" obsession with washing and grooming. They never traveled anywhere without soaps, combs and skin-buffers and in Scandinavian languages to this day, terms such as *laugardagur* ("washday") still denote Saturday because of the Viking habit of bathing once a week, something quite unheard of among the peoples with whom they interacted. Aware that blonds have more fun, those not so blessed used bleaches on their hair, which gave rise to the notion that all Vikings were blond.

Although some Norse groups who went a-Viking were most certainly brutal raiders, preying on monasteries and any other easy targets, most were far more industrious. They settled and farmed vast areas of Scotland, with the Orkneys and the Shetland Isles still provinces of Norway until the fourteenth century. They established Dublin, Lincoln and York; they had thriving settlements in America five hundred years before Columbus got here, and their influence spread across Europe and into Russia, itself named from the Finnish *rus*, in turn from the ancient Scandinivian *ruotsi*, meaning "the oarsmen." The main Viking bases were Kiev and what is now St. Petersburg and they traded the length of the Volga. They also settled much of northern France, hence Normandy, the land of the Norsemen, and when arch-Viking William the Conqueror thought it time to pay the English another visit, he did so in spades in 1066. Another Viking on the Nor(se)man invasion was Robert de Bruis, a family name which was modified by the birth of his descendant, Robert the Bruce.

Polka-Rot

In the early hours of September 1, 1939, the Germans invaded Poland, creating three myths in one day.

The first, which was exposed as a lie in 1945, was that Poland had attacked Germany to prompt Hitler's invasion. On the night of August 31, a motley crew under the command of SS officer Alfred Naujocks dressed up as Polish officers and attacked the Gleiwitz radio station on the Polish border, delivering an anti-German rant over the airwaves. They also dragged along several undesirables who, dressed as Polish soldiers, were machine-gunned and left at the scene. Just one of twenty similar incidents along the border that night, these activities earned Naujocks the epithet of "The Man Who Started the War." He later helped to set up the Organisation der ehemaligen SS-Angehörigen (ODESSA; Organization of Former Members of the SS) and helped his old comrades to escape to a life of comfort in Latin America.

The second myth that the Germans unleashed told of their having destroyed the entire Polish Air Force on the ground, bombed to oblivion in its hangars and on its airstrips. But the Poles were not as stupid as Hitler would have the world believe. Knowing that something was sure to happen soon, they had dispersed their planes to unknown locations, and most of these flew punitive missions against the invader and cost the Luftwaffe dearly.

The third myth, widely believed to this day, is that the Poles actually mounted a cavalry charge against the invading German armor, thinking their lances would penetrate the plating, which they believed to be wafer thin. Even the acclaimed correspondent and historian William Shirer—who really should have known better for reasons explained below—wrote in his enormously successful *The Rise and Fall of the Third Reich* (1959): "Horses against tanks! The cavalryman's long lance against the tank's long canon! Brave and valiant and foolhardy though they were, the Poles were simply overwhelmed by the German onslaught." Not only was Shirer wrong, but he was wrong on all counts; the Poles did indeed run cavalry attacks on the Germans, not against the tanks but against the advancing infantry, and these were so successful that the invader in that sector stopped in his tracks and actually thought about turning back.

By the afternoon of the first day, the German 20th Motorized Infantry Division was headed for the city of Chojnice, about 170 miles to the north-west of Warsaw, with the objective of gaining control of the railway junction of Krojanty, located in the Tochola Forest and about 4 miles outside that city. The only Polish forces in the area consisted in the main of two squadrons of cavalry from the 18th Lancers under the command of Colonel Kazimierz Mastelarz, who thought that attack was now the only option. He led his force of 250 lancers through the forest to come up behind the enemy and, when the Germans began to move out into open ground, the Poles attacked with devastating effect. Suddenly under saber attack from all sides, the German infantry was thrown into complete confusion by such outmoded tactics and were in full retreat when, unluckily for Mastelarz, some armored cars arrived to lay sufficient machine-gun fire to drive the cavalry from the field. The remnants of the 20th Division hurried back to the safety of the treeline and were still skulking there, debating a tactical retreat, when Panzer commander General Heinz Guderian arrived ahead of his armored columns and threw a fit when he heard his advance was being held up by men with swords and pointy sticks. But, by the time he had kicked sufficient butt to get the 20th moving again, Mastelarz, who died in the engagement, had bought enough time for Polish units in the next sector to withdraw southwards unopposed.

The next day, the first German tanks arrived in the area and parked up on that same open ground, still littered with dead Polish cavalry, giving Guderian the chance to twist things around and hide the shame of his advance being foiled by cavalry. A flock of foreign correspondents, including Shirer, was invited to the site and fed the yarn of backward Poles thinking they could take on tanks with lances. Shirer and his colleagues were allowed to take photographs of dead cavalrymen lying among the tanks, and were then ushered away to write their stories. Just to make sure the story got international exposure, Guderian himself issued dispatches telling how "The Polish Pomorska Cavalry Brigade, in ignorance of the nature of our tanks, had charged them with swords and lances and had suffered tremendous losses."

All said and done, the word "cavalry" is misleading in that it conjures up images of anachronistic brigades belonging to another era. Mastelarz had opted for a saber charge in that one instance for reasons of its speed, silence and fearsome efficiency, but all Polish cavalrymen carried modern weapons, and each detachment was issued with Bofors anti-tank guns. Horses were still a better way to move quickly through rough terrains; they didn't run out of gasoline and there was always grass for them to eat.

At about the same time as Mastelarz was giving the German 20th Division something to think about, their comrades in the 4th Panzer Division had the misfortune to run into the Wolynska Cavalry outside the village of Mokra, about 130 miles to the south-west of Warsaw. The 4th lost 52 tanks and about 60 other armored vehicles, and in the thirty-six days it took to subjugate Poland the Germans lost 674 tanks and 325 armored cars, and by far the majority of these to Polish cavalry brigades. No wonder the Nazis felt the need to belittle such men in the eyes of the world.

San Juan, Two, Three, Four

The myth of Theodore Roosevelt's taking of San Juan Hill in Cuba in 1898 with his Rough Riders was enough to propel him to the presidency, but

Rough Riders they were not and Roosevelt charged the wrong hill. Originally mocked as "Wood's Weary Walkers," the 1st U.S. Volunteer Cavalry Regiment raised for the Spanish-American War was initially under the command of Colonel Leonard Wood and their troubles began before they even left American soil. A motley crew of drovers, drifters and desperadoes, they gathered beforehand at San Antonio where the residents thought it might be a nice idea to give them a send-off party. Then-famous bandleader Carl Beck was hired to provide the music. Given the martial nature of the event, he thought it might be a nice touch to have cannon fire at a particularly rousing moment of the concert and so organized an "1812 Overture moment" without telling anyone. At the appointed moment the lights went out and the cannons fired, leaving the more trigger-happy of the Rough Riders presuming some sort of attack by Spanish-sympathizing Mexicans. They began firing wildly into the dark, wounding quite a few of their startled hosts who, having dusted themselves down, suggested an early night might be in order. Interviewed shortly after, Beck himself said, "I was in the Franco-Prussian War and saw some hot times, but I was about as uneasy last night as I ever was in battle." The next morning, a restrained and tight-lipped delegation wished Roosevelt et al. a swift departure on trains laid on for the four-day ride to embarkation in Tampa, Florida.

On arrival at the quay, it soon became apparent that not only had they failed to make transport arrangement for their horses, but the ship assigned to carry them had also been slated for two other regiments. Not big in the sharing department, Roosevelt boarded the USS *Yucatan* on June 7, 1898, and secured it for him and his men alone, albeit without horses. He was still crowing about this being his first victory of the war when reports of Spanish warships waiting for them offshore caused a delay of nearly ten days. Trapped on a ship by their reluctance to disembark and leave it vacant, the Rough Riders' lot was not much improved by the routine appearance of those they had usurped, raising glasses of chilled beer. After six days in the Florida heat with no fresh supplies and the harbor waters about them resembling an open sewer, the entire fleet set sail for Cuba on June 13.

Chaos, however, was not yet through with Roosevelt. As they bobbed in the frisky waters off the shores at Daiquiri, it dawned on those in charge that no one had found the presence of mind to ensure that their number included someone with experience of disembarking into surf. When the time came, and with most of the men already in the water, some idiot thought it might be the right moment to drive the transport mules into the water to see if they would instinctively swim ashore. Some swam away, some kept swimming from boat to boat and some, in panic, attacked the men by now desperately trying to avoid them. Many mules that did not drown were shot by the panicking men.

Once ashore, the Rough Riders were introduced to infantry life and did not like it one little bit. The first day's march was not over before most had thrown away their packs, equipment and rations, thinking it easier to loot food en route. Within days of arrival Wood was promoted and command of the Rough Riders passed to Roosevelt in time for the much-vaunted assault on San Juan Hill. In preparation for the infantry attack, artillery under one Captain George Grimes opened up on the Spanish emplacements, but as he had forgotten to arrange for the shipment of smokeless rounds, he presented the Spanish with an easy target of which they took full advantage. Ordered to cease fire immediately, Grimes stormed off in a sulk. But worse was to come. To lead the infantry through the dense jungle to their destination, the eccentric Lieutenant-Colonel George Derby went aloft in his hot-air balloon to act as guide. The trouble was, this elevated position also gave the Spanish gunners a good idea of exactly where the American column was located, so they simply fired blind into the foliage below the balloon.

When advanced contingents of Americans made it into the lowlands near the foot of the hill, they encountered barbed wire. This was a bad time to find out that no one had brought any wire-cutters. A battery of gatling guns turned up on the scene, prompting the 71st New York detachment to let rip a great roar of approval from where they hid in the foliage, and the Spanish, still sniggering from their previous salvos, aimed their guns in the direction of the cheering. By now,

Grimes was over his tantrum and was back at his battery in time to see the Americans breach the wires and begin their advance. Unfortunately, he mistook these men for Spanish forces and began shelling them until they withdrew. The Spanish, almost unable to see for tears of mirth, did not fire back at Grimes' smoke-puffs this time, as they now regarded him as something of an ally. While all this was going on, Roosevelt and his footsore Rough Riders were busy charging up nearby Kettle Hill by mistake. By the time this had been secured, the action on San Juan was drawing to a close, but Roosevelt decided to charge over for the last knockings anyway. However, in his excitement he foolishly rushed off without giving any clear and concise commands, resulting in his rushing up San Juan screaming "Chhhaaaarge!" all by his lonesome. By the time he had made his way back to Kettle Hill and marshaled his puzzled men, the Spanish on San Juan were in a rout, which was hardly surprising, given that they were outnumbered 15:1. So effectively did Roosevelt capitalize on his ill-deserved publicity, few know that the bulk of the action on Kettle Hill was valiantly fought by the African American 10th Cavalry under the command of "Black Jack" Pershing.

Saving Ryan's Privates

Saving Private Ryan (1998) has a determined Tom Hanks under orders to scour war-torn Europe to find and bring home safe the last remaining son of a family that has lost another three boys to enemy action. The instigation for the action is a misty-eyed reading of the so-called "Bixby letter" that Spielberg, like everyone else on the production crew, believed to be a genuine letter sent by Abraham Lincoln to "a great Bostonian lady during the American Civil War."

The "widow" Lydia Bixby of 15 Dover Street, Boston, was by all accounts a pretty bad lot. Known to the local police as a petty crook and brothel keeper, she was constantly presenting herself to various organizations as a deserving case for a handout, but she had not the wit to recognize her big score when it came. Bixby wheedled her way into the office of William Schouler, Boston's adjutant-general, who was left with the impression that the old girl was "the best specimen of a true-hearted Union woman I have yet seen." Totally swallowing her sob story, he then wrote on to Governor John Andrew: "About ten days ago Mrs. Bixby came to my office and showed me five letters from five company commanders, and each letter informed the poor woman of the death of one of her sons. Her last remaining son was killed in the fight on the Weldon railroad." In fact, only two sons, Charles and Oliver, had died in action. Of the remaining three, one had been captured at Gettysburg but subsequently made it home safe and sound; one had deserted and joined the Confederacy following his capture; and the third deserted the Northern Army. Unaware of this, Schouler told Andrew that nothing short of a letter from Lincoln himself was called for.

Now things get a bit cloudy. Lydia Bixby most certainly did receive a handwritten letter ostensibly signed by Lincoln but, as were the five letters she showed Schouler, this too was a forgery. But who wrote it and why? The letter was dated November 21, 1864, and read:

Dear Madam: I have been shown in the files of the War Department a statement of the Adjutant-General of Massachusetts that you are the mother of five sons who have died gloriously on the field of battle. I feel how weak and fruitless must be any word of mine which should attempt to beguile you from the grief of a loss so overwhelming. But I cannot refrain from tendering you the consolation that may be found in the thanks of the republic that they died to save. I pray that our Heavenly Father may assuage the anguish of your bereavement, and leave you only the cherished memory of the loved and lost, and the solemn pride that must be yours to have laid so costly a sacrifice upon the altar of freedom. Yours very sincerely and respectfully,
A. Lincoln.

Schouler delivered the letter in person to the rapacious Bixby who, a supporter of the Confederacy and no admirer of Lincoln, sat around bitching about the absence of any money or promise of pension. Within a few months she would burn the letter in a drunken rage, ignorant of the fact that she could have sold it for a small fortune in the months following his not-too-distant death.

The Internet is awash with analysis of the 130-word missive, which is indeed loaded with phrases frequently used by Lincoln in other letters known to be genuine. The best guess as to authorship is that the Bixby letter was penned by John Hay, Lincoln's secretary, who would have been sufficiently familiar with his boss's turn of phrase to conjure forth a passable forgery. Hay no doubt thought Lincoln too busy with the war to be approached with the request, and his actions were but a harmless deception designed to bring comfort to a bereaved mother. Who would ever know?

The nature of the paving on the road to Hell is well known, and Hay could not possibly have imagined the fuss his good intentions were to unleash. Within a couple of days of the letter arriving at Old Mother Bixby's, two Boston newspapers, *The Transcript* and *The Traveller*, carried transcripts in their editions of November 25 and in no time at all it was the talk of the nation, leaving Hay and Lincoln with no option but to keep quiet. Framed copies sold like hot cakes and, after Lincoln's death, subsequent presidents had replicas hanging in all the White House guest rooms. The true nature of the letter was not exposed until the mid-twentieth century, by which time the Bixby letter had become an accepted part of American heritage.

Shale Seizure!

The time and nature of the Roman invasion of Britain are not widely appreciated, but much can be said for the extent of its influence in those isles when the Romans did finally get their act together. Scottish historians never tire of claiming that the Scots were too wild a prospect for the Romans, who built Hadrian's Wall against them between AD 122 and 128 and then cowered on the English side for the next three hundred years. Many in England happily accept the notion that the Romans simply stopped at the northern borders and built a wall. Not only did the Romans mount several punitive missions into Scotland, penetrating as far north as the River Tay in the Highlands, but Hadrian's Wall was never intended to be a defensive line between the cultured south and the savage north. As for the Scots, they were not even there at the time; it was the Picts who held sway north of the wall.

The Roman invasion of Britannia did not begin with the arrival of Julius Caesar in 55 BC when it was a case of veni, vidi, screw up and go home. Almost as soon as he set foot on the beach, his epilepsy returned and his recurring fits and the determined attacks of the locals convinced him to go home again. He did have another half-hearted go the next year, but became bored with the whole idea, leaving the invasion to founder for a century until Claudius turned up in AD 43 with forty thousand men to do a proper job. They pushed relentlessly north and by AD 79, forces under Agricola were north of Aberdeen; he finally defeated the Caledonii, as he called them, at the battle of Mons Graupius (perhaps at modern Inverurie) in AD 83 or 84. This was a major engagement in which Agricola inflicted over 10,000 deaths at a cost of only 360 Roman casualties, so it is safe to say that neither the Highlanders nor the Lowlanders were any match for the Roman Army.

No one can build a seventy-mile-long wall with forts and lookout points in hostile territory, so the very existence of Hadrian's Wall indicates that Roman control extended many miles to the north of that Tyne–Solway line. Upon completion there were about eight thousand men garrisoned there, which works out to about one hundred per mile, so it is clear that the wall was never intended to be defended but to act as an early-warning line and a point from which the Romans could monitor and tax the movement of people and goods from one side to the other through its many gateways. Countless individuals and small raiding parties crossed and recrossed the wall with impunity. The wall was quite incapable of resisting even a minor assault at any point along its length, and archaeological evidence asserts that no fighting of any consequence ever took place at Hadrian's Wall.

In AD 138 construction began on the more northern Antonine Wall, which ran across the Clyde–Forth line at the central belt of Scotland to make a division between the Highlands and the Lowlands. Completed in 142, this wall included numerous forts and garrisons, the major ones being at Ardoch, Strageath, Perth, Dalginross and Cargill. In 208 the short but brutal Emperor Septimius Severus and an army of perhaps forty-five thousand pushed right through to the tip of Scotland, inflicting withering defeats wherever they went. The Scotti tribe did not move across from Ireland until the early to mid-fourth century and the Romans had quit Britannia by 410, so there was little time for them to interact either on or off the battlefield. But modern Scotland does have the Romans to thank for the haggis that they introduced as marching rations and the closest thing to canned food at the time, and the bagpipe, which was the standard marching instrument of the Roman infantry. (The singular is the correct form, never *bagpipes*, as there may be several drones—the stems propped over the shoulder—but only one pipe or chanter.)

The enduring myth of the Romans in Scotland concerns that of the Lost Legion; the suggestible to this day claim to have seen the ghostly souls of the 9th Hispana trudging through the misty glens. Some versions of this old chestnut say the men of the 9th marched into oblivion as they headed south from Mons Graupius, but all versions of the tale are crushed by the fact that the 9th Hispana was without a shadow of a doubt in York in 108, after which it swapped duties with the 6th Legion at Noviomagus, now known as Nijmegen in Holland, and elements of the unit were still there in 121. After this they seem to have left the stage, probably assimilated into other depleted legions as there is no record of any major disaster or disgrace befalling the 9th.

Sic Transit Old Gloria Monday

Dear, if not essential, to the core of American tradition is the notion that the first national flag was designed by a small group headed by George Washington and made by Philadelphian seamstress Betsy Ross.

Born Elizabeth Griscom, Betsy married one John Ross, who opened an upholstery shop in Philadelphia not long before being killed in a munitions explosion while serving in the militia in 1776, leaving Betsy to run the business alone. According to her grandson, William Canby, she was visited in the June of the same year by Washington and prominent patriots Robert Morris and George Ross, her late husband's uncle. Washington spread out on the counter what he claimed was his design for the flag under which he would fight the Revolutionary War and asked her if she could run up a prototype. Betsy herself made some design changes, to which Washington agreed before he and his compatriots toddled off to sign the Declaration of Independence, which is the first big hole in his story (see "Hancock's Half-Hour," page 147). Betsy set about sewing and christened her efforts "Old Glory" to ensure herself a place in the American heart forever.

All stirring stuff to be sure. But the first time this yarn was trotted out was on March 14, 1870, a Monday, when Canby addressed the Pennsylvania Historical Society as it prepared for its 1876 centennial, so the notion that one of the state's very own daughters had made the first national flag was not a hard line to sell. Wholly unchallenged, the story was soon appearing as established fact in reference books, and by the time the centennial celebrations were under way it had become an accepted fact. The building now standing as a museum at 239 Arch Street in Philadelphia is trumpeted as the house in which history was sewn; it is a major tourist attraction despite the fact that in 1949 the Joint State Government Commission of Pennsylvania pronounced that "there is no proof that Betsy Ross ever lived here." In 1892 the building was actually scheduled for demolition, but was saved by an art competition, run by the city, which offered $1,000 for "the best rendition of a local historical event." Supporters of the Betsy Ross myth got minor artist Charles Weisgerber to do a painting of the house entitled *Birth of Our Nation's Flag*, which won the competition hands down, leaving the city fathers somewhat hog-tied as to what to do with the house. Ultimately, it was another writer and artist who had designed the first flag; it was nothing to do with either Washington or Ross.

Francis Hopkinson was not just a leading figure in the run up to independence, but also a writer, composer and artist of no little renown. It was Hopkinson who designed not only the flag but also the Great Seal and other icons of American politics. The records show that in May 1780 he submitted an invoice of sorts to be compensated for his time and effort spent in the design of the Stars and Stripes, the Great Seal and the Naval Ensign for the new navy. Although he had willingly engaged in these "three labors of fancy," he expressed the thought that a quarter of a cask of wine might not go amiss as a gesture of gratitude. Hopkinson and Ross aside, there was no single fixed design for the flag until the Flag Act of January 13, 1794, and no one spoke of Old Glory until 1831, when the epithet is noted in Salem, Massachusetts, not Philadelphia. Until then a profusion of designs is recorded; the stars appeared in a circle, in one or more rows, they had anything from four to eight points and the bars varied in color and ran vertical or horizontal depending on caprice.

Sieg Heil America

It is but modern myth that the stiff-arm Nazi salute originated in the Roman Army. No one knows if or how legionary soldiers saluted; the Romans were meticulous recorders of detail, so the absence of any mention of a formal and official salute would strongly suggest that they did not. The origins are far more recent—the Nazis actually adopted the American salute as used until 1942 by those intoning the Pledge of Allegiance.

The pledge was written in 1892 (possibly) by Francis Bellamy, a prominent American national socialist, as was his equally famous cousin

Edward, an admirer of Prussian militarism and author of the utopian novel *Looking Backward* (1888). Both men's ideas of national and military socialism were widely published at home and across Europe. Subject to minor alterations over the years, the original pledge read: "I Pledge allegiance to my Flag [changed to "the Flag of the United States of America" in 1923] and to the Republic for which it stands, one Nation ["under God" added in 1954], indivisible, with Liberty and Justice for all." (Although Bellamy is broadly credited with authorship, the family of his associate, James Upham, has always maintained that he was the author and Bellamy merely the promoter.) Either way, the pledge was published in *The Youth's Companion* in the run-up to the celebration of the 400th anniversary of Columbus' stumbling across America.

Feeling the need to impose more militaristic ritual, Bellamy discussed this with Upham, who suggested that pledge takers come to attention with an audible click of the heels and commence the pledge with right hand over their heart before slowly extending the arm outward and upward toward the flag. Bellamy thought this was just perfect and so advocated its adoption. The erroneous notion that the salute had Roman origins was born of early cinema's love of Roman epics such as *Ben Hur* (the silent version of 1907), based on the book by Lew Wallace, the Union Army general who later, as governor of New Mexico, dispatched Pat Garrett to bring down Billy the Kid. Characters in *Ben Hur* and other celluloid romps such as *Nerone* (1908), *Spartaco* (1914) and *Cabiria* (1914), all employed the Bellamy salute, as the directors rightly thought that this would strike a chord with the audiences. After German and Italian fascists hijacked the salute, it was abandoned by Americans who opted instead to keep the right hand over the heart from start to finish. With the American abandonment of the Bellamy salute, there was left behind the notion that the salute had Roman connections, as it continued to be used on screen.

The main conduit carrying the Bellamy salute into European fascism was Gabriele D'Annunzio, novelist, dramatist, fighter pilot and war hero, an extraordinary character who, as Italy's most flamboyant fascist, was also Mussolini's mentor. As the author of the original novel, D'Annunzio also wrote the screenplay for *Cabiria*, a sword-and-sandal epic that was hugely influential, and the inspiration for D. W. Griffith's white supremacist *Birth of a Nation* (1915). Thus familiarized with the Bellamy salute's popularity in such films, when D'Annunzio and his fascist army took control of the troubled Croatian city of Fiume in September 1919 and declared it a free state, he and his cohorts were all using the Bellamy salute. Mussolini immediately adopted the gesture, dubbing it the *Saluto Romano* (Roman Salute) and the goose-step the *Passo Romano* (Roman Step), even though that uncomfortable march is a nineteenth-century Prussian invention. Hitler simply followed suit.

Those uncomfortable with the birth of such an infamous salute still try to establish a pre-Bellamy provenance and frequently cite the famous painting, *The Oath of the Horatii* (1784) by Jacques-Louis David. But even a glance at the painting shows one man on the right holding aloft three swords, and his three sons on the left reaching out for them; they are not saluting—their fingers are spread and thumbs almost at right-angles to their palms.

Singapore Sling

The loss of Singapore to the Japanese in 1942 was a tremendous blow to the British. It seems to have been Churchill himself who invented the myth that the city fell because all the defensive batteries were pointing seaward, while the sneaky Japanese emerged unexpectedly from the jungle to the rear. But then the whole sorry affair was his fault, so he had a personal interest in diverting attention from this awkward fact and did so by blaming those on the spot for failing to anticipate attack from such a direction. They *had* anticipated this attack, however, and Churchill had stymied their plans.

It is a simple matter of fact that the vast majority of guns on Singapore had a 360-degree pan, and had shelled the invaders incessantly for days; Johore and Connaught batteries fired every shell they had. The only guns incapable of firing inland were a couple of old naval guns with arcs dictated by the stops on their mounting plates; hardly enough to seal the fate of the entire peninsula. It is also a myth that the British Malaya Command in Singapore comprised a bunch of complacent and chinless wonders who could not see past the next pink gin at the Raffles hotel. Instead, they had fully anticipated a Japanese thrust down the Malay Peninsula and had a contingency plan in Operation *Matador*, which had been endorsed by Whitehall in 1941. Yet the aircraft and reinforcements allocated to make *Matador* possible were redirected to the Middle East on Churchill's explicit instructions. He greatly underestimated the Japanese threat and was convinced they would not enter the war at all unless Germany successfully invaded Britain.

When the British finally threw in the towel, the atrocities inflicted on all and sundry by the Japanese beggar belief. They covered ANZAC prisoners with petrol and burned them alive, and they raided every military hospital to bayonet staff and patients—even those on the operating tables at the time—before murdering and raping upward of fifty thousand civilians for the hell of it. Thousands of surrendered troops were then marched off to their own private hell on the Burma Railway.

According to Correlli Barnett, eminent British military historian and former keeper of the Churchill Archives: "I have no doubt that the sole author of this complete disaster was Winston . . . who had a remarkable capacity for distancing himself from mistakes and disasters that had his name written all over them."

Slaves and Knaves of the Civil War

Ask anyone the cause of the Civil War and they will confidently say it was slavery, this view compounded into "truth" by films such as *Gone with the Wind* (1939). But this is simply not the case. The war was really about the preservation of the Union—slavery was not even on the agenda. Just to confuse matters further, not all slaves were black nor were all blacks slaves. Many blacks were slave-owning and slave-trading freemen, in both the Southern and Northern states, and the greatest opposition to the revolting trade was in the South, not the North.

As the colonies had expanded, so too had the requirement for cheap labor and, right up until the nineteenth century, no one gave a damn what color the slaves were just so long as they were plentiful. In 1670 in the Virginias, the House of Burgesses, the first legislative assembly in the New World, enacted slavery-for-life legislation for blacks, while white slaves had to be released after twelve years' service, providing they had not racked up extra time for bad behavior. It was also proclaimed that "no negro or Indian though baptized and enjoined their own freedom shall be capable of any purchase of Christians [whites], but yet not debarred from buying any of their own nation." The Virginia Slave Code of 1705 firmed this up with the provision for enslavement of black freemen caught trading in whites. In reality, the twelve-year restriction on the enslavement of whites meant nothing; owners simply kept imposing extensions of service for transgressions, real or invented. The most celebrated non-white slavers were, Chang and Eng Bunker. They settled in White Plains, North Carolina, to operate as slavers and timber merchants, marrying the Yates sisters, Adelaide and Sarah, and had twenty-one children between them. The Bunkers, and hundreds of others like them, were trading slaves right up to the Civil War in which, surprisingly, about fifty thousand blacks fought for the South, some doing so to protect their business interests and coercing their "property" to do the same.

In antebellum America, slaves were far too valuable ($1,600 for a healthy male on the New Orleans block in 1860) to be routinely beaten, raped and maltreated, as is the common perception. There were most certainly incidents of vile brutality from the worst of the owners, overseers and recovery patrols, but they differed little from the kind of punishment meted out by gangers and overseers in the Northern factories wherein the "free" white workers were no better than slaves themselves.

The average lifespan of a slave, whatever his or her color, often exceeded that of his or her owner. They ate better than the average free white, with an average daily intake of 4,000 calories; their accommodations, health care, working hours and time off (that's right) were far better than that of any free white laborer, and family groups were often kept together, as contentment led to loyalty and less chance of runaways, mainly the province of single males. The average birthing age of a female slave was twenty-one, far higher than any free white girl, and sexual exploitation was rare—only two percent of births resulted from master and slave interaction, which was frequently consensual. (This certainly appears to have been the case with President Thomas Jefferson and his slave, Sally Hemings, who had five, possibly six children together. She spent two years with him in France, where she knew full well she was classed as free and could have kicked him out of bounds at the drop of a hat, but they seem to have enjoyed what was a marriage in all but name.) If slaves were leased out to other labor situations, the contracts always stipulated they had to be kept clear of dangerous work, such as blasting areas if working on the railways, when Irish immigrants were used in preference. Far from holding the power of life and death over their "chattels," owners were open to criminal prosecution for the killing of any slave. Of course there was corporal punishment directed at slaves, but it is fair to say that the average British or American sailor or soldier was far more at risk of a whipping than any slave, and that the labor force of the British-American Industrial Revolution were themselves effectively slaves of their employers, in whose dark and satanic mills children as young as five were routinely chewed up in the machinery with no redress. Apart from the freedom issue, slaves had it better than most working-class whites and free blacks.

Equally awash with slaves of many colors, the North, which had a far higher percentage of slave owners than the South, was largely unconcerned with the issue. (Although slaves made up about 30 percent of the Southern population and only two percent of the Northern, the bulk of the slave population in the South was concentrated in comparatively few owners, while in the North, ownership of perhaps one or two slaves was widespread.) Oddly enough, the largest anti-slavery lobby in pre-Civil War America was to be found in the South, where large-scale slave ownership was the province of the wealthy minority. Those against it complained not of the inhumanity, but of the unfair competition.

The whole country had long been comfortable with the idea of slavery. George Washington owned well over two hundred slaves; Patrick Henry was a slave owner all his life and thought blacks subhuman and thus excluded from his lofty ethos. Presidents Jefferson, Madison, Jackson, Taylor, Tyler, and Polk were all slave owners, and Lincoln happily married into the Todd family, whose money was largely slave based. In all, twelve antebellum presidents were slave owners, eight of them owning slaves throughout their tenure, and the last president to be an active slave owner in office was Zachary Taylor. Ulysses S. Grant, leader of the Union forces and later president, owned slaves, some of whom he had accepted as wedding presents in 1848 when he married Julia Dent of a prominent Missouri slaving family. Most Union generals were slave owners, none releasing their charges until the ratification of the 14th Amendment on July 9, 1868, three years after the close of the Civil War. On the other hand, Robert E. Lee, who was offered command of the Union forces before Grant, wrote that slavery was a "a political, social and moral evil." He did indeed own one slave, inherited from his mother, but the poor old chap was by then far too infirm for freedom, so Lee kept him in comfort until his death. Lee's only other brush with slavery came with the death of his father-in-law, George Washington Parke Custis; as executor of the will Lee had to make provision for the release of more than sixty slaves, in accordance with Custis' dying wish.

Contrary to popular opinion Lincoln was not the Great Emancipator, but went to war (some say precipitated it) to preserve the Union—that and that alone. In a letter of August 22, 1862, sent to Horace Greeley, editor of the *New York Tribune*, Lincoln stated:

> *My paramount objective in this struggle is to save the Union, and it is not to either save or destroy slavery. If I could save the Union without*

freeing any slave I would do it, and if I could save it by freeing all the slaves I would do it; and if I could save it by freeing some of the slaves and leaving the other alone I would also do that. What I do about slavery, and the colored race, I do because I believe it helps to save the Union; and what I forbear, I forbear because I do not believe it would help save the Union.

Lincoln had never made any secret of his views of white supremacy. In the Lincoln-Douglas Debates of 1858 he stated:

I will say, then, that I am not, not ever have been, in favor of bringing about in any way the social and political equality of the white and black races—that I am not, nor ever have been, in favor of making voters or jurors of Negroes, nor of qualifying them to hold office, nor to intermarry with white people; and I will say in addition to this that there is a physical difference between the white and black races which I believe will forever forbid the two races to live together on terms of social and political equality. And inasmuch as they cannot so live, while they do remain together there must be the position of the superior and the inferior, and I as much as any other man am in favor of having the superior position assigned to the white race.

From the early 1850s, Lincoln had been an ardent supporter of a succession of proposals to ship the blacks out lock, stock and barrel to South America, Central America, back to Africa, to Cuba, anywhere in fact but in his own back yard. On August 14, 1862, a delegation of black leaders was invited to the White House and told they were there to listen not debate. After informing them candidly that "Even when you cease to be slaves, you are yet far removed from being placed on equality with the white race . . . not a single man of your race is made the equal of a single man of ours." Going on to indicate that the white race was now irked by their continued presence, he outlined the Chiriqui Project, which would facilitate black resettlement in Central America and asked the delegation to spread the word among their "own kind' and make ready for the exodus. Lincoln's stated concern was that the blacks would, sooner or later, get ideas above their station, think themselves equal and start fighting for such status.

Not long into the war, Lincoln issued the rather cynical Proclamation of Emancipation, of which so much is made by those who have not read it. It freed no one. Released in two parts on September 1862 and January 1863, the document did not call for the release of any slave in the North nor any of those in the border states of Kentucky, Missouri, Maryland, Delaware and West Virginia, but only those in the South, so it freed no one immediately. It did, however, have the desired effect of enticing thousands of Southern blacks to head north for what they thought would be a better life. Once in the North, however, they were either herded into munitions factories or drafted into the forces on half the pay of their white counterparts; black soldiers netted $7 per month and whites $13. In all, there were about 20,000 blacks in the Union Navy and nearly 180,000 in the Union Army, where they were put into segregated regiments controlled by white officers. Barred from the saloons, brothels or any other establishments frequented by the white soldiers, blacks remained segregated in the U.S. Army until after World War II. The census of 1860 recorded 240,747 free black men in the South, thousands more than in the North, and many of these did indeed fight for the South.

If the conflict had been about the eradication of slavery and the elevation of black people American to any sort of equality, it would be reasonable to expect their lot to have improved in the post-bellum era, but we all know this is far from true. Even when *Gone with the Wind*, the classic Civil War drama, premiered in Atlanta, Georgia, prohibitions according to ethnicity were still going strong, so Hattie McDaniel, who played the portly Mammy, was not allowed to attend because of her color. When time came for her to collect her Academy Award for the role, she and her husband had to sit at the back of the room at a separate table for two, screened off by carefully placed plants. The female lead, Vivien Leigh, who had played Scarlett O'Hara, sat through both events knowing that her then-secret Anglo-Indian origins should have left her out in the cold as well.

Slaving Away in the Gallery

Cinema and television make so much of the Roman Army that few appreciate the size and significance of the Roman Navy, grossly misrepresented by films like *Ben Hur* (1959), a film based on the book written in 1880 by Lew Wallace, the retired Union general who sent Pat Garrett to kill Billy the Kid. For a start, the Roman Navy never used slave labor.

Until the close of the eighteenth century, Spanish and North African galleys used slave power—even Cervantes, author of *Don Quixote*, did a stretch on an Algerian galley—but this was not the case in the Roman Navy. The popular image of hundreds of emaciated slaves rowing to the beat of an enormous drum struck by a stern-faced Nubian is pure Hollywood. When coordinated rowing was required, time was kept with a high-pitched whistle that could be heard throughout the decks, above any general noise or that of battle. Drums of the day were of very poor quality and far too low of note. Galleys were under sail most of the time, since even a crew in peak condition would have been hard pressed to row more than ten miles without collapsing. Furthermore, they needed to conserve their strength for the considerable effort required to maneuver the vessel during battle or, rarely, to crank it up to ramming speed.

For the Romans, and for anybody else for that matter, ramming was very much a last-resort measure, just as likely to incapacitate the rammer along with the rammed. The Romans preferred to board and capture, as it was far cheaper to refit a captured vessel than to build one from scratch. The oarsmen (as many as two hundred in a trireme) formed the greater part of the boarding parties for such ventures, so no captain would be in a hurry to unchain that many resentful slaves with more reason to join the enemy than fight the enemy. The Roman Navy relied exclusively on free and highly trained men.

Far from a weapon of antiquity, the slow decline of the galley presented a curve cutting into the nineteenth century, when they were still a common sight off the North African coast. They last fought in the Mediterranean at the battle of Chesma in 1770, and the Navy used them to considerable effect during the Revolutionary War, most significantly at the battle of Valcour Island (1776), when Benedict Arnold chose to use the row-galley *Congress* as his command ship. Both the Russian and Swedish navies used galleys against each other during their scrap of 1808–09, after which Sweden lost a large tract of its territory to produce a new country called Finland.

Some Dirty Rotten Coward Has Shot Our Mr. Howard

Ever with us is the story that the Germans missed their chance to kill both Churchill and Roosevelt because of a silly misunderstanding of decoded signals traffic about their meeting in Casablanca in January 1943. The Germans, so the story goes, presumed Casablanca to be some pathetic linguistic pun intended to cover up the fact that the meeting was to be in the White House, and so never bothered to do anything about it. In fact, they knew all about the meeting and held it up to ridicule as futile in their propaganda which, of course, never reached Britain or the United States at the time. But the Germans would have a crack at Churchill (perhaps) later that same year, with someone else paying the price.

Of Hungarian-Jewish parentage and properly named Steiner, the slightly built English actor Leslie Howard is best remembered as Ashley Wilkes in *Gone with the Wind* (1939). He was invalided out of World War I with shell shock and was doing sterling service for the Allied cause in World War II when shot down by German raiders over the Bay of Biscay on June 1, 1943. Not insignificantly, he and his tubby manager Alfred Chenhalls looked a lot like Churchill and his slim bodyguard, Walter Thompson.

In the lead-up to and opening years of World War II, Howard had done much to promote the Allied cause and ridicule the Nazi regime, especially Goebbels, whom he parodied in one of his films. When not campaigning for American involvement in the war, he was flying in and out of neutral countries beating the Allied drum and carrying out more dangerous tasks as liaison between British Intelligence and friendly factions within those countries. Goebbels certainly regarded him as a spy and a "hostile Jew," and had issued orders for Howard to be "singled out for special treatment" if caught. At the same time as Howard was preparing to fly out of neutral Lisbon on KLM/BOAC Flight 777, Churchill was making his way back from a tour of inspection of North Africa and Gibraltar. Churchill was known to mingle with the herd on civilian flights; Chenhalls and Howard bore an uncanny resemblance to Churchill and Thompson and the Germans were watching all likely avenues of return, including Lisbon.

Churchill certainly thought Flight 777 was targeted in an attempt to get him, and in his post-war writings he expressed regret at the loss of Howard's life and the other sixteen passengers and crew. Whether Howard or Churchill was the target will never be known for sure, but there can be no doubt that the attack was planned and focused—the Germans set out to down that particular plane. The area where the strike occurred normally only attracted the odd, single-plane patrol, but on this occasion a flight of eight Ju-88s was dispatched to bring down Flight 777 by Oberleutnant Herbert Hintze of Staffel 14 based at Bordeaux. Equally unusual was the fact that several of the Ju-88s circled the floating wreckage to take numerous photographs that, after the war, were sent to Howard's family. How thoughtful.

Statues of Limitations

The notion that the position of the horse's hooves in a statue raised to a dead military hero indicates how the rider died is a reworking of an older but similar myth concerning the tombs of early English knights. The "rules" of this non-existent code vary, but all concern the position of the arms, legs and hands in the figure atop the tomb. If the arms are folded right over left and over a downward pointing sword, then the occupant of the tomb died in battle in the Crusades; left over right he died of wounds received in battle; left over right but no sword then he died of disease in the Holy Land, and so forth. And so it is with more modern equestrian statues, which are saddled with the same sort of nonsense. As with the "code" imposed on the knights, this too varies from teller to teller, but the most common version holds that one hoof raised indicates the rider was wounded in battle; two hooves raised show that he died in battle; and four hooves on the floor indicate a peaceful death of natural causes.

Recounted by tour guides and local historians on both sides of the Atlantic, the myth survives because there will always be the odd statue that, by coincidence, follows the "code," so the guide can point it out and trot out the old tale. But, according to Kathy George, Park Historian at Gettysburg, "Any relationship between the number of raised hooves on a horse-and-rider statue and the rider's actual experience in battle is merely a coincidence, as reflected in equestrian statues at Gettysburg National Military Park." The city of Washington, D.C., is home to more equestrian statues than any other city in the whole of the United States, yet here only seven out of about thirty statues follow the "code." For example, that of Andrew Jackson shows two hooves raised, yet he died in his bed at the age of seventy-eight.

Tale of Two Cities

An enduring myth of World War II concerns the night of November 14, 1940, when German bombers dropped 500 tons of high-explosive, 33,000 incendiary bombs and over 300 parachute bombs on Coventry. The story attached to that night maintains that Churchill knew of the raid in advance from decrypts of enemy messages, but deliberately refrained from organizing suitable defenses—doing so would have alerted the Germans to the fact that their "uncrackable" Enigma codes had in fact been cracked by the team at Bletchley Park. As recently as November 2008, Coventry's Belgrade Theatre hosted Alan Pollock's *One Night in November*, a play based on this false premise. Perhaps the myth endures because it is so plausible; had Churchill known that Coventry was to be the target that night, he could well have made such a decision. He could hardly phone the Germans and ask them not to come at all; Coventry was in for it that night, no matter what anyone did. But Churchill took no such decision because he didn't have to.

On November 9, a German pilot was shot down and taken for interrogation, "revealing" on the 12th that he was aware of rumors of an imminent and massive raid in which Coventry and/or Birmingham would be the target or targets, some time between November 15 and 20. This information was gleaned from taped conversations he had in a bugged cell he was sharing with a "plant"; had the pilot figured out he was being played like a fiddle and decided to reverse the game on his eavesdroppers? The Air Intelligence Officer at Bletchley summarized all the information into a report stating the German's information to be "doubtful and likely misleading," and that there was already "pretty definite information that the attack is to be against London and the Home Counties." These reports did not reach Churchill's office until late in the morning of November 14; he read them just after lunch. This same report also stated that if further information was received to indicate that Coventry or Birmingham was indeed a target, then the standard "Cold Water" instructions for counter-measures could, hopefully, be rolled out in time. Still convinced that London was to be the target, as he left Downing Street that afternoon for Ditchley Park, Oxfordshire, he was handed the latest intelligence box by his principal secretary, John Martin. By the time the car had reached the Albert Memorial, Churchill had read the contents stating London to be the target for an unusually heavy raid and ordered the driver back to Downing Street, where he arrived just after 4:00 p.m. He immediately ordered all female staff home and key personnel to secure bunkers. While he had been in his car, the Germans had switched on their locator beams for the raid and at some point just after 3:00 p.m. the RAF had ascertained that these did indeed intersect over Coventry.

By the time Churchill was made aware of this fact there was nothing anyone could do. Alerts had been sent out, but the Coventry defenses, even though they had been strengthened after previous raids, proved woefully inadequate on the night; but so were those of any other British city in 1940, and the Germans did send an awful lot of planes. That said, despite that perhaps seventy-five thousand buildings were destroyed, the civilian death toll was only 568 — a tragedy for them and their families, but not a bad ratio.

The originator of the "prior warning" theory was former RAF Group Captain F. W. Winterbotham in *The Ultra Secret* (1974). This was the first book to reveal that the Allies had broken the German codes, a fact that was a closely guarded official secret until then. Winterbotham claimed that it was he who personally telephoned Downing Street with the news that Coventry was the target and that he had done so at exactly 3:00 p.m., despite the triangulation of the German beams not having been fixed until a short time after that hour. Next up to bat was *Bodyguard of Lies* (1974) by Anthony Cave Brown, who raised the bar by stating that Churchill had received full notice of the real target on November 12. William Stevenson wove all this together to produce *A Man Called Intrepid* (1976), which claimed that as early as the beginning of the second week of November, intercepted Enigma traffic was stating "Coventry" in print as the target, and that Churchill was well aware of the fact but stated to close aides that protecting Coventry for that one night was far outweighed by the disclosure to the Germans that their precious Enigma had been compromised. None of this was true. Somewhat perturbed by these distortions and outright lies, John Colville, one of Churchill's surviving private secretaries, set down in 1981 an accurate account of what Churchill knew and, more crucially, exactly when he came by each piece of knowledge as it filtered through to him. Determined to leave nothing to forty-year-old memories, Colville resorted instead to the copious logs and diaries still in his possession. They confirmed the less intriguing reality that:

> *All concerned with the information gleaned from the intercepted German signals were conscious that German suspicions must not be aroused for the sake of ephemeral advantages. In the case of the Coventry raid no dilemma arose, for until the German directional beam was turned on the doomed city nobody knew where the great raid would be. Certainly the Prime Minister did not . . . The German signals referred to a major operation with the code name "Moonlight Sonata." The usual "Boniface" (Enigma) secrecy in the Private Office had been lifted on this occasion and during the afternoon before the raid I wrote in my diary (kept under lock and key at 10 Downing Street), "It is obviously some major air operation, but its exact destination the Air Ministry find it difficult to determine."*

Coleville went on to describe the course of events described above, with Churchill aborting his journey to Ditchley Park, returning to London and ordering various staff to positions of safety. Colville added:

> *Meanwhile Churchill, impatient for the fireworks to start, made his way to the Air Ministry roof with John Martin and saw nothing. For on their way to Coventry, the raiders dropped no bombs on London.*
>
> *There is not even the thinnest shred of truth in Group Captain Winterbotham's story of Coventry. It is to be hoped that neither this incident nor a score of others with which Mr. Stevenson's book about "Intrepid" is gaudily bedizened are ever used for the purpose of historical reference. To dispel such an unacceptable hazard is my excuse for this long digression.*

Colville was just one who came out to scotch the alternative version of events. John Martin himself had written much the same in *The Times* of

August 28, 1976, and others, from Downing Street, Bletchley Park and Air Intelligence, gave independent and cross-corroborating accounts. Throughout the 1970s and 1980s historians such as Norman Longmate, Ronald Levin, Harry Hensley and David Stafford dug into the issue and dismissed the story out of hand. War frequently calls for the making of decisions that, in the less demanding light of peace, can appear callous or downright criminal. No one, not even the most blinkered Churchill apologist, has ever said that he might not have left Coventry to its fate if presented with such a choice—the opening lines of Colville's statement above hint at this. He was just lucky not to have been presented with such a dilemma.

They Asked for It to Be Delivered

On June 30, 2007, the Japanese defense minister Fumio Kyuma made a very daring speech. He told his fellow countrymen that it was high time they abandoned their victim mentality over the atomic bombings of Hiroshima and Nagasaki (the district for which he himself was the representative). But Kyuma stopped short of mentioning what few in the West are aware of, that the Japanese themselves were trying to complete their own twenty-megaton device. Scientific opinion is still fiercely divided about how far down that road they were, but reading between the lines they could have been right down to the wire.

There really is nothing new under the sun. The history of atomic theory began with Democritus of Thrace, who hypothesized that the universe consisted of tiny particles of pure matter that were unchangeable and indestructible. He coined *atom* from the Greek *atomos*, that which can not be cut or split; on this he was proved horribly wrong, but nine out of ten is pretty good for the fifth century BC. By the 1930s many people were aware of the potential for weaponizing atomic reactions, Roosevelt giving the go-ahead in 1939 for the Manhattan Project and General Takeo Yasuda authorizing atomic weapons development to commence under Dr. Yoshio Nishina in July 1941. The Japanese Navy set up its own program under Professor Bansaku Arakatsu.

A close associate of Einstein and an internationally acclaimed physicist in his own right, Nishina had been researching high-energy physics since 1931 at the Riken Institute. He built his own twenty-six inch cyclotron in 1936, a sixty inch one in 1937 and bought a monster one from the University of California in 1938. Safe to say, the man was no stranger to the field and had been pushing for weapons development since the mid-1930s. After the attack on Pearl Harbor, the race was on with a new and deadly determination from all. Nishina and Arakatsu were both hungry for uranium and submarines were the favored method of long-haul transport for this material. General Toransouke Kawaishima managed to get the Germans to supply Czechoslovakian uranium in mid-1943 by telling them some cock and bull story about experimental jet fuel projects; the Germans did not believe a word of it, but made the deliveries anyway. Japanese subs also loaded up with more uranium at occupied French ports, especially Bordeaux, and a number of Italian subs under German command made similar deliveries to Japan. Just how many subs tried the journey and how many got through is unknown; the only shipment intercepted was on board U-boat 234 and even that is surrounded by mystery.

Having read the writing on the bunker wall, Hitler ordered a considerable consignment of uranium oxide to be loaded aboard the U-234, one of the largest subs of World War II, which was also carrying 240 metric tons of other cargo, including two disassembled Me-262 jet fighters. The vessel was joined by lieutenant-commanders Hideo Tomanaga and Genzo Shoji, after which Captain Johann Fehler went to sea on April 15, 1945, and set course for Japan. By May 4, they were picking up enough radio traffic to know that all was not well back home and on May 10 they heard Admiral Dönitz telling all subs to surface under a black ensign and surrender to the nearest Allied port or surface vessel. Fehler dithered; he was equidistant to the UK and the U.S., but considering his cargo thought he might get a better reception from the Americans. The crew held a vote and all agreed on America, which naturally distressed the Japanese who wished to continue as planned, as they were still at war. The dissenters were allowed to commit suicide and take a sharp exit out of tubes one and two before the U-234 made flank speed for America's west coast.

Fehler wished to avoid the British in any shape or form, but his main problem was now the Canadian Navy. He radioed his false intention to make for Halifax to surrender, after which he kept sending out bogus reports of his position as he made a dash for the New England coast. On May 14, Fehler surfaced to surrender to the USS *Sutton* off the Grand Banks of Newfoundland; both vessels were a bit twitchy, but the only incident involved one of the boarding party being fatally shot up the backside by the man preceding him down the conning tower ladder. Where the sub was taken next and what happened to its much-debated cargo is still argued. Velma Hunt, a professor of environmental health with a specific interest in uranium, now retired from Penn State University, maintains that the vessel made stops at Newfoundland and Portland in Maine, the cargo being offloaded in secret at each point. When the U-234 made its final stop at Portsmouth, New Hampshire, its cargo was seventy tons short of manifest and there was no sign of the two disassembled jet fighters, which are pretty difficult to lose on a submarine.

The officers were taken to Washington, D.C., for interrogation, with the exception of Second Officer Lieutenant Karl Pfaff who, with the uranium, found himself in a locked room at a U.S. Navy installation in Virginia, where he was ordered at gunpoint to open the coffer in case it was booby-trapped. Pfaff, who later returned to America to live, said that only when the safe was open and the internal canisters revealed did everyone return to join him, including Oppenheimer, although he did not know it was him at the time. Pfaff was whisked off to an internment camp and the uranium was shipped to Oak Ridge, Tennessee. Now the truth becomes muddy. Some say this consignment was pure weapons-grade material, but that seems unlikely as Germany's refining processes were not as technically or industrially advanced as America's. Had it been pure, that would have been enough for perhaps four bombs. If it was unrefined, its arrival in America was too late for refinement in time to be ready for the drops on Japan. On the other hand, there is yet another body of opinion holding that the batch of uranium did indeed make it to Japan, just not in the form that the recipients expected it to arrive.

The real significance of that shipment is that it indicates the Japanese bomb project to be in some measure advanced, as the uranium would be of little use to them were it not. Also, if Nishina was as far off track with his program as apologists maintain, how within minutes of "Little Boy" being dropped on Hiroshima could he figure out the number of neutrons fissioned at the bomb's core and the force of the blast? He apparently did this off the cuff with a slide rule, so he can't have been ignorant of the internal workings of such a device. Apologists also say that Nishina had made a mess of his calculations regarding the speed at which the two components in the warhead had to be rammed together; they say he had this down as being between 1/20th and 1/30th of a second instead of 1/200th and 1/300th.

Most curious of all, if the Japanese bomb project was so retrograde, why were the Russians so keen to get to Hungnam, the principal location of the Japanese nuclear program? Hiroshima was hit on August 6, 1945, Russia declared war on Japan on the 8th, and the offensive on Japanese-occupied China and Manchuria began the next day. As their comrades were busy flattening the Japanese Kwangtung Army, a special unit was heading for Hungnam in North Korea to remove everything from the heavy water to the last scrap of paper, all the Japanese men in white coats heading for a life back in the USSR. Up until then, American intelligence indicated that the Soviets would be twenty years in their development of a bomb; after Hungnam that figure was dramatically shortened. There is also an outside possibility, from statements made by Japanese personnel, that not long before the Americans hit Hiroshima a test was carried out in the seas off Hungnam. Although reckoned to be about a third of the power of the first Trinity test in the New Mexico desert, it still worked. The officers of the U-234 also stated that before their departure from

Germany, they had been told that such a test had been successfully conducted to impress upon them the urgency of their mission.

So, rather than being undeserving victims, the Japanese may have simply come second in a race they had willingly enjoined and desperately tried to win.

Turner's Prize

Lusitania was not an American liner; she was not sunk on her maiden voyage; she was not an "innocent" sunk without warning by the nasty Germans; the incident was not responsible for America's entry into World War I, and, as for British connivance in her sinking, the jury is still out on that.

Designated a Royal Mail Ship, *Lusitania* was a British ship of the Cunard Line which, along with her sister ship, *Mauretania*, was built with government assistance on the condition that they could both be pressed into service in the event of war; the structure and nature of the fittings of both ships reflected this dual-role intention. Even after their completion, the British government was paying Cunard an annual subsidy of £150,000 to keep both ships in a state of readiness for wartime roles. *Lusitania*'s maiden voyage began on September 7, 1907, and finished in New York on the 13th; she was on the last leg of her 101st voyage when she was sunk.

She began her last transatlantic run from Liverpool on April 17, 1915, to arrive in New York on the 24th, whereupon a delegation of German-Americans paid a visit to the German Embassy to express their concerns that any attack on such a ship would only stir up anti-German feeling in America and help the pro-war lobby. The embassy apparently concurred as they paid for announcements to appear on the travel pages of over fifty prominent publications and newspapers, to remind everyone of the state of war and the dangers of traveling on British shipping bound for the UK, then under a German blockade. For reasons never explained, the American State Department got wind of this and ordered the editors to pocket the money and "forget" to run the item. The only paper that the State Department missed was the *Des Moines Register*, which did run the announcement.

Everybody seems to have been quite happy for American citizens to board a liner that was carrying munitions and about to run the gauntlet of the German wolf-packs. Furthermore, people were aware that the Germans knew the liner was being used to transport munitions because the Germans had made no secret of the fact that they *did* know. Finally, the Germans managed to get their point across by publishing the following notice in leading papers in the space right next to Cunard's announcement of the imminent sailing of *Lusitania*. Headed with a bold "NOTICE!" The ad ran as follows:

TRAVELERS intending to embark on the Atlantic voyage are reminded that a state of war exists between Germany and her allies and Great Britain and her allies; that the zone of war includes the waters adjacent to the British Isles; that, in accordance with the formal notice given by the Imperial German Government, vessels flying the flag of Great Britain, or any of her allies, are liable to destruction in those waters and that travelers sailing in the war zone on ships of Great Britain or her allies do so at their own risk.
THE IMPERIAL GERMAN EMBASSY,
Washington, D.C., April 22, 1915

Three days later, U-20, U-27, and U-30 received their orders to proceed to British waters on April 30. On May 1 the Germans reprinted their notice next to Cunard's announcement of the sailing that day of *Lusitania*; the German Embassy staff could hardly have done more to make their point. Unimpressed, *Lusitania* slipped her moorings just as U-30 was sinking the American tanker *Gulflight* off the Scilly Isles. The Germans made a conditional apology for the action, but pointed out that, as the tanker was sailing under armed escort, it was a legitimate target.

Barely a day into the trip, *Lusitania* was found to be carrying three German spies who were immediately locked up, but alarm bells still failed to ring. Actually, these were not the first German spies to have displayed interest in *Lusitania*. Curt Thummel of the German Military Attaché's Office in America had previously managed to get a job on the liner as a steward. He had reported back to the German authorities regarding modifications to the twelve ring-plate mountings that had been installed for six inch naval guns and, according to his report, some of those guns were already on board. The Germans were also aware that on the day of her last sailing she was carrying over four million .303 rifle cartridges, 1,250 large cases of shrapnel shells, and assorted other cases of munitions and fuses. The ship was slated for conversion to her new role as a high-speed blockade-runner. The 1914 edition of *Jane's* and *The Royal Navy Officer's Pocket Book*, as carried by all good U-boat commanders, both had *Lusitania* and *Mauretania* listed as "armed merchantmen." Thus, with all due respect to the 1,198 lives lost (120 of which were American), it would have been dereliction of duty for the German Navy *not* to target and sink her.

The shadowy men of British Naval Intelligence's infamous Room 40 were aware of the U-boat deployment. They had long since cracked most of the U-boat codes and well understood the instruction issued by Commander Herman Bauer of the 3rd Submarine Flotilla, who ordered the deployment of the three aforementioned U-boats into the Irish Sea and the Bristol Channel. U-30 turned for home on May 4 to escort U-27, which had jammed bow planes, leaving U-20 on station and waiting. Still Room 40 said nothing. U-20 was under command of Walther Schwieger and, if as seems, the Germans had set out to take down *Lusitania* they could not have picked a better man for the job—in February that year he had torpedoed the British hospital ship *Asturias*. En route to his target area, Schwieger sank a couple of ships with neutral markings, and on May 6, just the day before he met up with Lusitania, he torpedoed the steamers *Candidate* and *Centurion* off the Coningbeg Light at the entrance to St. George's Channel.

Then came what he was perhaps sent out to sink, *Lusitania*, which for reasons later explored was holding a steady course at the reduced speed of 18 knots as she passed the Old Head of Kinsale to present Schwieger with a textbook target of which he took full advantage. At 2:10 p.m. on May 7, Schwieger gave the order to fire, but Quartermaster Charles Voegele refused to pass the order on to the torpedo room, saying he would have no hand in the murder of women and children. Not only does this make it pretty clear that all aboard U-20 knew exactly what they had in their sights, it also got Voegele three years in prison. The fateful shot was finally fired and, according to the U-boat's own log: "Clean bow shot at 700 meters. Torpedo hits starboards side right behind the bridge. An unusually heavy explosion takes place . . . followed by a second one—boiler or coal or powder?" So, one torpedo, two explosions.

Lusitania then descended into chaos. The crew and even some of the officers panicked, reducing the evacuation to a shambles. With the boat listing heavily to starboard, the lifeboats on that side swung out too far for boarding and those on the port side jammed against the massive and protruding plate rivets that either holed them or tipped them over, spilling the passengers into the water. By 2:25 p.m. Schwieger had seen enough and turned for home; by 2:28 p.m. *Lusitania* had hit the bottom, sunk in eighteen minutes.

And then the tongues started wagging. What had caused that second explosion? Why was the *Lusitania*'s captain, William Turner, a man of great experience, steaming a steady course at reduced speed if he knew hostile subs were in the area? Did he in fact know? Had Room 40 been mysteriously "forgetful" in alerting him? Was he himself a traitor, colluding with the Germans in the sinking of his own vessel? It is hard to know where to begin with all this, as the only sure facts are the sinking itself, but the presence of an extremely pungent rat cannot be ignored.

Best to start with Captain Turner. As one of Cunard's most senior captains, why did he behave in such a seemingly cavalier manner if aware of the very real danger in his path? Short of contacting U-20 by radio to convey his exact coordinates and speed, he could not have done more to present Schwieger with a sitting duck. Captain Richard Webb of the Trade Division went as far as calling Turner a traitor in writing: "One is forced to conclude that he is either utterly incompetent or that he has been got at by the Germans. In considering this latter possibility it is not necessary to suppose that he had any conception of the loss of life which actually occurred and he may well have thought that being so close to the shore there would be ample time to run his ship into a place of security before she foundered." First Sea Lord Fisher endorsed Webb's accusation: "Fully concur. As the Cunard Company would not have employed an incompetent man the certainty is absolute that Captain Turner is not a fool but a knave!" Everyone seemed extremely anxious for Turner to carry the can and, to this end, the Admiralty dispatched a deputation to Ireland, including spooks from Room 40, to keep Turner muzzled and on ice. Probably worried that it was their cargo of munitions that had been responsible for the second explosion, Winston Churchill (at the time first lord of the Admiralty) and company stuck rigidly to the story of multiple torpedo hits and branded the German version of events a face-saving lie. As it turned out, they needn't have worried; post-war exploration of the wreck revealed that all the *known* munitions were still intact. The alternative theory that the cold rush of water onto hot boilers caused the explosion can also be discounted so, unless there were other and more volatile munitions on the ship of which no one is now aware, it *might* have been a coal-dust explosion.

The main question mark over the whole murky business is: Did Winston Churchill, first lord of the Admiralty, actively conspire to have *Lusitania* sunk to bring America into the war? If he did then his plan failed; Roosevelt made all the right noises and fired off letters to Berlin talking of piracy, before letting the matter slide. It would be another two years before America got involved. But the lack of explicit content and the tardiness of the radio messages from Admiralty to Turner regarding the location and extent of U-boat activity do present a problem. That, in conjunction with the now certain knowledge that Churchill thought it highly desirable for citizens of other nations, particularly Americans, to be placed in danger of attack by the Germans, does pose a question or two. Churchill and Room 40 were aware of the deployment of the three U-boats and their destination on April 25, and *Lusitania* sailed from New York on May 1. On May 5 an alleged clandestine meeting was chaired by Churchill in the Admiralty, and on May 5 to 6, U-20 sank various vessels off the Old Head of Kinsale and the Coningbeg Light. At 12:05 p.m. on May 6, the Admiralty finally issued a blanket warning, which was relayed by Queenstown (near Kinsale in Ireland), and on May 7 at 11:52 a.m. *Lusitania* acknowledged she was now aware of the danger. Finally, on May 7 at 2:10 p.m., she was hit. Given the size of *Lusitania* and the number of lives at stake, it is more than strange that no one thought to radio Turner directly with something very explicit about the already active U-20 lying dead ahead. Why not tell him to make port in Ireland and wait for escort? Anything. And so to the alleged meeting of May 5.

It is stated as fact by some that *Lusitania*'s fate was sealed at a quiet meeting in an Admiralty map room, those present being Churchill, Admiral Fisher, Vice-Admiral Henry Oliver (chief of the War Staff) and Captain Reginald Hall (director of naval intelligence). That such a meeting took place to seal the fate of the *Lusitania* is far from impossible; war is nothing if not a dirty business, but those who state the meeting as fact have always over-egged the pudding with unnecessary and false embellishments. Colin Simpson, author of *Lusitania* (1972), not only claims that the ship was also carrying a large quantity of gun-cotton, which was responsible for the second and most devastating explosion, but he also places one Lieutenant-Commander Joseph Kenworthy at the alleged meeting and claims he was privy to the plot. In Simpson's favor is the fact that no munitions at all were listed on the ship's manifest, so why not indeed some gun-cotton as well? But as Kenworthy himself states— under his title of 10th baron Strabolgi, Kenworthy had published *Freedom of the Seas* (1927)—and his incontestable war record shows, apart from a year ashore in Greenwich (1906–7) he was away on active service at the time of the alleged meeting, in command of the destroyer *Bullfinch*. He did not join Admiralty War Staff in London until August 1916.

So, on the one side of the argument stand officialdom (which always tells the unvarnished truth) and the Churchill defenders who blindly resist any suggestion of his connivance. On the other side of the line stand conspiracy theorists determined to prove that the sinking was plotted down to the last detail by Churchill and Room 40. In the middle waters sit those who rightly question the two rather large elephants sharing the lifeboat. Why didn't the Admiralty cut to the chase and order Turner to feign mechanical problems and sit it out in New York until destroyer escort could be arranged? After all, Room 40 had decoded the German deployment signals to the three U-boats six days before *Lusitania*'s departure date. Also, if that was not an option, why wasn't Turner alerted to the danger directly by radio—not second-hand and vague through Queenstown—while a destroyer or two steamed out to meet the ship and escort her to safe haven. The second elephant represents Turner's seemingly criminal negligence on the day; why would such a man behave like a novice on a Sunday sail in peacetime if he knew U-boats were active in the area?

There is one possible scenario that fits most of the known facts, but this is only conjecture. Is it possible that Turner was approached in New York by men who were, or purported to be, from British Intelligence, who asked him to sacrifice his ship for the greater good of king and country? They might even have told him that the Cunard executive was in on the deal and that he had no option but to do their bidding. They would of course have assured him that he would be shielded afterwards and not held to account, and that he would have Churchill's undying gratitude and that of his country. Only that, or some similar pitch, could explain why Turner behaved as he did in such clear and present danger. He was on a strange course setting, close enough to shore for an effective evacuation of the ship, as observed by those who would brand him a traitor—it was as if he was expecting something to happen. He was holding that course as a steady line instead of zig-zagging, as would have been expected. True, six of *Lusitania*'s boilers had been shut down to save fuel, which reduced the ship's speed from 25 knots to 21 knots, but Turner, for reasons never adequately explained, had further reduced this to 18 knots as he steamed steadily past the Old Head of Kinsale, again in contravention of standing orders to stay clear of all landfall. Who knows? All in all it was "a damned dirty business," to quote Lord Mersey's closing comments at the inquiry he headed to clear Turner of any blame.

The Germans stood their ground and reiterated that if *Lusitania* was carrying munitions then it was her own lookout, and the responsibility of those who chose to use civilians as human shields for such a cargo in wartime. They did have a point; everyone has heard of *Lusitania,* but far fewer know of the sinking of the completely unarmed *Wilhelm Gustloff*, torpedoed relentlessly until she sank in the Baltic in January 1945, taking over ten thousand German women and children with her. That is nine-fold the death toll of *Lusitania* and six-fold that of *Titanic.* It's all a matter of who wins the war and gets to write the history books.

Tweedle-Dee and Tweedle-Dumb

It is believed by some that the town of Berwick-on-Tweed, by the Scottish border, is still at war with Russia and other European nations, as it was included in the declaration of the Crimean War in 1854 but omitted from the Treaty of Paris (1856). Some versions of the yarn include bogus accounts of Russian diplomats flying over in the 1960s to bring the bloodless conflict to a close.

Berwick is the only part of England that stands to the north of the Scottish border as formed by the River Tweed, and has a colorful history to say the least. Between 1296 and 1482 the town changed hands thirteen times before landing in England's hands for keeps. (There are still anomalies; Berwick Rangers is the only English soccer team to play in the Scottish League.) Matters were further complicated in 1503, when Henry VII of England and James IV of Scotland signed a treaty acknowledging Berwick to be "of but not within the Kingdom of England." This led to over-cautious legislators naming the town as specifically included in new laws or taxes, but no declaration of war from an outside party has ever cited Berwick as being included or excluded. All was ratified in 1746 with the Wales and Berwick-upon-Tweed Act, which stated: "in all cases where the Kingdom of England hath been or shall be mentioned in any Act of Parliament, the same has been and shall henceforth be taken to include the Dominion of Wales and the town of Berwick-upon-Tweed." Thus, it is pure invention that Berwick was still at war with Russia until the 1960s or still at war with Germany from World War I when round two broke out.

The myth seems to have been started by Archdeacon William Cunningham, who felt an affinity with the town. He was of English parentage, but born and educated in Scotland before lecturing in economic history at both Cambridge University and America's Harvard University. When discussing Berwick's inclusion or otherwise in laws and taxes, he did at one time ponder the possibility that until the Act of Union (1707) it might have been necessary to extend such niceties to declarations of war. And this seems to have been enough for Berwick to pick up on the whimsical conjecture and weave it into the history of the town, even claiming to have signed some sort of treaty with a Russian diplomat in 1963.

In fact, stories of missed treaties abound in military mythology, and the other two favorites relate to Andorra and the Isles of Scilly off the Cornish coast.

Andorra—at 181 square miles—is such a blink-and-you've-missed-it country that it is tailor-made for yarns and myths. The usual version of history recounts how plucky little Andorra was one of the first to declare war on Germany in 1914, but never got the chance to deploy its terrifying military machine comprising 10 men, seven of whom were generals. Come the Treaty of Versailles (1919), Andorra was omitted from the list of combatant nations and thus still at war with Germany when World War II broke out, leaving it the only nation to fight two world wars concurrently. Some versions of the myth have Andorra signing a separate treaty with Germany on September 25, 1939, nearly three weeks after the outbreak of World War II, while others claim that Andorra and Germany did not sue for peace until as late as 1958. Not bad for a nation whose defense budget today only amounts to about 15 euros for blank ammunition to blast off at state occasions.

It is a charming story, but it always lacks the specifics of truth, with plenty of unanswered questions. Who signed on behalf of Germany? Who were the Andorran representatives? Where did they meet? Where is the Andorran copy of this great document? Furthermore, Andorra could not declare war on anyone because it did not achieve independent sovereignty until 1993, prior to which responsibility for its defense lay with Spain; thus it was neutral for World War II.

And so to the longest war on record, the one that raged between Holland and the Isles of Scilly for 335 years. On March 30, 1651, the Dutch admiral Maarten Harpertszoon Tromp turned up with a dozen warships and a determination to wipe out the privateers using the isles as a base from which they plundered Dutch shipping. In the middle of what turned out to be a rather protracted stand-off, a British fleet arrived under the command of Admiral Robert Blake, who promised Tromp that he would sort matters out, once and for all. Accepting Blake's promise to regulate the privateers, Tromp sailed away without canceling the declaration of war he had made upon his arrival, or so the story goes.

In 1985, Roy Duncan, Chairman of the Isles of Scilly Council, made a formal approach to the Dutch Embassy asking if they could get together to bring down the curtain on their bloodless feud, and the ambassador, Jonkheer Rein Huydecoper, decided to run with the gag by attending the "peace negotiations" in St. Mary's the following April. (*Jonkheer* is the Dutch equivalent of Sir or Lord and produced the name of "Yonkers" in New York State.) Playing to the gallery, Huydecoper signed the peace treaty with a flourish and addressed the assembled press to the effect that Scillians and Dutch alike would be able to rest easy with the threat of attack now passed. It was a great PR coup for the island's tourist board, but no declaration of war had ever been made on the islands. Tromp was an admiral, not a nation, and Scilly part of England, so it would have been like declaring war on Rhode Island and expecting the rest of the United States to stay out of the battle. Besides, even if Tromp had made such a declaration or done so with the full backing of the Dutch crown, the treaty of 1654 at the end of the war between England and the United Provinces of the Netherlands would have sorted it all out with one fell swoop.

Victoria's Cross

Victoria's Cross . . . and so she should be, given the number of mistakes and misconceptions now attached to what she wished to be a dignified and understated award.

You could say that the Victoria Cross (VC) was a direct result of that new addition to war in the nineteenth century—the war correspondent, specifically William Russell. *The Times* of London had dispatched hacks to war zones before, the first being Henry Crabb Robinson, who wrote of Napoleon's romps along the Elbe in 1807, but he preferred to write up his reports in safety, gleaning what he could from second-hand sources. Russell, at the Crimean War in the 1850s, was the first proper war correspondent and a veritable thorn in the side of the military and the establishment at large. He wrote of the crass inefficiency of those in command, who guffawed over chicken and bubbly in their heated tents while ordinary soldiers lived in frozen filth and died of typhoid and cholera—twenty thousand to disease as against thirty-four hundred on the field. He also wrote of the courage and fortitude of the ordinary British soldier, although he never mentioned the "thin red line" so frequently attributed to his reportage. Russell gave the people back home the unvarnished truth instead of the image of jolly fine chaps in neatly pressed uniforms, charging across neatly mown meadows to give Johnny Foreigner what for. For once, the armchair soldiers could read about war as it really was—flies, filth and rotting flesh, and they didn't like it one bit. Neither did those on the corridors of power who, sensing the mood change, resolved to come up with something to placate the multitude.

Until the Crimean War, all the decent awards were reserved for senior officers. Junior officers and NCOs might get a field promotion, but the common soldier, whose bitter lot had been so graphically portrayed by Russell's reportage, was lucky to see a Distinguished Conduct Medal to use as a begging aid when he got home. Why not introduce a prestigious award that was open to all to show Joe Public how jolly egalitarian the British Army was? The duke of Newcastle, secretary of state for war, wrote to Victoria and her administration to suggest a new medal that would be open to the rank and file in recognition of their invaluable contribution. This was a change of stance indeed from a man who thought the great unwashed should be variously shot, flogged, transported or shoved up chimneys as deemed best by their betters. The royals went for the idea and became personally involved with the design and the inscription, which Victoria herself changed from "For the brave" to "For valor," as the former implied that only medal winners were brave. She also turned her royal nose up at the first dummies that, made of copper, looked dull and flat; bronze was required, she opined, and that takes us to the greatest myth of all—that all VCs are cast from Russian guns captured at Sebastopol on the Crimea.

That this was the intention is beyond dispute, but somehow the message was diluted in the chain of communication and the equerry dispatched to Woolwich Arsenal to requisition gun parts to be melted down was not quite as specific in his request as he might have been. As a result, he was fobbed off with bits from two or three clapped-out cannon the stores wanted rid of. It is known that two of these relics were Chinese, probably captured during the First Opium War (1839–42), but the provenance of the third is wholly unknown. And other guns must have been involved in later years; only the cascabels (the pommels at the rear of the barrel) were sawn off for use, and there have been 1,356 crosses awarded to date. With wastage, it takes fifty ounces to make a dozen crosses and it is known that the combined weight of the cascabels was 224 pounds, or, 3,584 ounces The metal used to produce the 1,356 crosses is known to have weighed just over 353 pounds, or 5,650 ounces.

The metal from the two Chinese cannon was not used up until 1914 and the last remaining VC ingot was lost during its transfer from Woolwich in 1942, so the origin of the metal involved is anyone's guess—X-rays of various crosses have confirmed multiple sources.

The first VC presentations were made in London's Hyde Park on June 26, 1857, when sixty-two recipients received their crosses from the queen herself for their actions in the Crimean War. Much against concerned advice, the queen insisted on presenting the crosses on horseback, which did prove a folly as she nearly toppled a couple of times. Unfortunately for recipient Lieutenant (later Commander) Henry Raby, one of these times was when she came to him and, losing her balance, lunged at him like a lace-trimmed lancer and, after an undignified struggle, managed to secure the pin straight through the poor chap's nipple. With the fortitude that brought him before her in the first place, Raby uttered not a sound and later expressed his relief that the blood did not show through his uniform until his beloved monarch had moved on. Lips don't come much stiffer than that.

To date, the youngest recipient was aged just fifteen, the oldest sixty-nine; there have been four cases of brothers attaining the award and three incidences of father and son. The largest number awarded for any single action were the eleven crosses dished out after the battle at Rorke's Drift (1879) in the Zulu Wars. And the weirdest of all, Company Sergeant-Major F. W. Hall, Corporal L. Clarke and Lieutenant R. Shankland were awarded the VC during World War I; it later transpiring that all three lived on Pine Street in Winnipeg. That thoroughfare is now known as Valour Street.

White House Whitewash

Still trotted out for an airing is the old chestnut about the White House originally being known as the Grey House, because of the color of its stone. So the story goes, the name was changed after the British burned

Washington in 1814, requiring the building to be painted white to hide the scorch marks. This is, of course, complete fabrication.

In America, the incident is remembered as an act of unwarranted vandalism by a jackbooted enemy, whereas it was a controlled retaliation for unwarranted vandalism inflicted by Americans on the Canadian town of York (modern Toronto), indiscriminately looted and burnt on April 27, 1813, by troops under General Zebulon Pike. Determined to repay the kindness, Admiral Sir George Cockburn and General Robert Ross led a force into Washington on August 24, 1814, having issued quite specific orders that no civilian was to be ill-treated or any of their property stolen or damaged. Only official buildings were to be attacked. True to their word, the only private residence that was destroyed was a house on the corner of Maryland Avenue, Constitution Avenue and Second Street North-East, from which partisans laid fire on the invaders, this being the only resistance met. Cockburn, who had a grievance against the *National Intelligencer* for branding him "the Ruffian," led a detachment to burn the newspaper to the ground, but was sympathetic to an appeal from a group of women who protested that the fire would spread to their homes. Cockburn agreed this would be the likely outcome and so ordered the office and printing house to be demolished, brick by brick, after which he strode away with the complete set of type for the letters C and c in a sack to hinder them from writing about him again.

With all in full retreat, President James Madison and his wife Dolley were made of sterner stuff. Long after every man had fled the presidential mansion, they beavered away to save as many treasures and sensitive documents as they could; the British were marching up the front steps as the Madisons fled out of the rear. Inside, the British found Dolley's table laid out for forty, and so they ate her food before burning her house to the ground. The thick sandstone (not grey stone) walls survived but were so weakened by the fire that they had to be torn down and the place rebuilt, so there were no burn marks to hide. Furthermore, since its original construction the place had been painted white, and was referred to as the White House long before 1814. The curator, Betty Monkman, has presented a barrage of pre-1814 references to the place as the White House, but admitted that the term was far more common after its restructuring than before. It was not until an executive order from President Theodore Roosevelt in 1901 that the name gained official recognition, known officially as the Executive Mansion before then.

Your Starter for Ten

Fort Sumter today is a massive tourist attraction, where visitors are told that here was fired the shot that started the Civil War. Not true—there were several engagements before the Confederates opened fire on Sumter on April 12, 1861, and the war began not in Charleston Harbor but hundreds of miles away in Florida.

The South seceded from the Union on December 20, 1860, and Fort Barrancas in Pensacola Harbor came under attack on the night of January 8, 1861, when the United States Army repelled an assault by Florida and Alabama troops. With the battery commander, John Winder, absent, Lieutenant Adam Slemmer was in command and, in the light of the attack of the 8th and the surrender of the Pensacola Navy Yard on the 10th, he decided to abandon Fort Barrancas for the deserted and slightly dilapidated but far more defendable Fort Pickens. Taking all the supplies and munitions they could carry and destroying what remained, Slemmer's decision proved sensible, as Fort Pickens remained in Union hands throughout the war. There were other scrapes at Forts McRee, Marion, Jefferson and Taylor, leaving events at Sumter well down the list.

One of three forts built on man-made islands in Charleston Harbor, South Carolina, Fort Sumter—like Fort Pickens—had seen better days and lay deserted. Major Robert Anderson, in a mirror decision to that of Slemmer, moved his command of eighty-three men from Fort Moultrie to Fort Sumter, spiking the guns and spoiling anything that could not be transferred. On January 9, 1861, the Union steamer *Star of the West* tried to get through with supplies and reinforcements but was forced to turn back by Confederate guns already in place on nearby Morris Island. The first shots actually fired on the fort came at 4:30 a.m. on April 12; a mortar round was fired over Fort Sumter from Fort Johnson to signal the commencement of a barrage that would not end until Sumter's surrender the next day. Not sure how to respond, the defenders of the fort did not return fire until 7:00 p.m., when Captain Abner Doubleday, later erroneously credited with the invention of baseball, gave the order to shell Confederate guns firing from Cumming's Point. But it was a very one-sided conflict and, after enduring a barrage of about three thousand Confederate shells, Anderson decided on the 14th that to surrender with honor was the only sensible option. He first secured permission to fire a hundred-gun salute to the Union flag before marching out to waiting transport. It was this well-intentioned act of gallantry that brought about the only casualties of the engagement. The salute was called short after the fiftieth blank showered a pile of ammunition with burning debris, causing it to explode and kill one Union trooper and wound five others.

SAD WARS AND
MAD WEAPONS

A-Pucker-Lips Now

It may be true that all is fair in love and war, but the two should not be confused.

In 1994 the Air Force Research Laboratory at Wright-Patterson Air Base in Ohio was busy disbursing over $7 million to explore the possibilities of developing some seriously strange non-lethal weapons. Apart from the halitosis and flatulence bombs, designed to create acute embarrassment among enemy troops, the main attention was focused on a biological weapon of such aphrodisiac intensity that it would make the enemy abandon their weapons and turn to each other with romantic intent.

Someone tipped off the Sunshine Project in Austin, Texas—an anti-biological weapons action group—who managed to get hold of a wealth of documents from the project and leaked them to the press in 2005. Two years later the bomb's development team were awarded the IgNobel Peace Prize, but the Air Force declined the invitation to attend the awards ceremony in Harvard University's Sanders Theater and accept their tribute.

Acoustic Kitty

Long before the advent of nano-spybots structured to look like dragonflies or other seemingly innocuous creatures, American and British Intelligence agencies recruited various small animals as spies, with predictably hilarious results. While MI5 was building its team of spy-detecting gerbils to sniff out traitors—apparently their olfactory system is highly sensitive to raised adrenalin levels in sweat—the CIA was working on an equally bizarre scheme involving the use of surgically modified cats to bug the Kremlin and Soviet embassies across the globe. Declassified documents from the Agency's Science and Technology Directorate (S&TD) reveal the full lunacy of Operation *Acoustic Kitty*.

In 1960, the fact that cats roamed the Kremlin in Moscow to control a significant rodent problem was perceived as an opportunity to bug the place, and by 1961 Operation *Acoustic Kitty* was up and running under the stern gaze of the S&TD. The idea boiled down to rigging up cats with microphones and internal power packs before "infiltrating" them into sensitive buildings or habituating them to external areas, such as parks and recreation areas around the same buildings where Soviet staff might take lunch or just chat on park benches, and then harvest the eavesdropped intelligence. There was also another team working on the obvious problem of how to recall these agents to get them recharged. According to retired CIA Soviet-specialist Victor Marchetti, author of *The CIA and the Cult of Intelligence* (1974): "They slit the cat open, put batteries in him, wired him up. The tail was used as an antenna. They made a monstrosity. They tested him and tested him. They found he would walk off the job when he got hungry, so they put another wire in to override that. Finally, they're ready."

After intensive training, one such modified critter was deemed ready for his first field trial, so a team of handlers drove him to a Soviet compound on Wisconsin Avenue in Washington and released him from their command van, which they had parked just across the street. At first all seemed to be going well; after preening himself for a minute or two the cat moved off in the right direction, but paused in mid-traffic just long enough for a taxi to turn him into $15 million worth of road kill. A member of the team retrieved the fallen agent in a plastic bag before the crestfallen team returned to base for a rethink.

The project limped on through a few more equally disastrous trials, but after the realization that, even without the unkindness of traffic, none of the cats would long survive the surgery, *Acoustic Kitty* was finally abandoned in 1967. Probably to reduce the embarrassment factor, some of the documents relating to the project are still partially censored or "lost," but the CIA does acknowledge that: "The work done on this problem over the years reflects great credit on the personnel who guided it, particularly [censored], whose energy and imagination could be models for scientific pioneers." This same memo goes on to defend the use of trained cats as "possible," while also acknowledging that "the environmental and security factors in using this technique in a real foreign situation force us to conclude that for intelligence purposes, it would not be practical."

And it seems our furry friends are not yet out of the woods. On July 12, 2007, *Sky News* in the UK picked up on an item run by Iran's official Islamic Republic News Agency, which informed a no-doubt alarmed viewership that Iranian Intelligence had "detained" fourteen squirrels suspected of being American spies, equipped with sophisticated miniature microphones and webcams. So far, neither the CIA nor the Pentagon has admitted recruiting Rocky and his cohorts, but time will tell.

Bat Bombs

Cry havoc and let slip the fruit bats of war lacks the ominous malice of Shakespeare's dogs, but America spent an awful lot of money on a World War II program to bomb Japan with bats.

As the Japanese headed to their date with infamy at Pearl Harbor, Dr. Lytle Adams, a dentist from Irwin, Pennsylvania, was up to his knees in guano in the Carlsbad Caverns of New Mexico, observing the millions of bats dwelling therein. Driving home in December 1941, he heard the news of the Japanese attack and, fancying himself as something of an inventor, resolved to take revenge on his nation's new enemies. With the bats still very much in his mind, he fomented a plan to start thousands of fires per day by using bats as tiny arsonists roosting in the eaves of Japanese traditional-style wooden buildings. He rushed back to Carlsbad to capture several bats and then headed home to learn everything he could about them. Having boned up on their hibernating habits, temperature tolerance and carrying abilities, he contacted his friend, Eleanor Roosevelt, for her to have a word in President Franklin's ear to pave the way for one of the most ill-advised and hare-brained schemes of the war.

On January 12, 1942, he sent his proposal in to the White House, where a primed president passed it on to the military with an endorsement that would come back to haunt him: "This man is not a nut." Shelving any normal skepticism from that point on, the Army Chemical Warfare Service felt it had no choice but to roll with the presidential endorsement and authorize Adams to recruit a team of naturalists from the UCLA to scour the countryside for "recruits." The team really liked the mastiff bat, which with a twenty-inch wingspan could fly quite happily with a one pound stick of dynamite, but fortunately for the mastiff bats they were not to be found in as great a number as the free-tailed bat, which lived in massive colonies of up to thirty million in the caves outside Bandera, Texas.

Although this bat weighed only a scant one ounce, it could carry up to 0.6 ounce of ordnance, so Adams turned to Dr. Louis Fisser of the National Defense Research Establishment, who came up with mini bat bombs filled with accelerant gel that would burn for four minutes with a ten inch flame.

Overjoyed, Adams was now ready to impress the military with a demonstration in a conference room in the War Department in Washington, D.C. When all were assembled, Adams thought it might be a crowd-pleaser to turn loose his bats without warning, prompting the attending high-rankers to dive for cover, unaware that the packs the bats were carrying were just dummies. Bats recaptured and generals placated, Adams was given the go-ahead for full trials, the first of which was an unmitigated disaster. On May 21, 1943, 3,700 bats were removed from artificially induced hibernation and fitted with dummy packs before being tossed out of a B-25 flying at five thousand feet; the pilot was Lieutenant Tim Holt, the actor who later starred opposite Humphrey Bogart in *The Treasure of the Sierra Madre* (1946). Not given enough time to recover from their torpor, the bats were still asleep when they hit the deck at terminal velocity. Back to the drawing board.

For his protégés' next outing, Adams built a mock Japanese village and, to be fair, the bats did manage to torch an impressive number of the huts. The trouble was, some decided to return to the hangar whence they came and burned that to the ground, while others decided that the visiting generals' cars would be a nice place for a snooze and incinerated them for good measure. Brushing aside these incidents, which to saner members of his team simply underlined the unpredictability of bats as carriers, Adams forged ahead with zeal. Dr. William Young, a UCLA hotshot involved with the program who had more than his own share of run-ins with Adams, submitted a report when made aware of Adams' next alarming trial:

> *Last Saturday Lt Charles J. Holt of the Marine Corps Air Station at El Centra came to Los Angeles to see me and we had a very interesting talk. Everyone in the project seems to be in agreement that Adams cannot accept responsibility for the project and have it function. For example, he ordered Lt. Holt to prepare for a test in the desert in which ten thousand armed bats were to be used. When Holt pointed out the tremendous hazard involved to the whole of Southern California by such a program, Adams was most indignant, and the lieutenant finally had to tell him that such an experiment would not be performed even if he, Holt, had to stand in front of the arsenal with a machine gun to prevent it.*

Lytle Adams now became something of a hot potato, along with his killer bats, until Fleet Admiral Ernest King, chief of naval operations, pulled the plug in mid-1945, by which time the project had cost millions of dollars and reduced grown men to tears. Unrepentant to the end, Adams derided the atomic bombs dropped on Hiroshima and Nagasaki, claiming his bats would have done a far better job: "Think of thousands of fires breaking out simultaneously over a radius of forty miles from every dispersal. Japan could have been devastated, yet with small loss of life."

Balloonacy

The first World War II American strike on Japan began at dawn on April 18, 1942, when sixteen B-25s cleared the decks of the carrier

Hornet to pay a little visit to Tokyo, Kobe, Nagoya and Yokosuka. Led by Lieutenant-Colonel Jimmy Doolittle, the purpose of the raid was twofold: to boost morale at home after the attack on Pearl Harbor and to let the Japanese know they were not beyond reach. That said, the raid was not particularly effective and ended badly for most of the crews, who knew when they took off that they did not have enough fuel to get back to *Hornet*. Doolittle ditched in China and was taken to an American missionary, who took him to the 1st American Volunteer Group (the "Flying Tigers") of the Chinese Air Force, where Colonel Claire Chennault recruited that same missionary as a spy. (This man was John Birch, later shot by Chinese communists and immortalized by the eponymous conservative U.S. organization the John Birch Society.) The secondary objective of the raid was achieved in spades—the Japanese military was furious that imperial territory had been desecrated (a bit rich after Pearl Harbor) and swore to respond in kind. But how? The distance from Japan to the United States was a massive problem solved only when the Japanese looked to their ancient history and found the answer in paper balloons.

Until Operation *Fu-Go* (Flying Fire) got its balloons off the ground, the Japanese did everything they could to hit the American mainland and claw back some face. On February 23, 1942, the Japanese submarine I-17 surfaced and shelled the Ellwood oil facilities at Goleta, Santa Barbara. Its captain, Nishino Kozo, claimed to have left the place in flames whereas he only managed to hit a decommissioned pump house and cause about $500 worth of damage. June of the same year saw the commencement of Alaska's forgotten war and on the 20th, an I-26 under Captain Yokota Minoru surfaced to let rip more than forty shells at the Estevan Point lighthouse on Vancouver Island. He failed to hit it even once; missing a lighthouse in operation takes the kind of talent you have to be born with, you just can't learn skills like that. The next night it was the turn of Tagami Meiji, who popped up in the Columbia River in his I-25 to take a fire a few shells at Oregon's Fort Stevens, but he managed only to make a few holes in a baseball field. He was back again on

September 9 to launch a Yokosuka E14Y1 seaplane piloted by Nobuo Fujita, whose attempts to start a forest fire on Mount Emily with incendiaries was a complete washout. Feeling that honor had been satisfied, the Japanese ceased these terrifying attacks on empty huts, baseball fields and other targets of strategic importance.

While all this was going on, Major-General Sueyoshi Kusaba was planning to attack the United States with paper balloons. Given the right size and design, Kusuba had figured out that a balloon in the atmosphere's jet stream would be over America within three days with a payload of one 33-pound anti-personnel bomb and four 11-kilogram incendiaries. Not bad. Having convinced his superiors that despite his proposal sounding a bit wacky the principles were sound, he was given the go-ahead to recruit an origami army of nimble-fingered schoolgirls to make the balloons out of large patches of *washi*, a tough paper made from the mulberry bush, which they stuck together in a cross-braced laminated pattern. While his youthful production crew cranked up production to hit a target of 10,000 units, Kusuba had a few technical problems to overcome.

The balloons could be dispatched only in the winter months, when the easterly winds predominate from October to March, but the cold caused a problem in that the balloons would shrink at night and drop down out of the jet stream. The Japanese team was nothing if not ingenious and, eventually, cheap, simple but devilishly cunning "Fu-Go's" were ready for launch on November 3, 1944. Without going into too much technical detail, this first intercontinental and autonomous weapon was suspended from a 32-foot, 9-inch diameter balloon with a 19,070 cubic-foot capacity filled with hydrogen, providing for a lifting capacity of 992 pounds at sea level and 298 pounds at 30,000 feet. Given that there would be no pilot to stabilize flight on the six-thousand-mile trip, the ballasting sandbag lines were linked up to fuse wire that, governed by an altimeter, would ignite to jettison ballast every time the balloon dropped to a pre-set minimum height. When the carefully calculated network of sandbags was spent, the balloon would be over

America, when the payload would be jettisoned and another fuse would ignite the gas in the balloon to leave no trace of the delivery vehicle. And it worked.

Bombs started cropping up all over the States, but caused more alarm than harm. Their appearance remained a frightening mystery until the turn of 1944–45, when duds were recovered intact to raise yet another specter: were these "Fu-Go's" a trial run for biological drops? America became very twitchy and ordered a press blackout on any and all incidents involving "Fu-Go's," which actually had more effect back in Japan than it did in America. The Japanese had no real way of establishing the effectiveness of Operation *Fu-Go*, and the deafening silence from America eventually persuaded them to abandon the launches in April 1945. As Kusaba himself would record after the war: "To my great regret, the progress of the war was faster than we imagined. Soon after the campaign began the air raids against our mainland intensified. Many factories that manufactured various parts were destroyed. Moreover, we were not informed about the effect of 'Fu-Go' throughout the wartime. Due to this combination of hardships we were compelled to cease operations."

After the war, the *New York Times* claimed that Operation *Fu-Go* had been a "humiliating failure" for the Japanese who could claim "first prize for worthless weapons of war," but was that entirely fair? The balloons cost only about $900 per unit and at least one thousand of them made it to target, which caused enough of a ruckus to tie up thousands of personnel on Operation *Fire-Fly* to watch the skies for silent incoming balloons. And there was one significant success that the Japanese never got to hear of. Hanford Engineering in the state of Washington was churning out radioactive material for the Manhattan Project and, when on-line, their worst nightmare was a power failure of the cooling pumps on the reactor. On March 10, 1945, their nightmare came true when a "Fu-Go" took out the transmission lines to the installation, which was only saved from destruction because the safety cut-outs worked faster than anyone could have hoped. Had the Japanese got wind of that result, they would have most certainly intensified the program with the thousands of bigger and better "Fu-Go's" they had waiting in the wings. Instead they ceased the operation in April 1945, just before the first and only American fatalities.

The same news blackout that discouraged the Japanese finally worked against the American public, who might otherwise have been very cautious around strange-looking things hanging from enormous balloons with Japanese symbols. In the course of a church picnic on May 5, 1945, thirteen-year-old Joan Patzke tried to pull a "Fu-Go" from a tree in the woods outside Bly, Oregon. The Reverend Archi Mitchell was transfixed with horror as his wife Elsie, aged only twenty-six, and five children were killed in the resultant blast. There were post-war recriminations against the military for their insistence on the blackout, and payments were made to the respective families but the court did rule that, on balance, the censorship was both warranted and for the "greater good."

The Japanese did not have the monopoly on freewheeling balloons. In the gales of the night of September 17, 1940, a large number of British barrage balloons broke their moorings and headed for Sweden, Denmark and Finland, where they brought down power lines and radio masts, prompting Churchill to order a team to explore the possibility of flotillas of incendiary balloons being sent over to Germany. Despite the RAF curling its handlebar moustache in derision at the plan, known as Operation *Outward*, the first killer blimps were turned loose on March 20 at Languard Fort near Felixstowe and started serious forest fires near Berlin and Tilsit. Assessment of the German power grid revealed it to be highly vulnerable to short-circuit, so the next wave of blimps, released from Oldstairs, near Dover, were fitted with trailing wires; some of these hit the grid outside Leipzig, causing such an overload that the Bohlen power station blew up. There were a string of lesser successes and, as it was calculated that it cost the Germans far more to cope with the balloons than it cost to make them, Operation *Outward* continued until late 1944.

Dogs of War

The very traits that earned the poor old dog its role as man's best friend left it wide open to abuse for the furtherance of war. The Romans used large mastiff-type dogs against infantry; the Spanish took similar dogs with them to South America; and the early settlers of what would become the United States used dogs against Native Americans, sometimes throwing prisoners to pit-dogs for entertainment. But for all-time cynicism, the Russian anti-tank dog of World War II takes some beating.

With the conditioning experiments of Pavlov very much in mind, the Russian military quickly hatched a scheme to use dogs to carry backpack bombs under German tanks. They repeatedly starved the dogs and then led them to food laid out under tanks to get the dogs to make the association between tank and food. Having also accustomed the poor animals to their suicide packs all they had to do, they reasoned, was starve the dogs before an armored engagement and then turn them loose.

The plan did have some limited success, but the main flaw was that the association training had worked too well; the vast majority of the dogs associated the underneath of *Russian* tanks with food. After 1942, when packs of hungry hounds forced three brigades of Russian armor into a panicked retreat, the scheme was abandoned.

Elijah Flies Back to Front

The mad scientists of the World War II British Department of Miscellaneous Weapons Development (DMWD) always enjoyed their most spectacular fiascos when rockets were involved. Such was the outcome when approached by the British Army bemoaning the inevitable compromise between speed of descent and safety of landing when dropping equipment and vehicles by parachute. Could there possibly be a way for a load to drop like a stone to minimize exposure time to enemy detection, yet still hit the ground like a feather at the last minute? Named as a reversal of the Biblical Elijah, because the team mistakenly thought the old chap had been propelled to the heavens by a pillar of fire, the DMWD soon had Project *Hajile* off the ground, in more ways than one. (Actually, Elijah was whisked away in a whirlwind that, as the last trial of *Hajile* turned out, was quite apropos.)

To be fair, what they came up with was the world's first retro-rocket device. Their idea was to drop the payload on a platform fitted with cordite rockets that would be triggered by a trailing plumb-bob when the whole device was a few yards from impact. Given that they would be playing with both propellants and explosives, the development team was exiled to the end of the pier at Weston-super-Mare, which was commandeered for the purpose and renamed HMS *Birnbeck*. Here they conjured forth their prototype, designed to be dropped from two thousand feet by a Lancaster bomber. On hand to film the trials for the benefit of those with more sense than to attend in person, was the same Louis Klementaski that the DMWD nearly killed with their *Grand Panjandrum* experiments (see page 240).

To begin with, Klementaski's main problem was that the pilot kept dropping the platform too far away from the end of the pier for his camera to capture the event with any clarity. So, perhaps irked by increasingly petulant demands for him to drop the payload ever closer, the pilot finally did just that. Necks craned back in anticipation, the party at the end of the pier watched and filmed as the platform with its payload of concrete blocks gracefully exited the belly of the Lancaster and abandoned itself to the embrace of gravity. It was Klementaski who, with the advantage of his camera lens, first figured out where the platform was headed and, pausing briefly to issue a warning cry, abandoned his post to run back up the pier as fast as he could. The last member of the party had only just made it to safety when the platform—all two tons of it accelerating earthward at forty feet per second—reduced their workshop to matchwood. Just to add insult to injury, once the dust had settled the rockets burst into life to set fire to all that remained.

The DMWD returned what was left of the pier to the overjoyed local community and relocated trials to terra firma, but things only got worse. As one ballast-laden platform after another embedded itself into the tranquility of the South Downs, the team tried to compensate by increasing the number and power of the rockets, but this only exacerbated the problems of instability. Indeed, everything was fine *until* the rockets fired, after which platforms either went into a spin before crashing or, worse still, flipped upside down to be powered into the ground by the rockets—hardly the ideal outcome. Sometimes, just to demonstrate a flair for the original, the platform would pancake and then ignite its rockets to perform a somersault and smash its cargo. The final straw came on the morning of the D-Day landings when, determined to help with the back-up, the team had made some "improvements." Knowing they were drinking in the Last Chance Saloon, they assembled about the rig to double-check every last detail. Unaware that the rockets had been fueled up, some bright spark thought it might be a good idea to test the igniter circuits, with predictable results. The platform leapt into the air and whirled round in blazing pirouettes to inflict assorted injuries and temporary blindness on all present. The project was then canceled.

Fantasy Island

The delightfully eccentric Pyke cousins were celebrated World War II researchers attached to various think tanks. While Magnus was alarming the Ministry of Food with his suggestions that, since the patriotic response for blood donors had produced a glut, the excess should be used to make black puddings to feed unwitting Londoners, Geoffrey was embroiling the British and American high commands in his free-thinking vision of icebergs being towed into the Atlantic to stand as mid-point bomber and fighter bases. He christened his brainchild Project *Habakkuk* after the biblical prophet who proclaims: "I will work a work in your days which you will not believe, though it be told to you."

All the subsequent paperwork spelled the name as *Habbakuk*, but this was the least of anyone's problems when dealing with Pyke and the products of his unlimited imagination.

Geoffrey Pyke had long been interested in the adoption of unorthodox materials for new uses. He greatly admired the ingenuity of the Germans in World War I for making their army uniforms out of nettles, and had developed an obsession with ice and super-cooled water by the opening of World War II. By 1942 he was attached to the staff of Lord Louis Mountbatten, chief of combined operations. He somehow managed to convince Mountbatten of the viability of capturing naturally carved icebergs or deliberately blasting them free of the ice caps to produce ice-crafted warships, aircraft carriers and airfields that could be towed into the mid-Atlantic to attack enemy shipping and the wolfpacks. The possibility of instant and free shipping was bound to attract attention and, superficially at least, to the unscientific mind the idea appeared to stack up.

Ice was of course unsinkable and icebergs are known to survive inconveniently long even in temperate waters; their sheer bulk had long since defeated all U.S. Coast Guard attempts to blast them out of shipping lanes, so bomb and torpedo damage would be negligible and repairable with more water. There was also absolutely no problem with evading magnetic mines, so why *not* fit them with engines and put them to use?

Pyke's greatest advantage was that he conformed to everyone's idea of the mad genius—unkempt beard, shabby clothes and quirky habits like always leaving his fly open for "health reasons"—so all dissenters were shouted down as hidebound conventionalists devoid of vision. Even Churchill joined the fan club suggesting, "Let us cut a large chunk of ice from the Arctic ice-cap, tow it down to Cornwall, fly on aircraft and then tow it to the point of attack." With Churchill's approval, Pyke was unassailable and shouted down all objections regarding the amount and cost of the cork insulation and steel structure that would be needed, the sheer size of the marine engines with enough power to drive the damn things, and the fact that, with 90 percent of their bulk underwater, none of these icebergs could ever enter shallows or harbors to be fitted out in the first place. None of this mattered; Project *Habbakuk* was sanctioned and Patricia Lake at Jaspar, Alberta, was identified as the ideal test and development site. A bit like building a boat in your basement, if the prototype was a success, it would be landlocked in Canada for ever.

No matter. Ice was cut from the lake and construction of a mini *Habbakuk* ice-ship was under way before the end of 1942. There were problems with the on-board refrigeration units and the ice itself which, although incredibly strong in some ways, once cut and shaped displayed a capricious propensity to fracture or shatter for no apparent reason. But more conventional scientists were already riding to Pyke's rescue, albeit unwittingly. Herman Mark, the father of polymer science, had cleverly escaped the Nazis in 1938 with his fortune converted into platinum wire bent into coat hangers. He made his way to America where, in 1943, he published a paper on the incredible strength of composite ice frozen with a small percentage of wood fiber or cotton wool. A copy of the paper was sent to Pyke, who passed the information over to Max Perutz, who later supervised Crick and Watson in their efforts to identify the structure of DNA. Conducting practical experiments in a butcher's walk-in freezer in Smithfield Market, Perutz established that about 4 percent fiber was the optimum, but when alerted to the full horror of Project *Habbakuk* he tactfully declined any involvement, insisting that the composition he had established be named "pykrete," before hurrying back to Cambridge. In the essay "Enemy Alien" in his published collection *I Wish I'd Made You Angry Earlier* (1998), Perutz branded the venture "absurd."

Perutz's findings sent Pyke hang-gliding over the abyss. If pykrete was stronger than concrete, which to be fair it was, why restrict the venture to mere ships and mini-airfields? Why not build a series of two-million-ton floating fortresses to take command of the whole of the Atlantic? Pyke was hailed as a man of even greater vision than first suspected. Mountbatten rushed off prankishly to toss a block of the pykrete into Churchill's bath to prove its resilience to melting. After recovering his composure from having his ablutions so rudely interrupted, Churchill sanctioned the idea in principle, but pointed out that Britain simply did not have the money for such a project. The Americans did, however. August 1943 saw Churchill and Mountbatten at the Quebec Conference, where the latter staged a somewhat theatrical demonstration for the assembled Allied brass in an attempt to convince the American contingent to stump up an initial $100 million. After a brief explanation, he whipped out a revolver and fired it into a block of ice, which promptly shattered. He next fired at a block of pykrete which, barely flinching, caused the bullet to ricochet past the ear of Sir Charles Portal, British chief of air staff, before inflicting a flesh wound on his American opposite number, Fleet Admiral Ernest King, who then had difficulty in sharing Mountbatten's boyish enthusiasm for *Habbakuk*.

It was left to the Americans to talk sense and pour cold water on *Habbakuk*. The range of carriers was increasing in leaps and bounds, and the sheer volume of structural steel and cooling pipes for such a monster as *Habbakuk* could build a dozen state-of-the-art carriers, which would be faster and more practical. If such a structure was needed, why not simply adapt and expand the existing Mulberry floating harbor concept?

This time even Mountbatten listened to sense, and Project *Habbakuk* was at last dead in the water. Deserted by his high-powered proponents, Pyke was left open to the ridicule some felt he justly deserved and this, along with other setbacks accompanied by similar pillory, plunged him into a state of depression from which he never recovered. On February 22, 1948, he shaved off his trademark beard, swallowed a bottle of sleeping pills and left a note to an unappreciative world. Cousin Magnus became a post-war television favorite in the UK, where he made science fun and accessible to the masses but also produced some quite serious works and studies on food and nutrition. Flamboyant to the end, he died at home, fending off an intruder with his cane at the age of eighty-four.

Grand Panjandrum

Had author Nevil Shute (full name: Nevil Shute Norway) not been on the development team for Panjandrum, this singularly ill-conceived device would have been a rose by another name. The term had been coined back in 1755 by Samuel Foote to tease an old actor named Charles Macklin, who was forever boasting about his ability to commit lines to memory after a single reading. Foote rose to the challenge and wrote a short piece of nonsensical text about a "Grand Panjandrum," and taunted Macklin to read it once and then repeat it. Famous in literary circles, this lampooning of Macklin gave the word "panjandrum" for anything ostensibly impressive but intrinsically useless, or anyone who is all front and no substance. The wartime Grand Panjandrum was both!

During World War II, the British DMWD was given the brief to come up with something that could breach the German Atlantic Wall, which in places was over ten feet high and seven feet thick. After a few *cogito ergo sum*s on their slide rules, Shute and his colleagues figured out that a payload of at least four thousand pounds was required to breach such a concrete wall and allow infantry to pour through unimpeded. The question was how to get it up the beach under fire? Some say it was one Captain Finch-Noyes who came up with the plan, but this is now impossible to ascertain; success has a thousand parents but failure on this scale is invariably a disowned orphan. But, one way or another, the team came up with what is best described as an unstable hybrid of a large empty cable drum and a Catherine wheel firework.

The two wheels were about ten feet in diameter, with a one-foot-wide steel tire and the explosive charge slung between them in a cage. The perimeter of the wheels was to be adorned with rockets, and the whole contraption controlled by a two thousand-foot trailing cable by which the operator could both steer and detonate the charge once Panjandrum was in place. All looked great on the drawing board and trials were scheduled to begin on the beach at Westward Ho on September 7, 1943. Shute himself took the controls for the inaugural run and on his signal the ramp of the landing craft was dropped and he hit the firing button. Panjandrum leapt from the DUK landing craft, into the water and was halfway up the beach when the portside rockets failed, causing the drum to capsize and drill itself into the sand. It was exhumed and dusted off for a second run with twice the number of rockets, but this too ended in failure.

The team returned to their London drawing boards only to return with Panjandrum Mk 2, which had seventy rockets and an improved guide cable with a break-strain of 1 ton. This time, with the visiting brass opting to disperse themselves throughout various places of safety, Shute et al. thought that they too would take precautions and this time activate their brainchild from inside the DUK and then stay there.

The new, improved and more powerful Mk 2 behaved perfectly. It emerged, leviathan-like, from the DUK at top speed and headed straight up the beach, to the nodded approval of all present. But with barely half the cable paid out, Panjandrum started to describe a large circle before retracing its tracks back down the beach, as if somehow homesick for the seclusion of DUK and the company of its creators. Shute's thumbs disappeared into a blur on his control box as his colleagues dived over the side, Shute holding his nerve until Panjandrum hit the bottom of the ramp and headed straight for him. Now inspired by sheer terror, he executed an abandon-DUK dive over the side that would not have disgraced a man half his age. Not knowing when to quit, the team brought out a standby device for another try.

The understudy was doing fine until Shute thought a touch of left brake was in order. Both brakes temporarily jammed, snapping the steel cable, which snaked back at alarming speed right over the heads of the terrified military onlookers. Panjandrum, enjoying its new-found freedom, took off along the beach at over sixty mph only to fall on its side and drill itself into the beach. Shute insisted on one last go, however, and the brass agreed, providing they pull back a bit and watch through binoculars. Needless to say, this last run was the most entertaining of all. Almost as soon as it hit the beach, Panjandrum began to shed rockets capriciously, which resulted in its veering about like a cobra looking where to strike. When it finally stabilized on an even course, it was left heading straight for the brass who, casting aside their binoculars, dived for cover along with Louis Klementaski, the motor racing photographer who was seconded to the DMWD to record their "triumphs." It was also Klementaski who took the old monochrome footage of the Barnes-Wallis "bouncing bomb" tests, but right then he had other things on his mind. Fortunately, in his panic to escape with his life, he left the camera running and the Imperial War Museum (IWM) still has the footage of Panjandrum disintegrating in a series of explosions as the only casualty, an Airedale dog called "Ammonal" owned by one of the VIPs, disappears out of shot, pursued by a couple of the detached rockets that gave him a serious singeing, but one from which he fully recovered.

Shute and his crew extricated the generals and admirals from their various bolt-holes and barbed-wire encounters, to be informed through gritted teeth that the Panjandrum project was to be scrapped. No surprise there.

Porker Wars

Pigs can indeed be troublesome creatures, as demonstrated by their ability to twice bring world powers to the brink of war and then to wipe out more people than died in World War I, which they also played a major part in starting.

First came the War of the Pig in 1859, which had Britain and America squaring up to each other over the death of a pig on land left in dispute by an ambiguity in the Oregon Treaty of 1846. Drawn up to settle the boundary between Oregon and Columbia, the agreement stated that the line would run along the 49th parallel of north latitude, down the middle of the channel that separates the continent from Vancouver Island, through the Fuca's Straits and on to the Pacific. But all this did was start Britain and America arguing about which channel was referred to; was it the Haro Strait that ran to the west of the San Juan Islands or the Rosario Strait to their east? In short, which of them held sovereignty over those San Juan Islands?

As the dispute rolled on, the Hudson Bay Company took over San Juan Island itself and ran it as an enormous sheep farm, much to the ire of the thirty or so American settlers scattered about the land. Everything was fine, however, until June 15, 1859, when a pig belonging to one Charles Griffin of the Hudson Bay Company wandered onto the land of American settler Lyman Cutler, and was happily rooting for potatoes when shot. Both men had been on friendly terms until this incident, but Griffin's demand for compensation of $100 was met with a counteroffer of a mere $10, as the pig had been trespassing at the time, and matters spiraled out of control from there. Each party demanded their respective governments take up the issue on their behalf, and before long the settlers of both sides were demanding troops for protection. In the end, there were nearly five hundred American troops dug in on the island with a battery of artillery, keeping an eye on a British force of over two thousand standing off in five warships with seventy guns between them. Both sides held discipline and, frustrated by no one taking the initiative, James Douglas, governor of Vancouver Island, ordered Admiral Baynes to land his marines to engage the Americans.

Thankfully for the Americans, Baynes refused to carry out the order, saying that he would have no part in taking "two great nations to war over a squabble about a pig." Although the islands were a mere trifle in the global scheme of things, the Civil War was just around the corner and if the pig war had come to shots then it would have been the perfect excuse for Britain to protect its supplies of cotton by throwing in with the South and altering the outcome of that particular conflict. As heads cleared on both sides, President Buchanan sent General Winfield Scott to negotiate with Governor Douglas. It was agreed that Griffin would be paid his $100 and that both sides should reduce their forces to a token military presence, the British to camp on the northern tip of the island and the Americans on the southern tip. Both groups lived in perfect harmony until Kaiser Wilhelm I of Germany was brought in to arbitrate in 1872, when he awarded the islands to America.

The next pig war was equally bloodless, but far more serious in its long-term implications. At the turn of the last century, Serbia was little more than a puppet state dancing on Austro-Hungarian purse strings; everything the Serbs needed they imported from Austria and their entire export of pork and live swine went back the same. The first indication of Serbian discontent came in 1904, when they started to buy their arms from France instead of Austria. They then struck deals with the Bulgarians to impose punitive tariffs on all goods from Austria, which responded in kind with a ban on Serbian pork and pig imports. Keen to find alternative markets for what represented a staggering 90 percent of Serbian-generated wealth, they leaned on Bosnia and Herzegovina to allow passage of their pork and livestock out to the Adriatic and on to new markets in Turkey, Egypt, Germany and Greece. With the money they earned from their pork exports, the Serbs bought alarming quantities of arms from France and, supported by Russia, started talk in 1906 of a pan-Slavic state. This was just too much for the Austrians, who announced they would put a stop to Serbian plans by any means necessary. This belligerence prompted the Russians to stand up behind the Serbs and tell the Austrians to make a move if they dared. With a pan-European conflict very much in the cards, Germany again averted a porker war by telling Vienna it simply had to accept the changes in Serbia or find itself isolated and alone.

Everybody backed down, but there was still bad blood between the Serbs and their old masters, this peaking with the assassination of Archduke Franz Ferdinand, heir to the Austro-Hungarian throne, on his goodwill visit in Sarajevo in 1914. The Austrians invaded Serbia and everybody else picked sides and piled in for World War I. But the pigs had not yet finished. In the last year of the Great War they gave us swine flu. It took some time for doctors to realize what was happening, as the appalling death toll of the conflict masked the initial outbreaks which became pandemic with the movement of service personnel of all nationalities to and from the fronts, speeding that unwelcome plow.

The true virulence of this swine flu only became fully known in the post-war years, when it was revealed that over half of all the American casualties in Europe were attributable to the flu and not enemy fire. The pandemic went on to kill some 100 million people, tenfold the combined casualties of the war itself.

Because the disease was first observed in clinical isolation at Fort Riley in Kansas in March 1918, it is sometimes said to have started there with the fort's small pig-breeding program, but was more likely taken there by returning troops. It was also misnamed the Spanish flu, as the first reports of its ravages came from that country which, being neutral, had no embargo on its press.

The Rape of the Bucket

There is still serious rivalry between the Italian city-states of Bologna and Modena, but in 1325 they engaged in a twelve-year war over an old bucket taken from a well. During one of their spats, which resulted in the battle of Zappolino (1325), a group of Modenese soldiers decided it might be a jolly idea to nip into Bologna, about thirty miles away, and steal the bucket from the well in the main square. It was bad enough being beaten by the Modenese, but when the defeated army got back to their city to find out about the bucket, they declared all-out war. Over the next twelve years thousands died in what came to be known as the War of the Bucket, which Bologna eventually lost. Modena still has the old wooden bucket in the town hall and a replica on show in the cathedral; mention of it can still raise feelings in both cities.

The stupidity of a war over an old bucket appealed to the Italian political satirist, Alessandro Tassoni, who wrote *The Rape of the Bucket* (1622), a mock-heroic yarn that would later inspire Alexander Pope's parallel *The Rape of the Lock* (of hair), first published in 1722. Long before "rape" acquired the specific meaning it holds today, it meant to carry away or steal, as in birds of prey being collectively known as raptors.

A Right Howdah-Do

Size, as they say, isn't everything, and the modern perception of the war elephant as an invincible battle wagon, stomping great swathes through the opposing ranks, is wide of the mark. Like any animal, elephants can be panicked easily, becoming more of a danger to those who had brought them to the party than to the enemy. King Porus lost to Alexander the Great because his war elephants were panicked into tap-dancing all over his own infantry; Pyrrhus, he of expensive victory fame, had to watch his army getting likewise depleted after similar attentions from his own elephants; and even Hannibal's father, Hamilcar, managed to drown on the back of one during his hurried retreat from his abortive siege of Helike in 229 BC. You just never knew how they were going to behave; all mahouts carried a hammer and chisel to cut the animal's spinal cord if it got out of control, but since the mahout was frequently thrown or dismounted as soon as the elephant panicked, this did not always happen.

The first name that leaps to mind when talking about war and elephants is that of Hannibal, but contrary to popular memory the beasts did not do him much good either. He started his transalpine trek with nearly forty elephants, but fewer than half a dozen made it to the other side; elephants are not very tolerant of high altitude and low temperatures. When the Romans paid him a return visit in 203 BC, Hannibal put his faith in his array of over eighty war elephants, which advanced like tanks with his infantry behind. The waiting invaders, however, were about to unleash their own zoological weapon—the hogs of war!

Elephants hate fire and they hate high-pitched noises. Ever the pragmatists, the Romans combined these two factors by covering pigs in tar, setting them on fire and then sending them screaming in agony into the ranks of elephants, which promptly stampeded back over the following infantry. The few that made it to the Roman ranks were neutralized by squads of men with axes to hack the poor brutes down.

Other nations' cavalry developed equally unpleasant ways of dealing with elephants, as witnessed by the modern cavalry sport of tent pegging, in which riders use a lance or sword to skewer a wooden peg on the ground while passing at a gallop. Big as they are, elephants do have an Achilles heel in that their toe-nails are particularly sensitive; lancers would always go for this target and honed their skills in practice runs that survive as the aforementioned sport.

Russian Roulette

In the 1860s, the Russian Admiral Popov came up with the doomed idea of circular ironclads and built two of them, one named after himself and the other called *Novgorod*, launched in 1873. Both were unmitigated disasters.

Among the many glaring drawbacks was the fact that the water-line was a scant 5 feet down from the edge of the deck, which was itself concave to the center. This layout was fine on a millpond, but on their first trials in the River Dnieper both ships succumbed to the mild current and began to rotate, and then kept rotating faster and faster as they were swept out to sea. The respective and hapless captains tried using the engines and even tried firing the guns like retro-rockets to halt the merry-go-round, but all to no avail. By the time more conventional ships were mustered to take *Popov* and *Novgorod* in tow, at least half the crew from each ship had been flung off into the sea and those with the presence of mind to lash themselves to something sturdy were still aboard but unconscious. Further trials were no less entertaining; even under the most ideal conditions a straight course was out of the question and every time either of the side-mounted twelve inch guns was fired the ships did their Frisbee act again. Both were withdrawn.

Smoke and Mirrors

It is still stated by some as fact that Archimedes used reflected and concentrated sunlight to set fire to the Roman fleet under Marcellus who lay siege to Syracuse from 214 to 212 BC during the Second Punic War (218–201 BC). A major flaw in any such assertion is the fact that the siege was recorded in great detail in Polybius' *Universal History*, Livy's *History of Rome* and Plutarch's *Marcellus*, yet none mention anything of the sort. Given ideal conditions, enough mirrors and a compliant target it is of course possible to pull off such a stunt, but not with a mobile enemy reluctant to co-operate in their own destruction.

The earliest mention of Archimedes going solar crops up in the writings of Lucian and centuries of repetition cemented this groundless assertion as fact. Come the seventeenth century several voices, including that of Descartes, were raised in open derision of the notion, so in the next century the French naturalist George-Louis Buffon set up an experiment on April 10, 1747, to settle the matter. And he did indeed successfully ignite several objects and planks of creosoted wood, but those who cite his results are shy of giving the full details of the display. Not only were Buffon's silvered mirrors vastly superior in their reflectivity than the burnished metal that would have been available to Archimedes, but in his first experiment to ignite a block of pine he used 168 specially produced mirrors, each measuring eight inches by ten inches and had them locked in stands and configured at the optimum range of 150 yards. Other trials impressed the assembled crowd, but Buffon had picked his day and focused a fearsome array of mirrors on a selection of inanimate objects at a fixed range before waiting quite some time for the predictable result. In short, he proved absolutely nothing.

A slightly more even-handed experiment was carried out in 1973 by the Greek scientist Ioannis Sakkas at the Skaramagas naval base, just outside Athens, where seventy coppered mirrors measuring five feet by three feet were configured on a plywood replica of a Roman warship anchored some 160 feet from the quay. As it had been given a healthy coating of tar, this too soon caught fire, as it would, and was left to burn to the triumphant cries of the onlookers. Next, a group from the Massachusetts Institute of Technology (MIT) set up an experiment in October 2005, when 127 mirrors measuring one foot square were locked onto a wooden ship at a range of around one hundred feet. Only after the ship had been "zapped" for over ten minutes did anything like a flame appear, but again only such fire as could be quickly doused by anyone on board. The group repeated the experiment on an old fishing boat in San Francisco for the popular television show *Mythbusters*, which deemed their efforts a failure in that they managed to inflict only some charring and a small amount of flame.

Just because something *can* be done today under ideal conditions does not mean it *was* done two thousand years ago. The optimum range for all such attempts seems to be a maximum of about 150 feet and the flashpoint of wood, depending on the type, is somewhere around 570°F (299°C), which would require a Roman crew to hold their ship perfectly still and remain oblivious to what was going on for about ten minutes, and then neglect to chuck a bucket of water over the flames. On top of all that, Syracuse is east-facing and owing to the shallows and rocks it would be impossible for a ship to get within 150 yards of the parapets for the defenders to pull off such a trick. Besides, the city had catapults with a range of about 600 yards and when the final assault came it was over land and from the rear; the Romans sacked the city, killed Archimedes and sailed home with their ships intact.

A War of Two Halves

By the end of 1968, there were some three hundred thousand Salvadorans living in Honduras, which although larger than El Salvador, had the smaller population. The Hondurans regarded these interlopers as illegal and deeply resented their setting up factories and sweat-shopping the local labor force. There were other petty squabbles between the two nations, but it would never have come to war had the two not been pitted against each other by the team draw for the soccer World Cup in 1969.

Their match was scheduled to be played on June 8 in the Honduran National Stadium at Tegucigalpa but, the night before the game, Honduran supporters set up a charivari outside the Salvadoran team's hotel to keep them awake all night, and the team blamed this for their 1–0 defeat the next day. In the unfathomable complexity of soccer results, this defeat counted as a draw, requiring a second match to be played in El Salvador, where things had already taken a sinister turn. Watching that first match on the television at home, and taking the result as an affront to her national pride, eighteen-year-old Amelia Bolanos wrapped her body in the Salvadoran flag and shot herself through the heart. Her funeral became a military state event, with the gun carriage followed by the Salvadoran president on foot and his entire cabinet bringing up the rear. By the time the Honduran team turned up to play the re-match in the Flor Blancal Stadium, Amelia had been declared a martyr and a national heroine and things were getting seriously out of hand. Needless to say, it was the Hondurans' turn for a sleepless night before being taken to the stadium under armed guard, where they saw their national flag burning in the middle of the field and a soiled bed sheet flying at half mast in its stead. With their goalkeeper left distracted and feeling decidedly vulnerable to well-timed small-arms fire, the Hondurans lost 3–0. The Fédération Internationale de Football Association (FIFA), oblivious to the wasps' nest it was blithely hitting with a very big stick, announced that in view of all the foul play and accusations of biased refereeing, the teams should play yet again but on neutral soil in Mexico. Here El Salvador notched up a 3–2 victory that qualified them through to the next round.

The next day, with borders already sealed, a Salvadoran plane flew over the Tegucigalpa Stadium and threw out a bomb to signal kick-off of the Central American Soccer War. The ground action began in earnest on the following morning, July 14, 1969. The Salvadorans made such a rapid advance that even they were surprised—it became known that many of the battalions listed for the other team existed on paper only; some of the Honduran generals had been working a scam and pocketing the budget allocated to these non-existent forces. Determined to make the most of such an unfair advantage, the Salvadorans advanced at full speed, but ran out of gasoline when just five miles into Honduras. In the air, American mercenaries were flying the Salvadorans' P-51 Mustangs in combat against the Hondurans' F4U Corsairs, which gives the conflict the added distinction of being the last in which piston-engined fighters went head to head.

It was all over in four days and, with about two thousand casualties apiece, both sides declared a draw. The Salvadorans went home to watch their team getting soundly thrashed in the next round of the World Cup, leaving the Hondurans to shoot a few of their own generals. The reason this conflict is still so little-known is because the world largely ignored this Ruritanian farce, concentrating instead on Apollo 11's first manned mission to the moon, launched on July 16.

The Zanzibar Express

The importance of Zanzibar (part of Tanzania) to the British in the nineteenth century prompted them to impose a condition that gave them final veto on ascendance to the Sultancy, because the last thing the British wanted was anyone pro-German on the throne. On August 25, 1896, that was exactly what they got. On this day, the pro-British Sultan Hamed died of poisoning by his pro-German relative, Khalid bin Barghash, who told the British just what they could do with their veto and proclaimed himself sultan of Zanzibar.

The British chaps on the spot, Sir Basil Cave and General Lloyd Mathews, fired off frantic cables asking for clarification of the British position and advice about what to do next. In due course they got their reply from Lord Salisbury: "You are authorized to adopt whatever measures you may consider necessary, and will be supported in your action by Her Majesty's Government. Do not, however, attempt to take any action which you are not certain of being able to accomplish successfully." Basically, this was diplo-speak for "succeed and we'll back you to the hilt; fail and we'll hang you out to dry."

While Cave was waiting for this less-than-helpful message, British warships began turning up in the harbor to anchor in plain sight of the palace complex, now occupied by the upstart, Khalid. Although he had assembled a few seven-pounders, some machine guns and armed his slaves, servants and even the ladies of the harem, Khalid was still sitting in a fragile refuge that was largely built of timber with plaster facing. At 8:00 a.m. on August 27, Sir Basil sent word to Khalid that he really ought to take a peek out of his bedroom window to see Her Majesty's Ships *St. George, Philomel, Thrush, Racoon,* and *Sparrow* sitting on his doorstep with their guns trained on his house of straw. At 8:30 a.m., Khalid sent out the reply that he refused to strike his standard as he did not believe for one minute that the British would dare open fire on him. Word was sent back that he had 30 minutes to change his mind or a state of war would exist and, at 9:00 a.m. precisely, Khalid was rudely disabused of any notions concerning British reluctance to fire on him—*Thrush, Racoon,* and *Sparrow* opened up and reduced the palace to dust. At the first salvo, Khalid ran to the German compound, leaving the slaves and ladies of the harem to bear the brunt of the barrage, which was called off at 9:35 a.m. when peace was declared in the shortest war in history.

The Germans refused to hand over Khalid, who was instead spirited away on a warship only later to fall into British hands in 1916, during World War I. He was put into exile on St. Helena which, although more famous for playing host to Napoleon, had also been "home" to Dinuzulu kaCetshwayo, king of the Zulu. Farcically short the war may have been, but the British were mortified to find that over five hundred people had perished in the fire that followed their bombardment, these unfortunates having been ordered to remain at their posts until death by the fleeing Khalid.

FURTHER READING

The following titles are recommended for further exploration of the myths and oddities of military history, and for providing additional perspectives on some of the more controversial aspects of this book.

Boller, Paul F., *Not So!* (Oxford University Press: 1995)

Boller, Paul F., and George, John, *They Never Said It* (Oxford University Press: 1989)

Burnam, Tom, *Dictionary of Misinformation* (Futura Publications: 1975)

——, *More Misinformation* (Lippincott & Crowell: 1980)

Chung, Dr. Ong Chit, *Operation Matador* (Times Academic Press: 1997)

Fogel, Robert William, and Engerman, Stanley L., *Time on the Cross: The Economics of American Negro Slavery* (Little, Brown & Company: 1974)

Harman, Nicholas, *Dunkirk: The Patriotic Myth* (Outlet: 1982)

James, Lawrence, *The Golden Warrior, The Life and Legend of Lawrence of Arabia* (Abacus: 1995)

Knowles, Elizabeth, *What They Didn't Say* (Oxford University Press: 2006)

Lively, Scott, and Abrams, Kevin, *The Pink Swastika* (Star Song Communications Group: 1998)

Loewen, James W., *Lies Across America* (Simon & Schuster: 1999)

——, *Lies My Teacher Told Me* (Simon & Schuster: 1995)

Marchetti, Victor, *The CIA and the Cult of Intelligence* (Alfred A. Knopf: 1974)

Perry, John C., *Myths and Realities of American Slavery* (Burd Street Press: 2002)

Phelps, Barry, *You Don't Say!* (Macmillan Reference Books: 1995)

Regan, Geoffrey, *Historical Blunders* (Guinness Publishing: 1994)

——, *Military Blunders* (André Deutsch: 2001)

Shenkman, Richard, *I Love Paul Revere Whether He Rode or Not* (Harper Perennial: 1992)

——, *Legends, Lies & Cherished Myths of World History* (Harper Perennial: 1994)

Shenkman, Richard, and Reiger, Kurt, *One-Night Stands with American History* (Harper Perennial: 2003)

Varasdi, J. Allen, *Myth-Information* (Ballantine Books: 1989)

Wahl, Jenny B., *Economic Analysis of the Common Law of Southern Slavery* (Cambridge University Press: 1998)

INDEX